Sustainability and Environmental Policy

Frank J. Dietz
Udo E. Simonis
Jan van der Straaten
(eds.)

Sustainability
and Environmental Policy

Restraints and Advances

edition
sigma

Further informations on environmental policy and other social science titles are available from
edition sigma   **Heimstrasse 14**   **D-1000 Berlin 61**   **Germany**

CIP-Titelaufnahme der Deutschen Bibliothek

Sustainability and environmental policy : restraints and advances / Frank J. Dietz ... (eds.). - Berlin : Ed. Sigma, 1992
   ISBN 3-89404-343-1
NE: Dietz, Frank [Hrsg.]

Cover Illustration: RB
Printing and binding: WZB   Printed in Germany

This is a story about four people: Everybody, Somebody, Anybody, and Nobody. There was an important job to be done and Everybody was asked to do it. Everybody was sure Somebody would do it. Anybody could have done it, but Nobody did it. Somebody got angry about that because it was Everybody's job. Everybody thought Anybody could do it, but Nobody realized that Everybody wouldn't do it. It ended up that Everybody blamed Somebody when actually Nobody asked Anybody.

Source: unknown

Contents

Introduction: The Concept of Sustainable Development

Frank J. Dietz, Udo E. Simonis, and Jan van der Straaten

Chronology of sustainable development

It is often supposed that the *concept* of sustainable development has been introduced by the World Commission on Environment and Development (the so-called Brundtland-Report) in 1987. This is far from satisfying the history of economic thought. The concept used by the Brundtland-Report is related to the idea of "good housekeeping" in such a way that economic possibilities in the future are not jeopardized by present economic activities. One could say that this is a normal way of doing business. In business economics safeguarding the future of the company is perceived as the ultimate goal of management. Should this not equally hold for society as a whole? A brief chronological overview on the history of economic thought can provide some insight into this (seemingly or factual) paradox.

Most classical economists were aware of the limited possibilities of the given natural resources to mankind. In particular, the "Law of Diminishing Returns" demonstrates that in this period natural resources or land were in the core of the economic argument. Using this law in his theory, John Stuart Mill (1848) came to the conclusion that a stationary state would be the ultimate outcome of the economic process. This is another way of saying that sustainable development can only be reached by aiming at a stationary state.

It is often argued, and for good reasons, that neoclassical economists have brought nature and the production factor "natural resources" to the margin of economic theory. By doing so, they introduced a system of analysis where the functioning of the market became the object of every economic theory. But, one cannot say that neoclassical economists hold the view that sustainable development is an irrelevant issue. On this point, the neoclassical argument cuts more ice.

Neoclassical economists are, generally speaking, of the opinion that scarcity is measured on the market. Natural resources are relevant, from an economic point of view, when they are bought and sold on a market. By contrast, natural resources outside the market are "free goods," and do not have economic significance in this way of thinking. The difference with classical economists thus is found in the "locus economicus," i.e., the market will bring forward a permanent mobility of production factors, including priced natural resources. When resources are going to become scarce, substitution of production factors will decrease that scarcity again. It is this substitution process which is thought to result in an optimal production at lowest costs. Therefore, technological development and substitution are the cornerstones of the neoclassical paradigm.

One can argue that this way of thinking has dramatic shortcomings when unpriced natural resources become of importance in the production process, as will be demonstrated in this book. But this argument is valid only when arguing from outside the neoclassical framework. Within the neoclassical framework there is an assumption of sustainable development to be realized by the unhindered functioning of the market. This is why sustainable development in neoclassical analysis is seen as a "normal" result of the economic process. One may criticize this system by arguing that the preassumptions of the analytical framework do not work in modern societies, dealing with enormous environmental problems in an unpriced reality.

Juan Martinez-Alier (1987) has shown that already in the nineteenth century some ecologically oriented economists warned of the effects on nature if the concept of value is solely based on individual preferences which are supposed to be reflected in market prices. However, in mainstream economics hardly any attention was given to the issue. Only after the Second World War it became clear that mass production on a large scale was accompanied by severe environmental problems. This is the reason why some economists gave attention to the shortcomings of the neoclassical framework in this respect.

K. William Kapp (1950) wrote on the "social costs" of private enterprise, focusing particularly on environmental costs. Kenneth Boulding (1966) argued that current economics did not pay sufficient attention to natural resources and that modern society could be compared with a "cowboy economy," taking natural resources from everywhere and destroying nature by throwing away the waste and damaging the ecocycles with this behavior. The paradigm shift he was asking for was labelled "spaceship economy"; a spaceship has only a limited amount of resources and, given the limited space and possibilities to cope with waste in a spaceship, all resources should be reused. This is another way of saying that sustainable development can only be realized by a significant change of the economy, giving equal footing to production, consumption, and recycling, and making producers, consumers, and recyclers equal partners in society.

Herman E. Daly (1973) is another eminent author who challenged the view that traditional neoclassical economics will bring forward a sound environmental situation. He recently used the term "plimsoll line" to make clear that certain ecological limits should not be overrun (Daly and Dobb, 1990). Again this is another way of using the concept of sustainable development.

Donella and Dennis Meadows (1992) called their new book "Beyond the Limits." And in order to demonstrate that the present world economy is unsustainable they use the concept of "overshoot," indicating a situation that cannot be maintained because industrial society is overusing the sources and overburdening the sinks.

One may ask whether or not there are differences between these approaches and the concept of "sustainable development" as used in the Brundtland-Report. What are the reasons that this concept was introduced by a World Commission, and why has this concept, finally, got so much of attention after all the other formulations, synonyms, and ideas?

The Brundtland-Report

The Brundtland-Report defined sustainable development as "a process of change in which the exploitation of resources, the direction of investments, the orientation of technological development, and institutional change are all in harmony and enhance both current and future potential to meet human needs and aspirations" (World Commission on Environment and Development, 1987, p. 46). The huge contrasts between the developed and the developing parts of the world have inspired the Commission to these specific contents of sustainablility. The Commission argued that economic growth is a necessity in underdeveloped countries, as poverty in these countries causes environmental disruption and leads to an overuse of natural resources. In the developed countries the situation is somewhat different; here the expansion of production and consumption is the main push factor to environmental deterioration. This implies that economic growth has to be curbed in this part of the world.

One may conclude that the major difference with earlier authors and positions using similar concepts is found in the political implications. The

Brundtland-Report brought the problem of environmental deterioration and ruthless exploitation of natural resources in the broader context of the relations between North and South. By doing so, the Commission made the discussion on environmental problems a global discussion, and at the same time more acceptable for people in the poor countries. It is this political load of the concept of sustainable development which got massive support from all over the world.

One should not overlook, however, that in this way of reasoning the concept of sustainable development cannot be operationalized without strong reference to ethical and political arguments. This implies again that environmental policy comes into the core of the public debate. In our opinion this is an absolute necessity, especially as many environmental economists focus too much on theories and analytical instruments without paying enough attention to the difficult process of implementing a sound environmental policy.

The scope and organization of this book

The scope of the book includes theoretical, empirical, technological, and international aspects of sustainable development. Accordingly the individual contributions are grouped into four parts in which both the restraints and the advances of sustainable development are addressed, namely *Theory, Policy, Technology*, and *International Relations*.

In the first contribution of Part I *Dietz* and *van der Straaten* give an overview on the relevant contributions in economic thought in the course of time. They state that the process of the industrial revolution, by using natural resources in a completely different way than before, has had a decisive influence on the development of economic theories. The market came into the center of theory, using the concept of "negative externalities" as a means to analyze and describe environmental problems. Current environmental problems, however, are evident on such a scale and severeness that this theoretical framework does not have sufficient strength to deal adequately with these problems. The authors therefore develop an analytical framework in which nature and the environment are the starting points for new economic theories.

Opschoor and *van der Straaten* investigate the significance of institutional aspects in environmental economics. They show that in the neoclassical framework only insufficient attention is given to institutional factors. The assumptions about the behavior of producers and consumers, about economic growth and the role of state are so static that a rather rigid description of reality is the result. The authors argue that institutional factors cannot be neglected by environmental economics, as they cannot be separated from the functioning of the market.

Bains and *Peet* give a description of a framework for interpreting sustainable development and apply it to energy policy. The main idea of the authors is to integrate concepts and to link arguments that are usually treated in quite separate arenas. Social and economic development is possible as a result of managing the natural environment, but this environment itself is not under social control. Its manipulation involves risks. If society is to continue to benefit from exploiting natural resources, it must recognize the environmental repercussions of economic activities, and forcefully use ecological principles in its institutions for resource management. The conceptual framework developed allows to draw connections between the environmental, social, and political aspects of the development process.

In the first contribution of Part II *Dietz* and *van der Straaten* investigate the relationship between economic theory and environmental policy. They are of the opinion that not enough attention has been given to this relationship. The shortcomings in theory are reflected in the behavior of the economic and political agents. The authors demonstrate that the policy on acid rain in the Netherlands has been dramatically undermined by vested economic interests. Particularly, the influence of the ministers of economic affairs, agriculture and transport on the abatement policy has been much stronger than the influence of the minister of environment. There is a significant imbalance of power in society which favors vested polluting economic interests.

Everett gives attention to the groups which can counteract these vested interests, namely the environmental movement. As scientists and pressure groups time and again have reasserted their concern about the environmental limits to rapid economic and technological growth, a number of political issues arise. First of all, how do environmental movements come about? How do opposing forces arise and counter environmental movements? What net effect do these conflicting forces have on long run environmental quality? Economic models of political behavior can provide some insights into these questions. The author applies a basic model to the history of environmental movements to illustrate some of his points.

Streeten picks up the question "sustainable development for whom?" There are possible distributional conflicts not only between industrial and developing countries but also between the rich and the poor. What institutional innovations are needed to make the poor and the developing countries the major addressees of respective strategies, under what conditions can a global environmental agency be envisaged that takes special care of the environmental problems and the developmental needs of the poor?

Kasperkovitch investigates the arguments that had substantial influence on the formulation of an abatement policy on pesticides in the Netherlands. She shows how arguments in the domain of economics penetrated more easily into the legislation procedure than environmental arguments. In this case, more weight has been given to the vested interests of agriculture and industry than to environmental concerns. She discusses the question which strategy can be seen as most effective to give environmental concerns a better chance.

Dietz gives special attention to the possibilities of a sustainable use of nutrients in agriculture. The application of nutrients in agricultural production has caused serious environmental problems. In various regions of Europe eutrophication of surface water, high levels of nitrates in groundwater and acidifying depositions of ammonia have been related to the agricultural use of phosphate and nitrogen. The present application levels of these substances—contained in chemical fertilizers and animal manure—are not in accordance with an ecologically sustainable agriculture. The objective of sustainable agriculture can be obtained by developing standards for nutrient application which are in accordance with the carrying capacity of the local natural environment. The author demonstrates how the formulation and implementation of such standards can be realized. In this respect it is suggested that systems for nutrient accounting at farm level are being developed. This would provide necessary information about the magnitude of nutrient losses or emissions to the environment. Nutrient accounting could also serve as a basis for environmental policies containing a mix of charges, taxes, standards, and permits. The proposed approach is illustrated by an application for agriculture in the Netherlands.

In the first contribution of Part III *Angerer* gives attention to the role technology has played in environmental policy. In Germany air pollution by SO_2 and dust has been considerably reduced in recent years. A reduction of NO_x can be supposed in the forthcoming years, mainly because of the decision to enforce the use of catalytic converters in motor cars. But for other emissions and wastes the situation is not similarly favorable. In a recent study, the potential contributions of new environmental technologies to reduce emissions for a number of emissions have been investigated. The results are quite interesting. Though in many cases technologies are available to control emissions, there are technology gaps to be closed in the next years. New technologies will play a significant role in future efforts for preventing and curing environmental damages. Nevertheless, the development of technology has to be accompanied by changes of behavior. In addition, the use of new technology cannot be realized without considerable fiscal incentives.

Simonis investigates the role technology can have when aiming at sustainable development. Information about the issues at stake is of great importance. What are, for instance, the relations between the growth of the GNP and the emissions in different countries? Knowledge on environmental productivity is another important issue, as well as the construction of other indicators of sustainable development. In most cases environmental policy still relies on end-of-pipe technology. To realize a more demanding situation, technology-forcing regulations and economic instruments should be harnessed. A discussion about "green taxes" is important; the environment would especially benefit from "right prices" when trying to develop and promote low-emission technology and products. Some instruments used in Germany are discussed in this context.

Part IV is on restraints and advances in international relations. *Harris* discusses the importance of global institutions for sustainable development. The environmental problems of the late twentieth century have a common characteristic: they are increasingly global in nature. This is the case with problems like the destruction of the ozone layer, climate change, degradation of soils, deforestation, and desertification. These problems pose a threat to the stability of industrialized nations and the growth prospect of the developing countries. There is good reason to predict that these issues will be major factors in shaping economic activity in the next century. In this context, the analysis of the institutional basis of economic activity gains in importance. The concept of sustainable development has emerged as a response to the environmental costs associated with both market and planned economies. For the author the future world economic system will need to be based on a kind of "green Keynesianism," with a social direction of capital flows, demand management, and technological choices, to achieve ecological sustainability.

May elaborates the complicated questions around tropical forests. Improbable as they are, the recently emerging alliances between social movements of forest people and progressive international entrepreneurs investing in new markets for tropical-forest products represent an important phenomenon in the struggle to conserve the tropical forests and the indigenous cultures. This contribution traces trends and probable results of these alliances with regard to both tropical resource conservation and the participation of marginal social groups in national economic development. The trade-offs between capitalist objectives and distributive proposals of forest people illustrate possible contradictions in sustainable development. Nevertheless, these international alliances represent a new, perhaps replicable model of global cooperation to manage threatened common pool resources. Such alliances recognize the forces driving modern capitalism while at the same time respecting the value of conserving indigenous knowledge, irreplaceable gene pools, and pristine systems.

Oodit and *Simonis* give attention to the complicated relations between poverty, environment, and development. Normally, this relation is perceived as a "vicious circle." Poverty leads people to overutilize and overburden their natural environment on which, in the end, all development depends. In reality, however, there are certain structures behind the aggregates of this relation. And those structures should be studied when searching for solutions to escape vicious circles. In this contribution therefore both poverty and environmental problems are structurally defined in order to detect options for development that may simultaneously contribute to alleviate poverty and to prevent further environmental deterioration.

In the last chapter of the book *Simonis* defines the effort to implement a global climate convention as one of mankind's great endeavors—and a challenge to economists, development planners, diplomats, and politicians alike. The inherent linkages between climate and the habitability of the Earth are increasingly well understood and the climate convention signed in Rio de Janeiro could help to ensure that conserving the environment and developing the economy in the future must go hand in hand. One of the specific tasks in the future negotiations is how to share the duties in reducing climate relevant gases, particularly carbon dioxide (CO_2), between the industrial and the developing countries. While the negotiations will be about climate and protection of the atmosphere, they could lead to fundamental changes in energy, forestry, transport and technology policies, and to future development pathways with low greenhouse gas emissions, i.e., sustainable development.

References

Boulding, K. E. (1966). "The Economics of the Coming Spaceship Earth." In H. Jarret (ed.), *Environmental Quality in a Growing Economy*. Baltimore.

Daly, H. E. (ed.) (1973). *Toward a Steady-State Economy*. San Francisco.

—— and J. B. Cobb (1990). *For the Common Good*. London.

Kapp, K. W. (1950). *The Social Costs of Private Enterprise*. Cambridge, MA.

Martinez-Alier, J. (1987). *Ecological Economics. Energy, Environment and Society*. Oxford.

Meadows, D. et al. (1992). *Beyond the Limits*. Post Mills.

Mill, J. S. (1848). *Principles of Political Economy*. Harmondsworth, Middlesex, 1970.

World Commission on Environment and Development (1987). *Our Common Future* (so-called Brundtland-Report). Oxford.

Part I.

Restraints and Advances in Theory

Sustainable Development and the Necessary Integration of Ecological Insights into Economic Theory

Frank J. Dietz and Jan van der Straaten

Introduction

The long-standing concerns of biologists and ecologists for the natural environment and their warnings that it was being seriously threatened by human production and consumption were increasingly heeded by society in the late sixties and the early seventies. These signs of public interest stimulated economists to pay more attention to environmental problems. They observed that what had formerly been free goods, such as clean air, clean surface water, unpolluted soil, silence, and natural beauty, had become scarce. Thus, the problem of "new scarcity" was analyzed by economists like Mishan (1967) and Hueting (1970 and 1974/1980).

However, in the second part of the seventies environmental problems were pushed into the background again. Instead, economic recession, increasing unemployment and the growing financial deficit of the public sector dominated social as well as scientific debates. At the end of the eighties the ever-worsening environmental problems attracted a good deal of attention again; first in national politics and in the media, then by economists. The general impression is that this renewed interest on the part of economists could be of a more permanent nature than it was before.

This gives rise to several questions. To us, the most crucial question is to what extent sustainable development can be adequately analyzed and implemented using existing economic theories. We try to answer this question by reviewing the development of economic thought. While doing so, we come to the conclusion that mainstream economics is only of limited use to analyze environmental problems. This relates to the period in which these theories were developed as well as to the opinions society held concerning the use of natural resources. We conclude the chapter with a sketch of a theoretical economic framework, in which ecological insights are included.

Following Opschoor (1990, p. 11), we define "natural resources" as the materials which can be taken from nature by reaping plants and animals, by mining ores and fossil fuels, and by draining flow resources like water and wind. Moreover, various buffers present in nature neutralize the pressure of human activities on the environment. If that pressure exceeds the buffering capacity, a substantial change in the environment occurs. This means a loss of environmental quality if the change is evaluated negatively. The buffering capacity can also be defined as a stock of environmental goods, which forms part of the natural resources available.

In the past, quite different terms were used to define the potential which nature possesses for human production and consumption. Classical authors often used the term "land" to indicate the production potential of arable land. In using this term they were alluding specifically to the ecological complex which makes agricultural production possible. This is currently expressed by referring to concepts like ecocycles, ecosystems and natural resources. All these concepts can be precisely defined by reference to the existing biological and ecological literature. Although we are of the opinion that ecological concepts used in economic contexts should be carefully defined, in the following we will use them rather loosely. When using the terms nature, environment, natural resources, ecosystems, and ecocycles, we have in mind the opportunities nature offers for human production and consumption.

Classical economic thought

Classical authors had different views in dealing with natural resources. There are authors who were of the opinion that there is no limit to the availability of natural resources. Adam Smith is the most well-known author in this group. He held an optimistic view of the possibilities for production and consumption in the future. This opinion was reinforced by social developments in the time in which he lived. The rapid advancements in science and technology, as well as the economic and military subjection of the New World, served as a confirmation of human capabilities. According to his line of reasoning, the relative scarcity of natural resources would be transformed into a relative affluence. The struggle with nature would be resolved in favor of mankind.

According to Smith, economic development, that is, production growth, originates from both the increasing division of labor and the free play of markets. Division of labor increases labor productivity, subsequently increasing total production and the need for (international) trade. This process should be stimulated by breaking down the social and political barriers erected to stop this development (such as opposition to the concentration of production in factories as well as mercantilist trade policy).

Smith illustrated the growth potential of production with the example of the manufacture of pins. At his time, however, England was much more an agrarian than industrial country, and the possibility of increasing production in the agricultural sector was considerably less than in the industrial sector. Dean and Cole estimated that the production of corn in England and Wales increased in the first half of the nineteenth century by 11 percent and in the second half by 28 percent. In the same periods the population increased by 5 percent and 49 percent, respectively. The increasing tension between the supply of and demand for corn in the second half of the eighteenth century had led to continuously increasing corn prices. While the corn price decreased between 1700 and 1750 by 16 percent, between 1751 and 1800 the price of corn rose by 133 percent (Dean and Cole, 1967).[1]

The continuous tension in the corn market and the resulting upward pressure on corn prices stimulated the nobility to look for ways in which to increase their acreage of arable land (Turner, 1984, pp. 47-51). The English landed nobility succeeded by appropriating formerly common land. English law gave landlords the opportunity to appropriate cultivated common land and to cultivate and to subdivide noncultivated common land. This process is known as the "enclosure movement" (Turner, 1984, p. 11). But in spite of the increase in the acreage of arable land, the growth of agricultural production continued to lag behind the population increase.

This discrepancy influenced classical economists around 1800 strongly; they therefore had a less optimistic world view than Adam Smith. The issue was raised of whether the quantity and the quality of arable land would be sufficient to meet food demand (Malthus, 1798/1982, p. 71,

---

1 The continuous rise of the corn price in the second half of the eighteenth century was constantly higher than the rise of the general price level. Subsequently, the Napoleonic wars pushed the corn price even higher (Dean and Cole, 1967, p. 91; Turner, 1984, p. 48).

pp. 75-6). Economists started looking for an explanation as to why the increase in agricultural production had fallen behind. The result was the simultaneous development of the differential rent theory (to which Ricardo's name was connected in a later period) and the "Law of Diminishing Returns" (Blaug, 1978, pp. 79-80).

The "Law of Diminishing Returns" states that agricultural production increases less than proportionally when additional production factors are applied. Classical economists derived this "law" from the phenomenon that the physical yield of newly cultivated arable land was lower than that of arable land which had been cultivated for some time. The diminishing returns worried the economists, as the population increased during this period at a pace never seen before. Given the poor fertility of waste land still to be cultivated, they predicted a structural shortage of food supplies in the long run.

It is remarkable that classical economists at the beginning of the nineteenth century hardly paid any attention to the possibility of technological improvement for increasing agricultural production (see, for example, Ricardo, 1823/1975, pp. 42-5). They could not conceive of extracting considerably more agricultural products from the ecological cycles than was already being done at this time.

We may conclude that classical economists in the first half of the nineteenth century gave the production factor "natural resources" a central place in their theoretical reasoning. This implies that they had an integrated picture of economic and ecological processes. The limits to production and consumption were thought to be determined by the extent to which raw materials could be extracted from the land (currently we would say from ecological cycles) without adversely affecting agricultural production in the long run. In other words, both nature and economy were seen as parts of the same closed system. The start of the "industrial revolution" at first did not change this view of the character and quantity of the natural resources available. This changed however in the second half of the nineteenth century when economists focused on the market mechanism and used the utility concept as the basis for value.

The industrial revolution

The start of the "industrial revolution" lent increasing importance to the quantitative aspects of the market. The production of goods took on an increasingly industrial character, whereby the necessity for trading these goods on international markets also increased. Due to this, a shift of interest occurred toward the observable economic and technical progress and the application of "positive" science as a tool and as a measuring instrument of that progress ("science as measurement") (Goudzwaard, 1978, p. 101).

In the same period, the concept of value changed. Classical economists held the view that the labor needed for producing a particular good objectively determined the exchange value. Publications by Menger (1871/1968), Jevons (1871/1924), and Walras (1874/1954) heralded, however, a paradigm shift. The satisfaction of individual needs, provided by the goods and services available, in their view was decisive for determining the exchange value.[2]

In the golden age of neoclassical theory (1870-1920), refinements on marginal analysis, the elaboration of the subjectivistic concept of value, and the extension of the general equilibrium analysis vied for attention. The problem of the restricted availability of natural resources, an important issue for classical economists, was no longer relevant for neoclassical economists. Marshall (1890/1925, p. 180), for instance, stated quite explicitly that technical development proved that Malthus was wrong. No attention has been paid, however, to the fact that this much-applauded technical development is based on the large-scale use of "stock" resources, such as iron ore and coal. Before the industrial revolution the actual use of natural resources was based almost exclusively on "flow" resources (muscle power, wind energy, wood, wool). Since then the wealth of a nation has been based increasingly on the use of natural resources with a stock character. This had two effects, closely connected to each other. Firstly, ores and fossil fuels are only present in the earth's crust in limited quantities, i.e., sooner or later these stocks will run out. Secondly, after being used in production and consumption processes, these materials are

---

2 Later, Marshall (1890/1925) connected the concept of value based on the production costs principle with the concept of value based on the principle of marginal utility. According to Marshall goods have value because, on the one hand, they satisfy human needs. On the other hand, the production of goods and services needs sacrifices in the form of the quantities of labor, capital, and natural resources used.

discharged into the ecological cycles, as is the case with metallic compounds, fumes, and synthetics. These are not naturally-occurring substances in ecological cycles, or, in any case, not in such large quantities. The result is the disruption and, at worst, the destruction of ecological cycles. The industrial revolution thus marks the transition from a more or less closed system of production and consumption to an open economic system, characterized by an increasing use of natural resources with a stock character.

As already stated, Marshall paid little attention to natural resources. Though he analyzed the price-making forces of land, ecological processes were only dealt with to the extent that they are expressed in some way or other in the market. For example, he mentions soil fertility while discussing agricultural production processes (Marshall, 1890/1925, p. 146). Moreover, Marshall makes the remarkable observation that there is "a growing difficulty of getting fresh air and light, and in some cases fresh water, in densely populated areas." In addition, he concluded that "the natural beauties of a place of fashionable resort have a direct money value which cannot be overlooked" (Marshall, 1890/1925, p. 166). However, Marshall did not elaborate on these ideas. In the context of the price mechanism as he described it this was hardly possible.

More as a matter of perfecting his theory than as an issue of empirical interest, Marshall introduced the concept of "externality." As suggested by the name, externalities or external economies concern the effects of actions of individual economic agents on the production possibilities of other economic agents, occurring *beyond* the market. As an example Marshall names the unintended influence an expanding company has on the production possibilities of other companies. These last also benefit from the presence of the expanding firm, from the increased level of training and education of the labor force available in the area, the growing supply of workers, or the increasing number of supply companies in the vicinity. This improvement of the investment climate occurred at no cost to the established companies (Marshall, 1890/1925, p. 314). It is striking that Marshall did not take external *dis*economies into account. Apparently, he had no reason to suppose that the process of industrialization would also create economic disadvantages, such as depletion of natural resources and the disruption of the environment.

Neoclassical environmental economics[3]

During the last thirty years of the nineteenth century the subjectivistic concept of value won ground at the expense of the objectivistic concept of value of the classical economists. Scarcity as an *individual* experience was given a much more prominent place in neoclassical theory than in classical theory.[4] Economic analyses were focused on the question of how scarcity relations are expressed in terms of price relations on the market. The choices economic agents have to make under relative scarcity are portrayed as optimization problems. Economic agents in their role as consumers or producers are expected to seek maximum realization of their goals within the usual constraints, such as a limited income or limited production possibilities. This assumption is typical of rational choice theory.

These developments in economic theory had substantial effects on the possibility of analyzing the relative scarcity of natural resources. Firstly, by putting market processes at the center of the theoretical system, unpriced but scarce resources are ignored. Many natural resources are not exchanged in a market, as a result of which they have no price and, hence, do not seem to be scarce in a world in which the market is the central institution.[5] Secondly, in neoclassical theory valuations made by individual

---

3 In this section only a brief review of the relevant neoclassical publications on environmental issues can be provided. This implies that we cannot deal with the problem of the optimal exploitation of nonrenewable resources. Most of these studies fit within the traditional neoclassical starting-points, which are dealt with in this section (see for a recent neoclassical study on nonrenewable natural resources Neher, 1990). We also do not deal with the discussion about the correction of GNP for environmental deterioration (Hueting, 1970; 1974/1980). After having died down at the end of the seventies and the beginning of the eighties, interest in this debate recently increased again (see, among others, Ahmed, Serafy, and Lutz, 1989), and has been supplied with new dimensions (see, among others, Kuik and Verbruggen, 1991). Neither do we discuss the position of the "new institutionalists," who consider the absence, transfer, and distribution of property rights of natural resources the ultimate cause of environmental problems. We cannot discuss models which quantitatively describe the relation between the economic system and the ecological system (see for a recent overview Hafkamp, 1991). All these topics and approaches deserve attention which we, however, cannot give them owing to lack of space.

4 Based on publications as such, for example, by Lionel Robbins (1935), the concept of relative scarcity became the cornerstone of contemporary mainstream economics.

5 It must be said, however, that unpriced forms of scarcity are not totally excluded in mainstream economics (Robbins, 1935; Hennipman, 1945). Nevertheless, before the 1960s only a few economists attempted to analyze the unpriced scarcity of natural resources in a neoclassical framework.

economic agents form the basis for the value of the production factors available (priced and unpriced). Those early critics whom we nowadays would call "ecological economists" held the opinion that considerable ecological risks were being run if the value of nature was seen as being dependent on the (short-term) needs of people. As early as a hundred years ago they argued in favor of using the (objective) amount of energy needed as an indicator of the value of goods and services instead of the (subjective) needs of people (Martinez-Alier, 1991). This ecologically based early critique of the subjectivistic concept of value however passed into oblivion in this century.

Externalities

Pigou was the first neoclassical economist who paid attention to environmental problems based on the concept of external diseconomies or negative externality. In order to indicate the significance of the concept, Pigou distinguished the social from the private product. Between these two a divergence may occur "out of a service or disservice rendered to persons other than the contracting parties" (Pigou, 1920/1952, p. 192). In other words, the actions of market parties may influence the welfare of non-market parties. This influence may be positive or negative.

The examples given by Pigou of "uncompensated services and disservices" partly concern environmental problems, which are so common nowadays. He mentions, for example, the emission of smoke by factories causing negative externalities, "for this smoke in large towns inflicts a heavy uncharged loss on the community, injury to buildings and vegetables, expenses for washing clothes and cleaning rooms, expenses for the provision of artificial light, and in many other ways" (Pigou, 1920/1952, p. 184).

In Pigou's view externalities create a difference between the social and the private cost price of goods and services. For example, in the case of a firm which discharges processing water containing heavy metals into a river, the discharging producer passes a part of his production costs on to society (in this case, the costs of restoring the quality of the river water). In such a situation market prices do not reflect the actual relations of scarcity, as the increased scarcity of clean river water is not taken into consideration in consumer decisions. This means that the factors of production are not optimally allocated.

According to Pigou (1920/1952, p. 192) it is the task of government to ensure that the externalities are passed on to the buyers of products. He proposes the imposition of a levy on activities causing negative externalities, such as a levy on the discharge of polluted waste water, and to subsidize activities producing positive externalities. The installation of purification equipment could, for example, be subsidized. The externality will therefore acquire a shadow price, which economic agents will take into account. Negative externalities will no longer be transferred to society; the optimal allocation of production factors will have been restored.

Despite Pigou's intellectual innovation discussions about the problem of externalities remained in the periphery of economic science, probably due to the very nature of the social problems in the first half of the twentieth century. Two world wars, the stagnation of production and large numbers of unemployed were the prevailing social concerns during this period. In the literature externalities were regarded as a theoretical refinement without much practical significance. Blaug (1978, p. 404) states that there was "a common tendency in the interwar literature to regard external economies as economic curiosa."

Apart from Pigou, King was the most important exception. He analyzed the concept of "social income," known as "national income" since World War II, and concluded that there is only a partial correspondence between a high level of national income and a high level of wealth, because high income in an industrialized society is accompanied by a rising scarcity of environmental goods, which were freely available before. The examples he mentioned are game, fruit, a beautiful landscape, a decreased availability of natural resources like ores and coal, and the disappearance of complete ecological systems caused, for instance, by the cutting down of a forest (King, 1919, pp. 5-49).

After World War II, Fabricant (1947, pp. 50 ff.) brought King's ideas up again, when a discussion started around the issue of how the concept of national income should be operationalized. In his opinion the depletion of fossil and nonfossil natural resources should be included as a cost factor, the level of national income being reduced by the equivalent amount. Denison (1947) and Kuznets (1947), by contrast, were of the opinion that such a correction was unnecessary. They saw nature as an infinite entity, the yields of which could be used without restriction. This discussion between Denison and Kuznets on the one hand and Fabricant on the other hand ended in accordance with the dominant opinion at that time:

Nature is such an infinite entity that depletion of certain natural resources is not an issue to worry about.

At that time, social concern was focused on recovering the production capacity, which had been largely destroyed during the war in Europe, and preventing mass unemployment, which was still fresh in everyone's memory from the economic crisis of the 1930s. Growth of production was thought to be the right means to achieve these goals. The emphasis on production growth also accorded very well with the atmosphere of the Cold War. In both Western Europe and Eastern Europe production growth was a political and military strategy, also serving ideological ends. In this climate there was no chance to discuss environmental problems. Such a discussion could only jeopardize the social concensus of striving toward maximum production growth. As a matter of fact, in the 1950s environmental issues were consciously and unconsciously kept on the periphery of social and scientific debates.

With the acceleration of industrial production in the course of the 1960s the increasing environmental problems that accompanied production growth were experienced by large sections of the population. Air pollution became more and more a normal phenomenon. "Smog" emerged as the unpleasant side effect of traffic; during such smog episodes asthma sufferers had to be evacuated to less polluted areas. Swimming in lakes and rivers became more and more dangerous. As a consequence of pollution and intensive farming practices, certain species of flowers and animals dramatically decreased in number. In spite of the continuous construction of new motorways, roads became regularly congested with motorcars. New industrial and residential areas were developed, criss-crossing rural areas and reducing their space. The enormous growth of the petrochemical industry increased the risk of calamities. In short, a situation arose in which many people were daily experiencing the degeneration of the environment. As a rather late consequence, scientific interest in environmental problems increased at the end of the 1960s or early 1970s.

Economists with a neoclassical background took their lead from Pigou. Situations of nuisance could be satisfactorily described using the concept of "externalities." However, this concept is less useful for analyzing problems concerning the depletion of resources, because depletion is not restricted to a limited number of individuals. Depletion affects society and mankind, and can be perceived as a "public bad." This does not necessarily detract from the relevance of the externality concept as a tool of analysis, but it reinforces Pigou's argument of state intervention. But the collective nature of externalities raises additional questions regarding their valuation.

The depletion of fossil resources is not in all cases an acute phenomenon; it is especially future generations who will be the victim of the current excessive use of fossil resources. And as we are not familiar with the preferences of future generations, the concept of externality loses its analytical strength. In fact, according to the definition of externalities, all effects of current economic activities on future generations could and should be regarded as externalities, since future generations are not involved in any of the present market transactions, although they will enjoy or suffer the effects of these transactions on their production and consumption possibilities. It is for this reason that neoclassical economists were initially inclined to interpret environmental problems only as a pollution issue, excluding the more wide-ranging problems like the depletion of fossil natural resources.

In the second half of the 1960s, economists began to write about environmental issues. These publications were dominated by what is called the Pigovian tradition. One of the most remarkable publications was Mishan's book *The Costs of Economic Growth* (1967). Mishan wanted to demonstrate that the industrial production had been accompanied by a decrease in welfare caused by the increasing number of external diseconomies. In his opinion too much attention is given to quantifiable economic variables in an earlier publication, such as export growth and growth of GNP. Explaining the overvaluation of quantifiable economic variables in an earlier publication, Mishan points to the social pressure for increasing production constantly: "For as we become richer, surely we shall remedy all social evil" (Mishan, 1960). In this context he stated that it is absurd that the right to pollute is given higher priority than the right to live in a healthy environment. His proposal is to protect these amenity rights by civil law. In that case, a producer who initiates or extends a production process which generates pollution first has to buy (additional) pollution rights. If the costs of the necessary pollution rights were so high that the additional production would not pay, it can be concluded that society gives priority to environmental quality. In this way, externalities can be completely internalized in conformance with the Pigovian tradition, and in doing so, the optimal allocation of factors of production would be restored.

There is, however, a certain inconsistency in Mishan's approach. Frequently he argues for a reallocation of production factors, for which he thinks of as creating incentives to adapt individual behavior via the price mechanism. Elsewhere, however, he states correctly that in many cases it is not possible to quantify external diseconomies, that is, to find an expression in money terms. When trying to bring this reality to economic theory, he gets stuck in fictitious and highly stylized arithmetical examples from welfare economics.

Mishan's doubts concerning the possibility of internalizing externalities can also be found elsewhere in the literature. Hueting (1974/1980, p. 185), for example, after a thorough attempt to quantify the national effects of environmental deterioration concluded that

> the crucial question "What is nature worth to us?" cannot be answered by means of the instruments available to us. But ... at the same time another question remains unanswered, namely "What is the worth of goods that are produced and consumed at the expense of the environment?" For when the value of the environment cannot be determined in the conflict between production and environment, the market price of produced goods may no longer be accepted as an indicator of the economic value of these goods.

Here, Hueting touches upon a fundamental shortcoming of the neoclassical approach. The fixation on priced forms of scarcity, that is, scarcity manifested in the tension between supply and demand on markets, more or less excludes the unpriced forms of scarcity.

This problem has also been recognized by other authors. Goudzwaard, for example, raised the question of whether economists should deal with unpriced scarcity. His answer is affirmative, since economic theory would lose its predictive capability if the coherence between priced and unpriced scarcity were excluded (Goudzwaard, 1970, p. 106). He suggests considering the problem of unpriced scarcity an element of *economic policy*, where other subjective elements can already be found. Doing so, however, would exclude the production factor natural resources from *economic theory*. In our view, this position can hardly be defended, given the long tradition among economists of distinguishing three equivalent factors of production. There are no fundamental grounds for excluding either labor, capital or natural resources from economic theory.

Obstacles to the internalization of externalities

The neoclassical strategy for abating environmental problems boils down to the internalization of externalities. The idea is that after internalization the preferences for *all* goods and services, including those that cannot be supplied via the market, can be expressed. However, internalization meets with fundamental obstacles. These obstacles will be discussed here with the intention of evaluating the strengths and weaknesses of neoclassical environmental economics.

The first fundamental problem concerns the *benefits* of avoided environmental damage. These benefits should be weighed against the *costs* of avoiding environmental damage. In monetary terms, estimates for the latter can be made easily and quite accurately. For example, the costs of decreasing the pollution level of a river which contains heavy metals from the effluents of firms along that river equal the costs of purifying the polluted river plus the costs of adapting the polluting production processes. Problems arise, however, when the benefits of a clean river have to be estimated. Some benefits can be expressed in market prices, such as the lower costs of producing drinking water and the higher proceeds from fishing. Many benefits, however, cannot be expressed in market prices, simply because there are no markets for public goods such as ecosystems and landscapes. What, for example, is the price of a square mile of wetlands? In conclusion, by weighing the known costs against the partly unknown benefits there is a considerable risk that the costs of environmental measures will be overestimated and not undertaken.

In the absence of markets, other evaluation methods are needed to estimate the benefits. In the last decade or so, a great deal of research has been done on alternative evaluation methods, including "hedonic pricing" and "contingent valuation"; surveys can be found in Freeman (1985), Anderson and Bishop (1986), Pearce and Turner (1990, pp. 141-58). Although some progress has been made, these methods only *indicate* individual preferences for a particular environmental quality. It is, for example, not clear whether the contingent valuation method underestimates the "willingness to pay" for a particular environmental quality (Hoehn and Randall, 1987) or overestimates it (Crocker and Shogren, 1991). Moreover, the crucial problem of how to aggregate individual preferences into a collective statement cannot be solved satisfactorily. Attempts at aggregation meet with problems of cardinal measuring of utility and of interpersonal comparisons of utility.

The second fundamental problem is that the preferences of future generations for natural resources and the environment are unknown. The depletion of nonrenewable natural resources (such as fossil fuels and minerals), the overexploitation of renewable natural resources (such as the cutting down of tropical forests), and the irreversible pollution of ecosystems (by chemical and nuclear wastes) indisputably reduce the "stock" of natural resources available for future generations. It is not possible to deal with this problem satisfactorily using currently known evaluation methods. Consequently, the evaluation of natural resources on the basis of the preferences of individual economic agents is myopic.

Where the preferences of individual economic agents are not or only partly known, the preferences of chosen policy-makers are often used to evaluate the environment and the natural resources available.[6] Of course, this offers politicians the opportunity to tighten up or to relax environmental standards according to their own preferences. Such high-handed behavior could cause them electoral losses at a later date if the environmental standards they choose deviate considerably from the preferences for environmental quality of the voters. Public choice literature shows, however, that there are certain circumstances (such as the short memory of voters, incomplete information, and coalition formation after elections) which would leave politicians a certain degree of latitude to act on their "own responsibility" (van den Doel and van Velthoven, 1990, pp. 99-163; Mueller, 1989, pp. 277-86, 344-7).

On the basis of estimated preferences of citizens for the quality of the environment or on the basis of their own preferences politicians could design an environmental policy consisting of levies on polluting activities and subsidies on environment improving activities. Such changes in relative prices could induce economic agents to altered behavior and to switch to less polluting technology.

However, the desired altering of behavior is not guaranteed, because politicians are still not familiar with the *real* preferences of the economic agents for environmental improvements as well as their *real* interests in environmental degeneration. A levy on petrol, for example, imposed with the aim of substantially decreasing car use, will hardly have the desired effect if politicians underestimate the willingness to pay for car use. The risk of incorrectly assessed preferences and, hence, of ineffective environmental policy measures, seems at least rather high.

Attempts have been made to resolve this problem with the help of econometric research. When the price fluctuations from preceding years are combined with the generated changes in supply and demand, the supply and demand elasticities of goods and services that cause pollution

---

6 In the welfare economics literature this is called the "Bergsonian approach." Because of the above-mentioned problems with interpersonal comparison of utility, social welfare is assumed to be dependent on the interpersonal valuations of utility by policy-makers (Boadway and Bruce, 1984).

in production or consumption can be calculated. The decrease in pollution desired by politicians can then be converted into necessary changes in particular production and consumption patterns. Subsequently, the necessary price increases or price reductions can be calculated. These price alterations could be put in effect by means of levies and subsidies.

This strategy, unfortunately, is more attractive in theory than it is in reality. In a country such as the Netherlands, for instance, the emission reductions required for a sustainable development vary from 70 percent to 90 percent (Langeweg, 1988). If such large adjustments in production and consumption are to be accomplished by means of levies alone, the prices of relatively polluting goods and services will have to increase dramatically, often several times their actual prices. No doubt, price increases of this magnitude will change the preferences of economic agents and, hence, change the supply and demand elasticities of goods and services. If these elasticities become subject to substantial changes, politicians lack essential information concerning the behavioral adaptation that may be expected *after* the imposition of levies.

Since Pigou several variants of economic instruments have been developed, such as deposit systems and marketable pollution rights. These instruments are aimed at influencing individual behavior indirectly by using financial incentives. In particular, marketable pollution rights are being increasingly advocated in economic literature. One of the advantages mentioned is that the environmental effects of marketable pollution rights are not as uncertain as those of levies (Baumol and Oates, 1988, pp. 178-80; Nentjes, 1990, pp. 159-65; Pearce and Turner, 1990, p. 115). The maximum amount of polluting emissions which politicians consider "permissible" are sold to the highest bidder in small, well-defined emission units. If strict enforcement is practised, total emissions in the "bubble" will not exceed the previously specified ceiling (environmental quality goal).

At first sight, the environmental effects of a system of marketable pollution rights would seem to be entirely predictable. On further consideration, however, they appear less sure. Especially, undesirable regional concentrations of emissions can hardly be prevented (Baumol and Oates, 1988, p. 184; Pearce and Turner, 1990, p. 116). In addition, it is difficult to see why the previously mentioned emission reductions of 70 to 90 percent needed to establish ecologically sustainable production and consumption processes should be more easily attained, that is, with less social resistance, using marketable pollution rights than by imposing regulatory levies.[7]

To summarize, the preferences of economic agents are not known (future generations) or only partly known (current generation). This knowledge is, however, indispensable for the design of an effective environmental policy based on the Pigovian internalization method.[8]

Ecological uncertainties

Internalization of externalities thus appears to be difficult, because we lack sufficient knowledge concerning individual preferences. But even in the hypothetical case that we were familiar with all individual preferences and, subsequently, able to aggregate them into a collective decision on the desired environmental quality, this would still not preclude ecological disasters. This problem is linked to a fundamental limitation of rational choice theory in the context of environmental issues.

In general, the optimization strategy of rational choice theory implies that the production factors available—in most cases only labor and capital are implicitly meant—are allocated according to the preferences of the economic agents, satisfying as many needs as possible. The same strategy applies to the management of the natural resources available. The diagnosis is simple: The present allocation of natural resources is not optimal, as is demonstrated by the unwanted environmental deterioration. The neoclassical remedy is to restore optimal allocation by price alterations. However, there is doubt as to whether this optimization philosophy is feasible for the management of the "ecological utilization space" (Opschoor, 1987).

A striking example of this is forests dying on a large scale as a result of acid rain. One of the most important causes of acid rain is the emission of large quantities of sulphur dioxide (SO_2). Some 20 years ago, in Europe

---

7 It is not possible to elaborate here on the pros and cons of marketable pollution rights. For economic contributions see, for example, Baumol and Oates (1988, pp. 155-296); Nentjes (1990); Pearce and Turner (1990, pp. 84-119). For a legal contribution on the choice of economic instruments in environmental policy see, e.g., Peeters (1991).

8 Although the debate regarding the problem of which instrument is the most efficient is not unimportant and attracts much attention in economic literature, we will not discuss this issue. Here the central point is the integration of ecological insights into economic theory, so the question is how far current economic theory provides the possibility of *analyzing* environmental problems.

first measures were taken to reduce the harmful effects of SO_2. These measures included the switch to natural gas and nuclear energy and, especially, the construction of tall smokestacks. It seemed that adequate measures had been taken, because air pollution in urban areas and industrial regions did decrease. However, the tall smokestacks have only dispersed the acidifying substances over large parts of Europe. Acid deposition beyond the industrial areas increased rapidly, deteriorating forests especially in Central Europe and Scandinavia. The acidification of ecosystems was probably foreseeable. Biologists warned at an early stage that tall smokestacks would at best shift the problem elsewhere. Society, however, was easily able to dismiss these warnings as exaggerations, because it was not known for certain what the effects on nature would be.

Another example is the extensive ecological damage caused by the use of DDT and other persistent agricultural pesticides. The emission of carbon dioxide (CO_2) will lead to unpleasant surprises later, when the effects of climate change become significant. The same holds for the relation between the emission of CFCs and the stratospheric ozone layer. From these and other serious examples we can see that again and again the effects of human (industrial) actions on nature are underestimated, minimized or even neglected.

If the effects of so many interventions in and influences on nature are not sufficiently known or are consistently disregarded, an optimum use of natural resources, as neoclassical analyses and policy recommendations presuppose, becomes a problem. The point is that neoclassical optimization requires insight into the effects of alternative actions on nature (or into the availability of natural resources) with a probability bordering on certainty or at least with a probability that can be calculated using the theory of probabilities. The former is the familiar assumption of the existence of fully-informed agents whereby the problem of inadequate ecological knowledge is simply neglected. The latter seems more advanced, but still needs far better ecological knowledge than we generally have (cf. Drepper and Manson, 1990).

In general, processes in nature, and hence human interventions in these processes, appear to be hardly predictable for at least three reasons. First, synergetic effects increase the impact of separate emissions on the environment. For example, the combined impact of the acidifying substances SO_2, NO_x, NH_3, and O_3 on plant growth is substantially more severe than the (linear) total of the impacts of each of these substances (Tonneijck, 1981). Second, thresholds are very common in ecosystems.

Again acidification serves as an excellent example. The sudden acceleration of the deterioration of forests and the subsequent dying-off of large parts of European forests at the beginning of the 1980s came for most people (including scientists!) like a bolt from the blue. It appeared that the buffering capacity of the soil had protected trees from serious damage for decades. Once saturation point had been reached, acidifying substances can damage trees considerably and kill them within a couple of years. Third, many emissions have a delayed effect on the environment. It may take decades, for example, before the nitrogen from manure and chemical fertilizers is washed from the top soil into deeper layers, causing severe nitrate pollution of the groundwater. Even if nitrogen leakages into the groundwater could be prevented as of today, nitrate pollution of groundwater will continue to increase considerably for decades to come.

In short, synergetic effects, thresholds, and delayed reactions cloud the issue of the relations between emissions and environmental deterioration. As a result of human actions ecosystems change far more capriciously than economists normally assume. The neoclassical approach to optimizing the use of the natural resources available is unsatisfactory as long as we cannot accurately assess the quantity of natural resources we have. In other words, we cannot optimize our "ecological utilization space" without knowing the concrete limits that must not be crossed if irreversible effects on nature are to be avoided.

Marxist-oriented approaches

One conclusion to be drawn from the preceding section is that for a long time neoclassical economists neglected the "third production factor." The question arises of whether alternative approaches in economic theory have dealt more adequately with the effects of production and consumption processes on the availability and quality of natural resources. Marxist-oriented authors have been the keenest critics of mainstream economic theory. Therefore in the following we will examine this "natural" antipode of neoclassical thought for its sensitivity to and treatment of environmental problems.[9]

---

9   We will not discuss institutionalist analyses of environmental problems here. For
    such an approach see, for example, Söderbaum (1987) and Swaney (1987a and

Unfortunately, it must be stated that during the last hundred years Marxist and Marxist-oriented authors have paid even less attention to environmental problems than neoclassical authors. K. William Kapp is the most important exception to this rule.[10] As early as 1950 he pointed out the great economic significance of environmental problems. Kapp stated that the capitalist mode of production is accompanied by a large number of adverse effects. In addition to phenomena already mentioned in the literature, such as unemployment, accidents in factories, and the loss of know-how caused by new developments in technology, he described air pollution, erosion of the soil, the deterioration of flora and fauna, and the wasting of energy as negative effects generated by the capitalist mode of production.[11] He stated that companies try to transfer as many of their production costs as possible to other economic agents or to society as a whole (Kapp, 1950, p. 200).

Hueting was one of the first who gave comprehensive attention to the work of Kapp. The way he evaluated Kapp's work illustrates the contrast between the neoclassical approach and Kapp's viewpoint. According to Hueting (1974/1980, p. 72), Kapp however presents only a simplistic view of the environmental problem,

> in which the business firm acts as a kind of exploiter, loading the burdens of environmental deterioration on the shoulders of its employees, the consumers and society as a whole. In my opinion it is inconceivable in the social order of today that each of these categories would passively accept these burdens unless there were for those groups compensatory advantages in the form of products at a price considerably lower than if the external effects were to be included in that price.

In contrast with this view Kapp stated that ". . . the more the social costs of private enterprises increase in significance and size, the more society will

---

1987b). We made some comments on this approach elsewhere (Dietz and van der Straaten, 1992).

10   One may argue that Kapp is much more an institutionalist than a Marxist author, as institutional issues are central in his work. However, with respect to the analysis of environmental problems Kapp tends to a Marxist position. His critique of the neoclassical approach of environmental problems is part of his criticism of the capitalist mode of production in which the controversy between labor and capital plays a dominant role.

11   Kapp calls all these adverse effects "social costs." It is clear that Kapp's definition of social costs is much broader than the concept of externalities. Not only the effects of economic activities on parties not involved in the market transactions, but *all* failures of the capitalist mode of production are incorporated in this concept.

become aware of them, and will learn to think of value in non-monetary terms" (Kapp, 1950, p. 200; translation by the authors). Instead of learning to think in non-monetary terms, Hueting wants to quantify the costs of environmental disruption in monetary terms.

Apart from Kapp, Marxists hardly paid any attention to environmental problems. This is not surprising, as the work of Marx deals—first and foremost—with the exploitation of labor by capital. In handbooks accepted by Marxists hardly anything can be found that could be called a theory of the environment or natural resources. The fixation upon the exploitation of labor had the effect of making environmental problems seem irrelevant. In the 1960s and 1970s, most Marxists regarded environmental problems as artificially constructed by bourgeois economists to distract attention from the class struggle. For this reason Marxists had no appreciation of, for example, the reports to the Club of Rome.

This attitude, however, became untenable. All sections of the population suffer to some extent from increasing environmental problems. Both capitalists and workers have to deal with or suffer from problems like acid rain, nuclear waste, holes in the ozone layer, climate change, pollution of ground and surface water, and so forth. Ultimately, these important problems could no longer be neglected by Marxist authors. Moreover, discontent with the deterioration of nature led to the rise of environmental interest groups. Forced by this social development, Marxists have recently started to develop a position on environmental problems.

Initially, the orthodox approach dominated analyses of environmental problems. This approach is, in a nutshell, based on Marx's idea that the capitalist mode of production destroys the basis of life, while a socialist mode of production would not have these failings (Marx, 1867/1977, pp. 474-5). Authors in this orthodox tradition suggest that man's alienation from nature has the same root cause as man's alienation from labor. The abolition of the alienation of human labor by transferring the control of the means of production to the working class will, at the same time and more or less automatically, put an end to man's alienation from nature and the environment (cf. Heise and Hembold, 1977, pp. 22-38; Romören and Romören, 1978, pp. 35-47; Krusewitz, 1978, pp. 81-108; Gärtner, 1979, p. 70).

This literature suggests that Marx had a comprehensive framework within which the analysis of environmental problems and the depletion of natural resources had been foreseen. However, this is not the case. An in-depth perception of the relation between nature and society hardly was an issue in the period in which Marx lived. The rise of the industrial revolution and the accompanying technological development generated a widely-held belief in the potential of technical progress. This idea can also be found in the work of Marx; the development of the forces of production were, in his view, a necessary condition for realizing a socialist society. Marx did not develop systematic ideas regarding the relation between nature and society; sporadic remarks on this matter, however, are scattered throughout his work.

Marx held the opinion that nature and labor are two components of a dialectical unity and paid a great deal of attention to the value of labor (Marx, 1867/1977, p. 172; 1844/1964, p. 112). But what value is derived from nature—the other component of the dialectical unity—remains obscure. He only stated (should we better say: he even stated) that nature has no value in itself. Natural materials acquire value only by their mingling with human labor: "The purely natural material in which human labour is objectified, to the extent that it is merely a material that exists of labour, has no value" (Marx, 1857-1858/1973, p. 366).

Marx focused on the contradictions between labor and capital. Analyzing these contradictions he used, among other things, the labor theory of value originating from Ricardo. Using this theory gave Marx the opportunity to demonstrate and criticize the mechanism of the creation of surplus value and the exploitation of labor. It also led, however, to a split between economy and nature. Hence, nature appears to be no longer a source of value in Marx's theory. This result must be attributed particularly to the assumption implicit in the labor theory of value that the resources nature offers are inexhaustible (Immler, 1983a and 1983b). As an unconscious result of using the labor theory of value Marx discarded nature as a source of value, although this is contrary to his own starting-point, i.e., that labor and nature are two components of a dialectical unity and thus *both* sources of value. It is not clear whether Marx was aware of this inconsistency, but it is certainly connected to the almost exclusive attention he paid to the labor factor.

The division between man and nature in Marx's theories has strongly influenced the view of Marxist authors concerning environmental problems. Harmsen states that this explains why Marxists have for so long refused to recognize the social importance of environmental problems. Marxists continued to take for granted that the abolition of classes in society would automatically generate a rational environmental management (Harmsen, 1974, p. 15).

At the end of the 1970s the first critical remarks about the orthodox approach were heard among Marxist authors. Several attempts were made to construct alternative theories about nature and the environment using Marxist starting-points (cf. Ullrich, 1979; Ernst Pörksen, 1984; Govers, 1988). One can conceive of concepts like "exchange value" and "use value" to describe the overexploitation of the environment. However, these attempts are not really convincing, and this can mainly be attributed to the fact that Marx' theories lack sufficient categories for analyzing current environmental problems.[12]

Summarizing, we may say that there is no Marxist theory specifically dealing with the "ecological question." But even if such a theory existed, it would not give us an answer to the crucial question as to the extent to which the pollution of the environment should be reduced. Until now, neither neoclassical nor Marxist theories have offered a satisfactory solution to this problem. This is partly due to the origin of these theories.

Both neoclassical and Marxist theories originate in the second half of the nineteenth century, describing and analyzing the same market processes. Neoclassical economists emphasized the issue of efficient use of the production factors labor and capital, while Marxist economists stressed the unfair distribution of power and income between labor and capital, resulting from the same market processes where, according to neoclassical economists, an optimal allocation of production factors is realized. The structure of both range of ideas are such that the level of socially acceptable environmental deterioration (or quality) cannot be determined. In addition, determining the borders of the "ecological utilization space" is hampered by a lack of knowledge about essential ecological relations, as already discussed in the previous section.

Sustainable development as a starting-point

The preceding sections have shown that alternative theoretical concepts are needed. In neoclassical theory no special attention is paid to natural resources. Too much reliance is placed on the idea that the use of natural resources is a normal optimization problem. Internalization of externali-

---

12 Elsewhere we have presented a more comprehensive review of Marxist analyses of environmental problems (Dietz and van der Straaten, 1990).

ties is the key to an optimum use of the natural resources available. In Marxist theories there is also too much dependence on ancient doctrines, in which it is assumed that the quantity and quality of natural resources are constant factors. In contrast to classical economists of the nineteenth century, regarding the availability of natural resources as an explicable variable, twentieth century economists consider the environment as a datum (neoclassicals) or as a constant factor (neomarxists). This change of attitude is closely connected to the switch from the use of natural resources with a flow character to the dominating use of natural resources with a stock character. This switch enabled economists to push nature as a factor of production to the periphery of economic theory and to focus attention almost exclusively on the analysis of the market mechanism. The current environmental crisis demonstrates that this attitude is untenable.

Various alternative starting-points for the adaption of economic theory have been suggested in the literature. Boulding (1966) has the concept of "spaceship earth" in mind, Goudzwaard (1974) proposes to economize within the limits set by nature, Sachs (1976, 1984) advocates ecological development, Söderbaum (1980, 1982) suggests ecological imperatives for governmental policies, Opschoor (1987; 1990) wants to keep economic activities within the ecological utilization space, and Brundtland, *et al.* (1987) opt for the by now famous concept of sustainable development. All these views have in common that ecologically bounded possibilities for using natural resources are taken as a starting-point for the development and refinement of economic theory. In this respect we have returned to the viewpoint of the classical economists of the beginning of the nineteenth century.

Sustainable development is a normative concept. Indeed, the heart of the argument is about a fair distribution of natural resources among different generations, as well as among the populations of the First, the Second, and the Third World of our own generation. Though the concept is given massive support throughout the world, particularly since the UN Conference on Environment and Development in Rio de Janeiro in June 1992, the realization of sustainable development is highly problematic (Opschoor, 1990). One of the major problems is the operationalization of the concept. In this respect many questions arise. What are, for instance, the limits nature sets to human production and consumption processes? Are these limits related to current ecological quality, which has already vastly deteriorated, or should we aim at an improved ecological quality? At what pace can we use stocks of exhaustible natural resources if we employ a maximum recycling of materials? Such questions can hardly be answered on the basis of current knowledge.

In our view, the character of the relations between the ecological system and the economic system determines the direction in which answers to these questions are to be sought. Particularly, a closer look at ecological cycles (or ecocycles) is needed. For too long production and consumption processes have been portrayed as completely closed cycles, suggesting they are independent of ecological processes. If ecological insights are to be integrated into economic theory—and we think this to be necessary in order to grant nature a better position in economic theory—the traditionally closed character of economic cycles in economic theory has to be opened up.[13]

In ecology, the notion "ecocycle" describes the character of ecological processes. In general, an examination is made of the course taken by various substances in an ecological process, at what point they accumulate or decompose and how substances get blocked in the ecocycle. The description of an ecological process is complete only if the flow of information and energy in the ecosystem is also indicated. Without energy from the sun the system would not function. Furthermore, some sort of information must be present in the ecosystem on the basis of which events can take place within the system. This information causes, for example, the decomposition of organic matter or the generation of new cells. Each economic model in which an attempt is made to describe how production and consumption could be fitted into ecological processes should take these relationships into account.

Figure 1 helps to distinguish between several kinds of effects of human production and consumption on the ecological system.[14] A system of human production and consumption is based, among other things, on the use of natural resources from ecological cycles—the active part of the ecosystem. Agricultural production provides a good example of this relation. Organic matter is formed under the influence of the sun and serves as

---

13 The following paragraphs are based on Dietz and van der Straaten (1988) and van der Straaten (1990, pp. 103-16).

14 Ecological systems can be described on a global level (higher air layers, including the ozone layer) where processes regulating radiation and temperature are located, on a continental level (continents and oceans) where processes take place, such as air and ocean currents, on a fluvial level (large river basins and coastal seas) comprising various processes related to the water ecology, on a regional level (landscapes) involving various processes within the soil, and on a local level (work and living environment) dealing with the environment made by man.

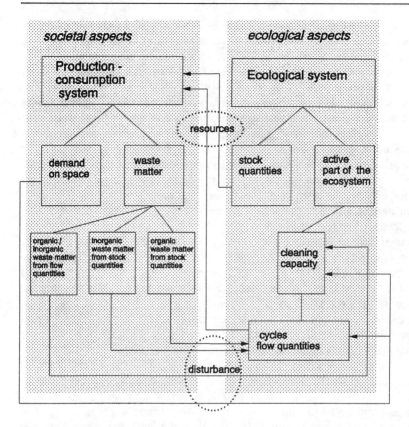

Figure 1:   The relationship between the system of production and consumption and the ecosystem

food for animals and humans. These natural resources are, in theory, inexhaustible and therefore flowing forever. In contrast, the fossil natural resources are exhaustible as is natural oil. The hydrocarbons of which it is composed are denoted as "stock quantities," because the stock of natural oil available in the earth's crust does not increase within a human time horizon. The fossil part of the ecological system is hardly, if at all, affected by the flow of waste products originating from the economic system. Pollution of the environment occurs in that part of the ecological system where cycles function. These cycles can be disturbed by the discharge of waste products.

There is a great difference between the dumping of organic materials and the dumping of inorganic and synthetic materials into the ecocycles. Organic materials are normal elements of functioning ecocycles, while inorganic and synthetic substances are foreign to them. Among the latter are the waste products from fossil resources. When dumped into the ecocycles they cause disturbances, even in low concentrations, because there are no mechanisms available to process or to decompose these waste products. On the other hand, the dumping of decomposable organic matter does not necessarily disturb the ecocycles. Such matter is already part and parcel of the ecocycles and can be decomposed by bacteria in the normal way. However, if too large quantities of decomposable organic matter are dumped into, for example, surface water, the water's self-cleaning capacity can be impaired to the extent that only stinking, rotting and deoxidized expanses of water remain. Similarly, pollution from fossil matter is worse than pollution from organic, decomposable matter. Whereas the latter occurs locally and may be neutralized after a certain time, pollution from indecomposable stock matter is irreversible. It is almost impossible to restore the cycle in this case. Substances foreign to ecocycles accumulate, causing long-term effects on the environment and across a large area. Thus, when heavy metals are discharged into surface water, the flora and fauna in it will be seriously affected. Heavy metals do not just disappear when the organisms die, but accumulate in the ecocycles.

Attention has not yet been paid to one category of effects on nature by human actions: the use of land. Yet this very seriously violates the ecocycles. The process began when people settled in one place, took up agriculture and began to change the natural layer of vegetation. In Europe the process has reached a point where hardly anything of the original vegetation is left. Modifications in the layer of vegetation do not necessarily lead to irreversible changes in the ecocycles, but they do interfere with the cyclical process. Further attacks on the natural vegetation by the building of houses and factories, the construction of roads and other material infrastructures have seriously affected the ecosystem. Their effect, however, is different from that of the discharge of waste products, in that they threaten the functioning of the ecocycles faster and more directly. For instance, ecocycles may be changed if natural woodland is turned into arable land or cut back because of road construction.

The box "production and consumption system" in *Figure 1* represents the human impulse to exploit natural resources. The price mechanism only partly informs individuals about the quality and availability of natural resources. The recommendation made by (neoclassical) economists to remedy this lack of information by price alterations using levies and subsidies appears to be hardly feasible (see above). This implies that the lack of information about the environmental effects of economic activities continues to exist. A (Pareto) optimum exploitation of nature seems to be hardly possible due to the unpredictable effects of human activities on nature. Under these circumstances there is a real danger that the "burden of proof" for the ecological sustainability of human activities rests squarely with nature. That being so, environmental problems are likely to increase rather than decrease.[15]

In our view, existing mainstream economic theory is not the proper starting-point for the development of theories concerning environmental problems. We would do better to take the insights of ecologists as a starting-point, despite the often imperfect nature of those insights. It is this very uncertainty concerning what and how much we can take from nature without creating irreversible effects, which should make us act carefully.

Concluding remarks

Aiming at an ecologically sustainable society, a prerequisite is to use the ecocycles in such a way that their functioning is not damaged irreversibly. It is not easy to operationalize this starting-point. In any case, the discharge of substances which are foreign to or rarely occur in the ecocycles and are mainly extracted from the stocks of fossil natural resources should be minimized or, even better, stopped. This imperative implies that the speed at which fossil natural resources are depleted needs to be considerably reduced by converting radically to the recycling of minerals and synthetics. However, it is impossible to recycle all materials completely. During production, consumption and recycling processes a part of the materials is always going to be "lost," that is, end up in ecocycles. Technological development should be directed towards a continuous decrease in the percentage of "lost" materials. Ultimately, the sustainable solution is to convert completely to renewable resources. Renewable resources can be

---

15   This is one of the explanations for the lack of linkages between mainstream environmental economics and current environmental policy (see Dietz and Van der Straaten, 1992).

extracted from the—on a human timescale—ever-functioning ecocycles (provided that exploitation is careful), and subsequently, after being used in production and consumption processes, can be disposed of without disturbing ecocycles (provided that the carrying capacity is not exceeded). The same recommendation applies to the extraction and use of energy; fossil stocks of oil, natural gas and coal will be depleted sooner or later. This means that a complete conversion to the use of energy derived from flow quantities is inevitable in the long run.

The process of conversion to an ecologically sustainable mode of production will have considerable effects on various social relations. In any case, sustainable development will attack historically vested interests. Partly owing to the market process a situation has come about which is far away from sustainability.

Unfortunately, one cannot expect that the reversing of the damage to the environment will be a spontaneous process. For the creation of a sustainable society there will be a strong need for collective strategies and decisions, resulting in a strict environmental policy. Decisions that effectively stimulate a sustainable development will not be received with great acclaim by those who privately benefit from the current degradation of the environment. Well-organized groups of polluting producers like the petrochemical industry, the transport sector and agriculture will certainly oppose strict environmental measures. In general, however, these interest groups do not contest the aim of sustainability but the pace at which sustainability is to be realized.[16]

Basically, there should be no limits set to the choice of instruments for attaining sustainability. In our view, the price mechanism can play an important role, although a different one than in neoclassical theories. Sustainable development implies that limiting conditions for production and consumption processes have to be formulated. Such limiting conditions cannot simply be derived from the internalization of externalities, as was demonstrated in previous sections. We should instead derive them from public debates and democratic collective decisions based on ecological insights. Subsequently, both legal and economic instruments will have to be used to steer all activities in society onto a sustainable course.

---

16 Recent debates, political decisions and the influences of interest groups concerning the reduction of acidifying emissions in specific sectors are described and analyzed in van der Straaten (1990 and 1991; especially oil refineries and electric power plants); Dietz, van der Straaten, and van der Velde (1991; traffic); Dietz and Hoogervorst (1991) as well as Dietz and Termeer (1991; agriculture).

Labor and capital will offer fierce resistance to the determination of ecological limiting conditions, especially when their short-term interests are jeopardized. In fact, a social struggle concerning the distribution of the "ecological utilization space" among the various production and consumption processes may be the result. In this social struggle national and local government will play a mayor role, but new institutions may have to be developed (cf. Harris, in this volume).

The picture sketched in the preceding paragraphs deviates from the ideas of economists such as Goudzwaard, reasoning back from *economic policy* towards *economic theory*. In this line of reasoning, the subjective element is assigned to economic policy in an attempt to keep economic theory free from value judgments. By doing so, however, a fundamental shortcoming of neoclassical theory is ignored, namely that the price mechanism lies at the center of neoclassical economics, relegating environmental deterioration to the periphery of economic thought. This is demonstrated by the use of the term "externality" for effects of production and consumption on the environment. One should be aware of this one-sided orientation of neoclassical economics, as well as the consequences for environmental policy based on this approach.

What is needed, instead, is an integration of ecological insights into economic theory. Despite the promising efforts of some authors to do so, adequate incorporation of natural resources in economic theory will not be an easy task. This holds particularly if mainstream economists continue to see the economy as a system operating independently of nature. If an environmental problem arises, its analysis and the development of an abatement strategy is left to the specialists in the subdiscipline of environmental economics. All critical comments on the nonincorporation of natural resources in economic theory can be neutralized by referring to this subdiscipline. In this way an alibi is created to maintain the closed system view.

The consequences of an adequate incorporation of natural resources into economic theory can hardly be overestimated. For instance, the traditional system of national accounts would be untenable in the long run, as it is based on measuring economic variables revealed almost exclusively on the market. Such a system cannot give any insight into the unpriced scarcity of various natural resources.[17] Also, cost-benefit analysis is only

---

17 Here we encounter the debate concerning the possibility of a green GNP (see for a recent state-of-the-art overview Ahmad, Serafy, and Lutz, 1989). However, attempts to calculate a green GNP meet with the fundamental problems discussed

partially useful for environmental problems as long as important benefits (e.g., environmental quality) have no market price. As a third example, the expression of the national debt in dollars without taking into account the national debt caused by the deterioration of natural resources is not an adequate indicator of the solvency of a country. Furthermore, accounts concerning industrial relations should no longer neglect the position of employees in industries which destroy or irreversibly affect the environment. And finally, the concept of the "optimal growth path," as defined in macroeconomics, should be regarded as a nonissue if the effects of environmental factors are not included in the concept.

To summarize, developing environmental economics is not enough; an adequate integration of natural resources into economic theory requires the rewriting of mainstream economics.

References

Ahmad, Y. J., S. E. Serafy and E. Lutz (1989). *Environmental Accounting for Sustainable Development*. Washington, D.C.

Anderson, G. D. and R. C. Bishop (1986). "The Valuation Problem." In D. W. Bromley (ed.), *Natural Resource Economics. Policy Problems and Contemporary Analysis*. Boston.

Baumol, W. J. and W. E. Oates (1988). *The Theory of Environmental Policy*. 2nd edition. Cambridge, MA.

Blaug, M. (1978). *Economic Theory in Retrospect*. Cambridge, MA.

Boadway, R. and N. Bruce (1984). *Welfare Economics*. Oxford.

Boulding, K. (1966). "The Economics of the Coming Spaceship Earth." In H. Jarret (ed.), *Environmental Quality in a Growing Economy*. Baltimore, pp. 3-14.

Crocker, T. D. and J. F. Shogren (1991). "Preference Learning and Contingent Valuation Methods." In F. J. Dietz, F. van der Ploeg, and J. van der Straaten (eds.), *Environmental Policy and the Economy*. Amsterdam, pp. 77-93.

Deane, P. and W. A. Cole (1967). *British Economic Growth 1688-1959: Trends and Structure*. 2nd edition. Cambridge, MA.

Denison, E. F. (1947). In *Studies in Income and Wealth*, Vol. 10. Conference on Research in Income and Wealth. New York, pp. 77 ff.

above. In our view, a much more promising initiative in this context is the attempt to develop indicators of sustainable development, by which the "extent of sustainability" of a whole nation, or specific sectors could be determined (cf. Kuik and Verbruggen, 1991, for potentials and pitfalls).

Dietz, F. J. and N. J. P. Hoogervorst (1991). "Towards a Sustainable and Efficient Use of Manure in Agriculture: The Dutch Case." *Environmental and Resource Economics*, Vol. 1, 3, pp. 313-32.

—— and J. van der Straaten (1988). "The Problem of Optimal Exploitation of Natural Resources: the Need for Ecological Limiting Conditions." *International Journal of Social Economics*, Vol. 15, Nos. 3-4, pp. 71-9.

—— and J. van der Straaten (1990). "Economic Analyses of Environmental Problems: A Critique of Marxist Approaches." In S. Brander and O. Roloff (eds.), *Politische Ökonomie des Umweltschutzes*. Regensburg, pp. 147-71.

—— and J. van der Straaten (1992). "Rethinking Environmental Economics: The Missing Links between Economic Theory and Environmental Policy." *Journal of Economic Issues*, Vol. 26, No. 1, pp. 27-51.

—— and K. J. A. M. Termeer (1991). "Dutch Manure Policy: The Lack of Economic Instruments." In D. J. Kraan and R. J. in't Veld (eds.), *Environmental Protection: Public or Private Choice*. Dordrecht, pp. 123-47.

——, Jan van der Straaten, and M. van der Velde (1991). "The European Common Market and the Environment: The Case of the Emission of NO_x by Motorcars." *Review of Political Economy*, Vol. 3, No. 1, pp. 62-78.

Doel, J. van den and B. C. J. van Velthoven (1990). *Democratie en welvaartstheorie*. 3rd edition. Alphen aan de Rijn.

Drepper, F. R. and B. A. Mansson (1990). *On the Role of Unpredictability in Environmental Economics*. Paper presented at the Conference "Economics and the Environment." 17-19 September, Tilburg.

Ernst-Pörken, M. (ed.) (1984). *Alternativen der Ökonomie—Ökonomie der Alternativen*. Argument Sonderband AS 104. Berlin.

Fabricant, S. (1947). In *Studies in Income and Wealth*, Vol. 10. Conference on Research in Income and Wealth. New York, pp. 50 ff.

Freeman, A. M. (1985). "Methods for Assessing the Benefits of Environmental Programs." In A. V. Kneese and F. L. Sweeney (eds.), *Handbook of Natural Resource and Energy Economics*, Vol. 1. Amsterdam, pp. 223-70.

Gärtner, E. (1979). *Arbeiterklasse und Ökologie*. Frankfurt a. M.

Goudzwaard, B. (1970). *Ongeprijsde Schaarste*. Den Haag.

—— (1974). *Schaduwen van het groeigeloof*. Kampen.

—— (1978). *Kapitalisme en Vooruitgang*. Assen.

Govers, H. (1988). *Natuur, techniek en milieupolitiek*. Utrecht.

Hafkamp, W. A. (1991). "Three Decades of Environmental-Economic Modelling: Economic Models of Pollutant Emissions." In F. J. Dietz, F. van der Ploeg, and J. van der Straaten (eds.), *Environmental Policy and the Economy*. Amsterdam, pp. 19-45.

Harmsen, G. (1974). *Natuur, Geschiedenis, Filosofie*. Nijmegen.

Heise, K-H. and M. Hembold (1977). "Umweltgefährdung und Kapitalverwertung." *Marxismus Digest*, No. 2, pp. 22-38.

Hennipman, P. (1945). *Economisch motief en economisch principe*. Amsterdam.

Hoehn, J. P. and A. Randall (1987). "A Satisfactory Benefit Cost Indicator for Contingent Valuation." *Journal of Environmental Economics and Management*, Vol. 14, No. 3, pp. 226-47.

Hueting, R. (1970). *Wat is de Natuur ons waard?* Baarn.

—— (1974/1980). *New Scarcity and Economic Growth*. Amsterdam.

Immler, H. (1983a). "Ist nur die Arbeit wertbildend?" *Sozialismus*, Vol. 5, pp. 53-8.

—— (1983b). "Natur ist wertbildend." *Sozialismus*, Vol. 10, pp. 27-30.

Jevons, W. S. (1871/1924). *The Theory of Political Economy*. London.

Kapp, K. W. (1950). *Volkswirtschaftliche Kosten der Privatwirtschaft*. Tübingen.

King, W. J. (1919). *The Wealth and Income of the People of the United States*. New York.

Krusewitz, K. (1978). "Opmerkingen over de oorzaken van de milieukrisis in historisch-maatschappelijke samenhang." In H. Verhagen (ed.), *Inleiding tot de politieke economie van het milieu*. Amsterdam, pp. 81-108.

Kuik, O. and H. Verbruggen (1991). *Search of Indicators of Sustainable Development*. Boston.

Kuznets, S. (1947). "National Income and Industrial Structure." *The Proceedings of the International Statistical Conference of the Econometric Society*. September 6-18, Washington, D.C., Vol. 5, pp. 218-19.

Langeweg, F. (ed.) (1988). *Zorgen voor Morgen*. Alphen aan de Rijn.

Malthus, T. R. (1798/1982). *An Essay on the Principle of Population*. Harmondsworth.

Marshall, A. (1890/1925). *Principles of Economics*, London.

Martinez-Alier, J. (1991). "Ecological Perception and Distributional Effects: A Historical View." In F. J. Dietz, F. van der Ploeg, and J. van der Straaten (eds.), *Environmental Policy and the Economy*. Amsterdam, pp. 117-37.

Marx, K. (1844/1964). *The Economic and Philosophical Manuscripts of 1844*. NewYork.

—— (1867/1970). *Capital*, Vol. 1. London.

—— (1857-1858/l973). *Grundrisse, Foundations of the Critique of Political Economy (rough draft)*, translated by M. Nicolaus. Harmondsworth.

Menger, C. (1871). *Grundsätze der Volkswirtschaftslehre*. Wien.

Mishan, E. J. (1960). "A Survey on Welfare Economics 1939-1959." *Economic Journal*, Vol. 70, pp. 197-256.

—— (1967). *The Costs of Economic Growth*. London.

—— (1971). "The Postwar Literature on Externalities: An Interpretative Essay." *Journal of Economic Literature*, Vol. 9, pp. 1-28.

Mueller, D. C. (1989). *Public Choice II*. Cambridge, MA.

Neher, P. A. (1990). *Natural Resource Economics, Conservation and Exploitation*. Cambridge.

Nentjes, A. (1990). "Economische instrumenten in het milieubeleid: financierings- of sturingsmiddel?" In P. Nijkamp and H. Verbruggen, H. (eds.), *Het Nederlandse milieu in de Europese ruimte*. Preadviezen van de Koninklijke Vereniging voor de Staathuishoudkunde. Leiden, pp. 145-66.

Opschoor, J. B. (1987). *Duurzaamheid en Verandering: over ecologisch inpasbare economische ontwikkeling*. Amsterdam.

—— (1990). "Ecologisch duurzame ontwikkeling: een theoretisch idee en een weerbarstige praktijk." In P. Nijkamp and H. Verbruggen (eds.), *Het Nederlandse milieu in de Europese ruimte*. Preadviezen van de Koninklijke Vereniging voor de Staathuishoudkunde. Leiden, pp. 7-41.

Pearce, D. W. and R. K. Turner (1990). *Economics of Natural Resources and the Environment*. London.

Peeters, M. (1991). "Legal Aspects of Marketable Pollution Rights." In F. J. Dietz, F. van der Ploeg, and J. van der Straaten (eds.), *Environmental Policy and the Economy*. Amsterdam, pp. 151-65.

Pigou, A. C. (1920/1952). *The Economics of Welfare*. London.

Ricardo, D. (1823/1975). *The Principles of Political Economy and Taxation*. London.

Robbins, L. (1935). *An Essay on the Nature and Significance of Economic Science*. 2nd edition. London.

Romören, E. and T. I. Romören (1978). "Marx en de ekologie." In H. Verhagen (ed.), *Inleiding tot de politieke economie van het milieu*. Amsterdam, pp. 35-47.

Sachs, I. (1976). "Environment and Styles of Development." In W. Matthews (ed.), *Outer Limits and Human Needs*. Uppsala.

—— (1984). "The Strategies of Ecodevelopment." *Ceres, FAO Review on Agriculture and Development*, Vol. 17, pp. 17-21.

Söderbaum, P. (1980). "Towards a Reconciliation of Economics and Ecology." *European Review of Agricultural Economics*, Vol. 7, pp. 55-77.

—— (1982). "Ecological Imperatives for Public Policy." *Ceres, FAO Review on Agriculture and Development*, Vol. 15, pp. 28-32.

—— (1987). "Environmental Management: A Non-traditional Approach." *Journal of Economic Issues*, Vol. 21, No. 1, pp. 139-65.

Swaney, J. A. (1987a). "Building Instrumental Environmental Control Institutions." *Journal of Economic Issues*, Vol. 21, No. 1, pp. 295-308.

—— (1987b). "Elements of a Neoinstitutional Environmental Economics." *Journal of Economic Issues*, Vol. 21, No. 4, pp. 1739-79.

Straaten, J. van der (1990). *Zure regen, economische theorie en het Nederlandse beleid*. Utrecht.

—— (1991). "Acid Rain and the Single Internal Market: Policies from the Netherlands." *European Environment*, Vol. 1, No. 1, pp. 20-4.

Tonneijk, A. E. G. (1981). *Research on the Influence of Different Air Pollutants Separately and in Combination in Agriculture, Horticulture and Forestry Crops*. Wageningen.

Turner, M. (1984). *Enclosures in Britain 1750-1830*. London.

Ullrich, O. (1979). *Weltniveau*. Berlin.

Walras, L. (1874-1877/1954). *Elements of Pure Economics or the Theory of Social Wealth*. Homewood, Ill.

World Commission on Environment and Development (1987). *Our Common Future*. Oxford.

Institutional Aspects of Sustainable Development

Johannes B. Opschoor and Jan van der Straaten

Introduction

In 1987 the World Commission on Environment and Development (WCED) advocated worldwide "sustainable development." The report documented that the prevailing patterns of economic growth would not be ecologically viable, and that this would not automatically be redressed from within the economic process and the economic institutions. Obviously, a new policy is needed. Would this new policy be compatible with predominant (neoclassical) economic views and practical approaches based on these views? For a variety of reasons to be reviewed below, the notion of sustainable development will have to be adequately incorporated into economic theory, with repercussions for the treatment of natural resources as factors of production and as welfare determinants, for valuation theory, and for the evaluation of market forces. These and related aspects are the subject matter of this chapter.

Sustainable development

Sustainable development has been defined as "a process of change in which the exploitation of resources, the direction of investments, the orientation of technological development, and institutional change are all in harmony and enhance both current and future potential to meet human needs and aspirations" (WCED, 1987, p. 46). Mäler (1990) refers to development as sustainable, "if the total stock of resources—human capital, physical reproducible capital, environmental resources, exhaustible resources—does not decrease over time." Pearce and Turner (1990) take it to mean "maximizing the net benefits of economic development, subject to maintaining the services and quality of natural resources over time." According to Opschoor (1990), development is sustainable "if the environmental impacts do not impair the present and future functioning of resource regeneration systems, waste absorption systems and the systems supporting flows of other environmental services and goods, and when use of nonrenewable resources is compensated for by at least equivalent increases in supplies of renewable or reproducible substitutes."

The latter two definitions represent a prudent approach to possibilities of substitution. Mäler's definition allows for such substitution and is in accordance with a dwindling natural capital, as long as human capital and/ or physical capital make up for the reduction in natural capital. Opschoor and others have argued that levels of environmental pressure be established that are considered as (proxies for the actual) thresholds for unsustainability: "safe minimum standards" or "critical loads."

No doubt, economists should assist in designing and evaluating alternative pathways towards sustainability, and help search for changes in institutions and instruments necessary for and sufficient to bringing the economic process onto a sustainable course. However, the notion of "sustainable development" poses many challenges to economic analysis, particularly critical questions regarding the mechanisms and processes dominant in current economic systems. We shall, therefore, present a broader, an institutional approach to environmental problems.

Institutional aspects of the interrelations between economy and environment

In this section we shall briefly outline what we mean by an institutional approach to environmental problems.[1] In the *Appendix* we provide a broad-brush comparison of neoclassical economics and its institutional counterpart in terms of a series of selected premisses.[2] In what follows immediately below, we shall indicate the significance of the institutionalist

---

1 The philosophical foundation of institutionalism rests on work by Veblen, Dewey, Clarence Ayres, and J. Fagg Foster; recent contributions were made by Tool (Dugger, 1988) and Hodgson (1988).

2 Traditionally, institutionalists have dealt with the main economic issues of the day, and—like their neoclassical colleagues—have analyzed environmental problems after these became manifest. In other words, there is nothing to suggest that institutionalist are intrinsically more environmentally aware than other economists.

premisses for the analysis of the economic process and structure, in terms of their environmental "performance":

1. The self-erected boundaries that neoclassical theory operates behind ("fixed context" or "Datenkranz") are crossed. The "fixed context" premiss is replaced by one of "circular interdependence." In analyzing environmental problems, circular interdependence means working from the notion of chains of triggering factors, causes, effects, responses, etc. that link the economy to the environment. Institutional economics thus employs a circular or "biological" approach to society (and hence to economy-environment interactions) rather than a mechanical one (see, for example, Wiseman, 1989).

2. Institutional economics studies behavior not exclusively from an individualistic, utility "maximizing" premiss as neoclassical analysis does, but allows for other values and approaches to decision-making. The maximization assumption on behavior is put in a wider range of possible behavior, including "satisficing" strategies, and by allowing for "nonrational" or "noninstrumental" modes of behavior.

3. Institutional economics deviates from the "weighing premiss" by allowing "values" to take precedence over preferences as manifested in market and quasi-market situations. The weighing premiss is replaced by a hierarchical approach to values with some continuity, or social reproduction-oriented values such as: "sustainability" or "environmental compatibility." The latter two values are regarded as representing more ultimate values such as the nonindividious recreation of the community, and the continuity of human life (Swaney, 1987). The continued existence of species and ecosystems may be in this category of societally relevant items where individual preferences or priorities for them remain low. This may, at the collective level, give rise to explicit *a priori* policies on nature conservation. All these arguments support the position that the environment is a "merit-good," not to be decided upon by aggregate individual economic values attached to it (Opschoor, 1974; Hueting, 1980). Institutional or evolutionary economics thus typically employs an ethical approach biased towards expressing itself in terms of "rights" rather than of "utilitarian values."

Neoclassical environmental economics relies on estimates of economic values as the sum of use values and nonuse values. Economic values of environmental changes can be deduced from their consequences in terms of alterations in market behavior or from surveys or experiments through which people are invited to express welfare or utility equivalents of environmental changes. There is a serious doubt as to the sufficiency of these variants, given the nature of environmental problems and the occurrence of unknown or uncertain effects, effects on other generations, effects on other species, etc. (Hoevenagel and Opschoor, 1990).

The role of values in institutional analysis has been outlined in the Appendix. Continuity of human life and the noninvidious recreation of community are two ultimate values in a hierarchy that puts such values beyond the wants, needs and preferences that are the stuff of mainstream microeconomics. When extrapolated to shed light on environmental issues, these two values imply as a corollary: environmental compatibility (Swaney, after Tool), or the principle of coevolutionary sustainability (Swaney, 1987). This can be illustrated as follows: We are looking at a system in which several subsystems or modules interact and reproduce themselves. Among these subsystems are: (i) population (composition, size, dynamics); (ii) technology and economic potentials and demands; (iii) the organizational/administrative structure of society; (iv) culture/worldview/ethics and the environmental base. As soon as incompatibilities arise, a process of structural adaptation will have to emerge within and between these modules. If this process is to be successful in terms of survival, it will have to lead to changes in several of them, and these adaptations must be mutually compatible. This in fact implies ecological sustainability, as otherwise the economy's material base will be insecure and cause future incompatibility.

This means that we postulate a third criterion, in addition to efficiency and equity, namely that of coevolutionary sustainability. A fourth criterion is inter-species equity: a societally accepted element of care for the prospects of other species, insofar as humankind can effect these prospects.

4. Finally, institutional economics would take Kapp's results on inherent tendencies towards "cost-shifting" as a point of departure. Externalities are an almost endemic disease in decentralized systems of decision-making. The causal links between the present institutional framework and environmental degradation thus must be an explicit area of study. Institutional economics looks at institutions and instruments in a much broader context than does neoclassical economics. Not only is there an explicit interest in the evolution and operation of nonmarket instruments in addition to market instruments, but there is also scope for an assessment of instruments in much more than its efficiency aspects,

namely its conformity with policy trends, administrative traditions, etc.[3] Also in terms of institutions, the scope is wider: property rights, cooperative rather than competitive organizational strategies, environmental impact assessment, societal decision-making on investments, projects and policies, etc.

Institutional approaches to regulatory (re)design to effectively deal with environmental problems follows the principle of the theory of regulation, as outlined in the Appendix. That is, realignment of rights, duties and incentives, information flows and (social) pressures, etc. are considered in terms of their impact on behavior and decision-making either directly or indirectly, and compensatory strategies are sought that could compensate or convince (sufficient numbers of) losers.

Economic performance and sustainable development

Modern economy and unsustainability

Economic activities are the most manifest sources of environmental stress. They are based on extracted raw materials and energy, they pollute, and they imply spatial claims damaging the integrity of natural environments. This stress is a problem insofar as environmental buffering capacities are exceeded, and this excess is not compensated by remedial activities. Economic activities as the main sources of environmental stress should not be regarded in any static sense, but rather as the substrates of larger societal processes. Amongst these processes there are three that have, since the early seventies, been singled out as the alleged main causes of environmental destruction: population growth, economic growth, and inappropriate technological change.

A comprehensive approach of environmental problems is important because in such an approach cultural and institutional aspects are to be analyzed explicitly within the framework of the economic theory applied. By cultural aspects we refer to norms, values, and beliefs that govern individual and societal perspectives, attitudes, and conducts. By institutional aspects we mean the set of formal and informal relations between

---

3 See, e. g., Kling (1988) for a theoretical analysis and J. B. Opschoor and J. B. Vos (1989) for a descriptive, empirical analysis.

individuals, the organization of societies in terms of customary or instrumental behavioral patterns, political organizations, etc. The processes of economic and population growth and of technological change are largely driven, or at least directed, by structures prevalent at the ideological (or cultural) and institutional (or systems') level (Opschoor, 1989; van der Straaten, 1990). The most important ideological aspects referred to include:

(a) a pervasive belief in "progress" reduced to material growth and dominance over "nature" by Homo sapiens;
(b) a dominant utilism reduced to exclusive concern for self-centered individual welfare;
(c) a reemerging faith in the properties of the market mechanism to bend individual nastiness to a maximal public good.

In the remainder of this section we shall deal with institutional aspects only.[4]

Cost-shifting: "distance"

It has long been established (Kapp, 1970) that the economic process as directed by decentralized decision-making based on market signals and competitive behavior, leads to "cost-shifting;" that is, to pushing part of the adverse consequences of one's behavior on to others.

Economic activities lead to effects that are external to those who decide over these activities in the first place. Major cases of such "external effects" include the environmental impacts of economic activities. In other words, economic activities lead to social costs (including the costs of environmental degradation) that are not fully translated into private costs, or internalized into the private decision-making mechanism. This phenomenon has long been recognized as one example of what has been labelled "market failure." Market failures are defects in the market mechanism that lead the economic process away of what would be societally desirable. Such failures necessitate government interventions.

The practice of cost-shifting is facilitated by what could be labelled the "distance factor." The consequences of environmental degradation in relation to economic activities manifest themselves at often large distances

---

4 We thus also disregard the implications of imperfect knowledge and imperfect information and similar effects. The reader is referred to literature on the "merit"-aspects of environmental goods (e. g., James, *et al.*, 1978; Hueting, 1980).

from the source or agent causing them; a distance both in terms of space and time (e. g., DDT in polar ice caps, chemical time bombs, and climate change). But there is another distance-related problem, namely that of the distance between the level of one's individual influence and the level at which a problem must be addressed for its solution. One could refer to this as: distance in decision level. Examples are countries sharing a common resource or individual fishermen exploiting a shared fish population (the "prisoners' dilemma" in the case of very few actors, or the "tragedy of the commons" in the case of many actors in a situation of open access to resources). In many cases, in the absence of intervention by national or international authorities, this leads to a destruction of a shared or common property resource, to ongoing pollution, etc. Distance between cause and effect, that is what combines these various situations. And if such distances become substantial, then what is optimal from an individual perspective may not at all be optimal from a social or collective perspective. Where such distance factors prevail and the party on which the burden is shifted cannot counteract this distance by pressing his interest, government intervention is needed. This is quite obviously the case with environmental problems.

Reasons why the interest of the "party on whom the costs are shifted" are not adequately reflected include:

(a) absence of legally based "property rights" protecting the damaged party, or of liability regulations enforceable upon the causal agent;

(b) absence of means to exert "countervailing power" (Galbraith) through the political system (i.e., lack of voting power as in cases of transboundary cost-shifting, or intertemporal cost-shifting, or cost-shifting onto other species), or through the market place (i.e., lack of purchasing power). Reasons why this situation is not easily changed by installing more appropriate institutions or legislation include the filtering process applied by any political system in responding to claims for systemic changes: the filters (again) of time preferences (whereby future effects and future interests are discounted away) and of present purchasing or voting power, both heavily biased in favor of the predominant economic interests.

Economic growth and its main motives

Economic growth may be beneficial for many reasons. One problematic feature of it, however, is that it tends to take economies beyond what is ecologically sustainable. This means that the growth tendency is likely to continue for too long if unchecked, or if its course is not corrected. Growth in industrialized countries during the past decades has brought the gross national product (GNP) up to levels 12 to 15 times as high as they were in 1900. Expected growth patterns in the same countries will lead to a further doubling in the next 25 years. Worldwide growth (basing ourselves on UN population extrapolations and the rise in material welfare of developing nations as expected by WCED) would lead to a rise in industrial production alone with a factor of 15 or so until 2050, if present tendencies prevail.

In order to understand the determinants of the growth process one normally points at the predominant value structure of economic agents, according to which more is preferred to less. This, however, is a far from complete analysis, and one that fails to come to terms with some more basic features. Amongst these are the following:

(i)   a structural tendency to bridge wealth gaps both within and between economies by striving for higher levels of satisfaction, the aspiration levels always being set at the levels of those that are materially "advanced;"

(ii)   the goal to ensure continuity in a competitive and uncertain context (especially at the levels of firms) entails a strive for growth, profit, market control, hence: inherent and unending strives for growth;

(iii) in attempting to maintain political security and continuity, states have preferred to accommodate the emancipating groups by providing them with more absolute and relative wealth and income, not by taking this from the privileged in absolute terms, but by redistributing from a growing national product;

(iv)   technological development has tended to be labor-replacing. In societies favoring full employment this implies a substantive push for continued economic growth at a rate beyond the technology-induced rate of growth of productivity.

Within the context of this chapter these points cannot be elaborated in detail. They may suffice in suggesting how formidable a task will lie ahead if ultimately, from an ecological point of view, it would not be sufficient to change the technologies or locations of our economic activities, but if the levels of these activities themselves (the scale of the economy) will have to be controlled and redirected.

Towards sustainable development: institutions and instruments

Now that we have identified some structural deficiencies of modern economies in terms of their staying within the boundaries of a sustainable economy, we shall try to address the second question, i.e., that of institutional reforms towards rendering socioeconomic development more sustainable.

The main lessons to be drawn in terms of desired institutional adaptation are that there is a need for (i) controlling growth and for (ii) redirecting it. Curbing economic growth is needed insofar as it would otherwise lead to an overall environmental stress beyond the limits the ecological buffers could stand. This implies that these limits be determined and translated into politically accepted threshold values beneath which the economy has to remain. Economic activities likely to bring society near or beyond these thresholds would have to be scrutinized for their economic significance and for possibilities to reduce their environmental impacts by using new technologies. Normally, technological development follows the demands of the market. But that will not always benefit nature and the environment. Hence, an appropriate technological development, based on the realization of the sustainable paradigm, is only possible by the interventions of authorities.

If the possibilities for improving the relevant technologies are coming to an end, then the level of economic activities may have to be subjected to societal control, as may be the case with energy production, pesticide use, private transportation, intensive farming, and the chemical industry. This may ultimately result in changes in overall patterns of consumption, but will certainly alter the pattern of production.

Such controls need not necessarily take the form of bureaucratically licensing industries, although sometimes they will take that form. As an alternative, government may wish to manipulate the economic process by putting a financial cost to environmental stress, i.e., shifting environmental costs back to the causing agents, which would indirectly change decisions on environmentally undesirable investments, raw materials, and final products. In any case, this would extent the powers of the state into areas (particularly economic planning and pricing policy) from where it has been actually withdrawing in recent years.

The above policy of curbing economic growth does not affect the basic forces underlying it. Depending on how far societies may go with curbing growth, more basic strategies may be needed. As we saw, growth tendencies are triggered by structural elements such as poverty, inequality, insecurity, wrongly oriented technological development. Hence, in the first place, innovation-oriented toward reducing the environmental burden and toward increasing demand for labor-intensive products needs to be stimulated much more than is the case already (some call this "green Keynesianism").

In the second place, poverty alleviation at the global level would both directly and indirectly (through its impact on population size) reduce long-term environmental stress. However, this is likely to come about only via economic development, and this implies a short-term additional environmental burden. Poverty alleviation without changing the quality of economic growth is a *cul-de-sac*. Such quality changes in East and South will only come about insofar as the consumption patterns in the West will manifestly reflect new environmental values. Enhancing quality in Europe in particular may be a *conditio sine qua non* for such new values to be adopted. This implies national and international institutions capable to change prevailing distributions of incomes and current distributions of access to resources.

Thirdly, the most profound policy to curb economic growth would be that of reducing (world) market insecurity and competition. As this comes close to the very essence of our economic system, and as faith in the existence of alternatives for that system has been dwindling rapidly, one cannot but hope that the environmental crisis can be resolved without having to consider changes as fundamental as these.

From a structural perspective, society needs also to prevent or reduce cost-shifting tendencies. As we already saw, this has to do with distances between cause and effect in space, time, and decision level.

Distances in space may lead to redistributions of environmental impacts either through transportation by air and water, or via redistribution of sources of environmental impacts by changing the patterns of international trade and investment. In cases of internationally shared environments (common property resources), new institutions may be needed for more appropriate management. This will include new types of jurisdiction at the international level and a partial transfer of national sovereignty (see the chapter by Harris, in this volume). In cases where environmental effects are redistributed via the world market (international trade and investment), these effects have to become known and visible, and (where needed) to be transferred into changing regulations on international trade (e. g., GATT-rules, international price regulations). This will especially be the case when North-South trade results in unsustainable patterns of production in developing countries, or when developing countries, as a consequence of international debt-servicing obligations, are forced to sell out natural resources on the world market at dumping prices. In fact, the environmental crisis is so intensically linked with other aspects of international relations (trade, debt) that the debate on a "new economic order" needs reopening again rapidly.

Distance in time needs to be overcome by lifting the veil of time preference. In concrete terms, the concept of "sustainable development" needs to be adopted by individual states and be made operational. One form this could take is the adoption of some type of "legacy principle" or "trusteeship," whereby societies oblige themselves to pass on to the next generation an environmental quality and resource stock at least as large as the one they found. Institutionally, this would have to be complemented by installing some authority to represent future generations' interests, e. g., an Ombudsman-type organization for this specific purpose.

Distance between decision levels (the "prisoners' dilemma") can be overcome by creating authority at the appropriate level, by exchanging information, and preferably to have some authority over the joint resource or environment. The International Rhine Committee is an example of such a platform (but one without enough authority), and so is the North Sea Conference. This leads to issues of sovereignty and jurisdiction, as have been mentioned already.

Furthermore, principles are needed to allocate management costs. The "polluter-pays-principle," as adopted by EC and OECD, is one example of such a principle, but one that increasingly proves untenable if continental and global environmental problems are to be coped with. This principle should be amended by one on sharing environmental costs, for instance, according to economic strength. Finally, new sources of financing such platforms/authorities and their activities need to be developed. Here one can think of international taxes based either on levels of environmental stress (e. g., an International Carbon Tax, a European Acidification Fund based on Acid Charges, etc.), on levels of development (e. g., GNP per capita), or on the use of natural resource (e. g., an International Fossil Fuels Tax).

Finally, an alteration of rights is needed, such that environmental stress is recognized as a new type of claim on livelihood or existence rights (of species) to be compensated for by those laying that claim, to those on whom the claim is being laid. This could be in the form of an extension of the "pollution-pays-principle" to not only the measures prescribed by environmental policy, but to damage costs in general. Another extension might be that noncompliance with agreed practices be punishable more heavily than is currently done, or that some *ex ante* "performance bond" be made possible (such as is the case in Australia) to be returned upon behavior according to agreement. Such fundamental reversals in the legal status of polluters vis-a-vis pollutees will not easily come about and may need political mobilization and coalition formation between various NGOs' "environmental countervailing power."

All these measures, regulations, permits, and principles are likely to be attacked by interest groups which have achieved their powerful position by cost-shifting. Often it is argued by these groups that consumers are not willing to pay a higher price caused by increasing abatement costs. Recent investigations in the Netherlands showed that some 70 percent of the consumers were willing to stabilize their earning power during a ten-year period, even in a situation of expanding production, if these surpluses of money were used to abate environmental pollution. They stated that environmental problems are more urgent than all other societal problems. These results may demonstrate that forming a coalition between environmental groups and consumer organizations could have a great impact.

Conclusions

Although many economists are more or less aware of the social and normative character of economic theories, this starting point is seldomly found in economic publications. Neoclassical economics may be seen as a scientific description of the expansion process of the industrialized world during the last century. This description is realized by using the categories relevant in this expansion process. New problems cannot be described when relevant categories are not present in the set of variables used in the system of thinking. From way back economists have distinguished three production factors, namely, labor, capital, and natural resources. But in the neoclassical tradition only the production factors labor and capital are really dealt with. Natural resources are only relevant as far as they are traded on a market, where price-making will take place. Environmental problems are dealt within neoclassical approaches by the concept of "external effects." Indeed, these effects are external, that is, external to the center of the theory: the market itself.

One should not be surprised that with these starting points it was not possible to address, let alone solve the growing environmental problems during the last decades. Nature and the environment are now in a worse state than ever before. Among other factors, this is surely connected with the existence of a dominant economic theory in which only insufficient categories are found to analyze environmental problems of a fundamental character.

In our opinion, this problem of insufficient scientific information in economic theories can be encountered in two different ways. In the first place, one may argue that the problems are outside the scope of economics and should be analyzed and solved by ecologists and biologists. Thus, Molle (1990) indicates the environment in a European context as "beyond economics." We will not follow such an approach. By doing so, an economist would lose his ability to make predictions about relevant economic variables such as the level of production and consumption in the future. Furthermore, by doing so, one leaves the economic tradition of dealing with natural resources as one of the three production factors. In our opinion, the only way out of this dilemma can be found in the incorporation of natural resources into economic theory itself; the acceptance of the concept of sustainable development undoubtedly implies this position. This choice makes clear that the deterioration of nature and the environment on a large scale is an economic, a social and therefore a political problem.

Appendix: Institutional and Neoclassical Economics—A Comparison

1. Neoclassical and institutional approaches: basic assumptions

Neoclassical economics analyzes what is regarded as the economic aspect of human behavior from a perspective characterized by four premises:

(a) The "fixed context" premiss:
The object(s) of studies are part of a large range of parameters, assumed to be static or "given," including:
- institutional arrangements (i.e., the economic system),
- preferences and wants,
- the state of technology, and
- the state of functioning of the natural environment.

Basically, the context that is considered as fixed consists of relevant variables that are actually recognized as such, but left out of the analysis which is to focus on more significant aspects. Thus, neoclassical economics is especially interested in exchange relations between different actors in situations of different factor endowments. Walter Eucken referred to these items as "Datenkranz," surrounding the object of economic analysis: they were "data," i.e., given.

(b) The "maximization" premiss on behavior:
This is the assumption that individuals and groups will try to maximize their objective function (i.e., welfare for individuals and profit for enterprises). In fact, it is utilities that are maximized. Neoclassical economics assumes: (i) that individuals independently form preferences reflecting individual values; and (ii) that individual values are to count exclusively in all matters.

(c) The "weighing" premiss on evaluation:
This premiss implies that all relevant changes as a consequence of economic choices can be expressed in a welfare-related, one-dimensional entity, so that the costs and benefits of all alternatives can be reduced to neat (ordinal) balance figures which can be ranked. Hence, all different types of value can be aggregated into one-dimensional entities such as "utility," "net benefit," or "welfare."

(d) The "(near) optimality" premiss on decentralized decision-making:
It is assumed that within certain boundary conditions, coordination of economic decisions and hence the economic process, are best (in the sense of "optimal") institutionalized if run via the market mechanism.

We now briefly review some features of an institutional economic approach:

(e) "Circular interdependence" replacing "fixed context"

This point goes against the alleged neutrality of economic activities vis-a-vis their natural, institutional, and cultural environments. Most neoclassical models fail as adequate descriptions of the physical realities which do form the constraints within which societies (and economies) must remain. Often variables in these "environments" are linked with those within the economic process and a full analysis of the system as a whole is needed, if all relevant feedbacks are to be considered. To do justice to these realities, the other subsystems must be described in terms of a reasonable model of their internal processes, with possibilities to incorporate all outputs including economically nonfunctional ones. Typical in the institutional approach also is the rejection of a reductionist view and the replacement thereof by a more integrated (some even advocate a "holistic" view) or "evolutionary" (sometimes labelled: "organic") approach.

(f) Behavioral pluriformity

Besides the maximization aspect there are more relaxed approaches, such as "satisficing," even "irrational," or nonfunctional ones.

(g) Coevolutionary instrument values

Society has values that deviate from individual values, e. g., on the basis of society's much longer life expectancy or on that of a paternalistic concern over individuals' well-being beyond their own concerns. Valuation approaches from an individual perspective may hold in a certain domain, but cannot be generalized to statements on public goods and merit goods. Institutionalists postulate the existence of a hierarchical value system. They see "wants" as drivers of the behavior of individuals, influenced by the economic process itself; it is these "wants" that are satisfied to a smaller or larger degree, thereby affecting welfare levels. Beyond wants and welfare, institutionalists perceive "values" as operators on human and societal behavior. In normatively assessing economic performance, institutionalists will use as a criterion the institutions' instrumental significance for realizing the deeper or more ultimate values such as: "sustainability" or "environmental compatibility." In fact, a social value hierarchy could be postulated in which societies, with the support of the individuals in their capacities as "citizens" opt for social states (in terms of allocation of private goods, public goods, and merit goods) that cannot be deduced as optimal from their market behavior.

(h) Regulation and markets

Kapp (1969 and 1970) has argued that the phenomenon of "externalities" is endemic and pervasive within any society with decentralized decision-making, including market economies. In such economies the "shifting of costs" to others is an institutionalized form of behavior to be expected by firms, as it is rewarded by competitive success. Kapp's theorem of "cost-shifting" was a fundamental critique of the neoclassical school. Markets are institutional arrangements associated with externalizing ("cost-shifting") behavior. Market-mechanism conformity, therefore, cannot be a criterion for judging the adequacy of new environmental policy instruments. The market mechanism itself should be judged instrumentally, in terms of its consequences for ulterior values.

2. Institutions and values: some institutionalists' views

Institutions (according to Veblen) are social arrangements serving productive and acquisitive purposes. They include allocative mechanisms such as the market, the plan, parliamentary budget decisions; rights, both customary and formalized; organizational structures; patterns of behavior, etc. There may be several arrangements, serving a given set of purposes. The main concern of institutionalism is to identify institutions that enhance progressiveness (i.e., productive purposes or values such as the fullness of life and continuity of culture).

In evaluating alternative institutions, instrumental criteria are used. In developing new institutions, one should look at social/institutional causes of socially undesirable performance of the current institutional structure, and adapt that structure from a value directed perspective. The question then becomes: which values? It is common to distinguish instrumental values (i.e., serving some end) from ceremonial values (references to tradition or custom). Veblen saw instincts as basic units of social development, and as the sources of values. Several instincts or "proclivities" such as workmanship, parental bent, and "idle curiosity" are regarded by him as contributing to the progressive development of human society, as they can add to the fullness of life and the continuity of culture. The "continuity of human life" and the "noninvidious recreation of community" are two ultimate values (Swaney, 1987).

Institutionalists generally hold that:
1. values take priority over "wants;" wants are determined within the economic and social processes and can be seen as transformations of underlying values by individuals and groups, given the context in which they find themselves;
2. values are no single level, fully separable entities, but form a hierarchical structure of separate and partly connected specific values at different levels;
3. this hierarchy cannot be reduced to a single common yardstick such as utility or welfare;
4. individuals, groups, and societies may have value structures, and they will not be identical.

3. Toward a positive theory of regulation

(a) Neoclassical theories: externalities, property rights, and public choice

Mainstream economics has recognized that regulating market forces is warranted when all competitive conditions do not hold or efficiency is not ensured (see, for example, Haveman, 1976). This may be the case with externalities and with common property resources.

The early answer to externalities was formulated by Pigou (1920): If (marginal) private net products and social net products do not coincide, the "free play" of self-interest will, in general, not lead to a maximal national dividend. In such cases, it is possible for the state "if it so chooses, to remove the divergence ... by 'extraordinary encouragements' or 'extraordinary restraints'," such as bounties and taxes (p. 192). This is the "Pigovian Tax," to be charged to the generator of an externality.

According to Coase, however, a Pigovian Tax is not necessary for efficiency. Coase proposed an approach centered around the concepts of "property rights" and "transaction costs." In cases when transaction costs are absent or low, Coase's analysis leads to the conclusion that the allocation of "property rights," such as rights to generate externalities, is irrelevant from the perspective of resource allocation or efficiency. Parties will bargain, and this will ensure an efficient solution. However, if transaction costs are a barrier to such bargaining, then property rights should be allocated in such a way that efficiency would be maximally enhanced.

Basically, Coase's theory was designed to deal with individual externalities. How does this theory relate to common property resources in a situation of open access? Common resources are scarce goods to the community. The individual user perceives them as free goods, the use of which by him depends on his own interests. Unless there is some person or institution capable of ensuring a sustained use of the resource the resource will be mined (Hardin, 1968: The 'tragedy of the commons'). This is all the more likely as traditional social restrictions on individual (egoistic) use are vanishing and/or overtaken by other interests and values. The alternative would be to privatize the resource.

The property rights theory defines property rights as sanctioned relations amongst people arising from the existence of things and pertaining to their use. It perceives property rights as developing in order to internalize externalities when the gains of internalization become larger than the costs of internalization. Such developments normally result from changes in economic values, new technologies, new markets, etc., to which old property rights are poorly attuned. The dynamics of property rights have been envisaged as being driven by the costs/benefits of different degrees of property rights development. Marginal costs of regulation are assumed to increase with the degree of regulation; marginal benefits are assumed to slope downward. The optimal degree of regulation is found where the marginal cost curve intersects the marginal benefits curve. This optimal point changes when the MC-curve shifts, or when the MB-curve shifts. New possibilities for hitherto not traded resource yields will imply a shift in the MB-curve; new techniques enabling regulation or control may shift the MC-curve. Often it will be impossible to practically determine the marginal costs and benefit in money terms. Yet, the model may succeed where Hardin's approach appears to fail. The property rights approach suggests that societies have an endogenous rationale for changing their traditional systems of resource use.

(b) Institutional approaches of regulation

The above approaches to regulatory change do not help in predicting the direction of change. A successful theory of regulation must account for benefits and costs to all involved, and take into account the mechanism by which interests are transformed into policy. Bromley (1989), Reynolds (1981), and Kling (1988) have attempted to develop such a wider reaching theory of regulatory dynamics.

Different institutional arrangements consist of different constellations of (constraints and) opportunities or "choice domains" (Bromley 1989, p. 741). New technological and economic developments may foster changes in these domains. Changes in relative prices induce institutional change if an institutional rearrangement can shift the possibilities frontier in such a way that a net improvement is possible. Changes in technologies induce institutional change to permit capture of new income streams. Changes in collective attitudes about income shares induce institutional change to modify the income distribution, and changes in collective attitudes about consumption patterns induce institutional change to modify the patterns. Note that environmental change may lead to shifts in this respect.

Reynolds defines regulations as sets of socially imposed bounds on the range of choices open to an individual. He distinguishes implicit regulation (part of the "fabric of society," e. g., the market) and explicit regulation. When society becomes larger or more fragmented in terms of values and interests, a process will start of replacing implicit regulation with explicit regulation. Explication begins with some interest groups gaining beneficial regulations of the "revenue augmenting" type (such as price support, entry control, incomes policies); in reaction to this, society may tip the balance and respond with "cost augmenting" controls (such as taxes, fines, etc.).

In King's synthesis four benefit/harm configurations are distinguished:
1. regulatory change that helps the public interest and helps regulated parties;
2. regulatory change that helps the public interest and harms regulated parties (cost-augmenting regulatory change);
3. regulatory change that harms the public interest and helps regulated parties (revenue-augmenting regulatory change);
4. regulatory change that harms the public interest and harms regulated parties.

According to Kling, regulatory evolution is likely to occur when new (potential) sources of costs and benefits are identified or recognized, and in cases of changes in information availability and in transaction costs barriers (e. g., new or more forceful pressure groups).

(c) Toward an institutional approach of common property

Historical and anthropological analyzes of typical cases of "common property" show numerous checks and balances, such as mutual obligations, prevent open and egotistic hunt for the common resource (see Quiggin, 1988). Institutionalists interested in the evolution of the structure of property rights in an historical context come to at least two conclusions:

- Property rights develop to internalize externalities when the gains of internalization exceed the costs. Randall (1983) distinguishes between a tradition focusing on flexibility and efficiency, and a tradition focusing on stability and security of rights. He emphasizes that instability in property rights encourage "rent-seeking" behavior aimed at securing a reassignment of rights.

- The dynamics of property rights involve far more than voluntary, rationally founded individual transfers (the "evolving elements theory"). Property rights will change if goals or requirements change, or contexts alter. It has been shown that the Coasian approach is only relevant in a limited sense (Swaney, 1987, p. 1766; see also the views [in Quiggin on actors: state, etc.] who use coercive power to enforce [new] property rights, in addition to consensual processes). Given the existence of transaction costs, changes cannot be adequately realized by voluntary exchange; state intervention is needed.

- Standard theory has advanced from Pigou via Coase to the creation of additional or new private property rights. Institutionalists point at possible collective property rights as alternative solutions. The collective property rights approach acknowledges that traditional collective-ownership systems were far more than open access-resource use systems.

References

Bromley, D. W. (1989). "Institutional Change and Economic Efficiency." *Journal of Economic Issues*, Vol. 23, No. 3, pp. 735-59.

Coase, R. H. (1960). "The Problem of Social Costs." *Journal of Law and Economy*, No. 3, October, pp. 1-44.

Dietz, F. J. and J. van der Straaten (1991). "Umweltökonomie auf dem Prüfstand: Das fehlende Glied zwischen ökonomischer Theorie und Umweltpolitik." In F. Beckenbach (ed.), *Die ökologische Herausforderung für die ökonomische Theorie*. Marburg, pp. 239-56.

Dugger, W. M. (1988). "A Research Agenda for Institutional Economics." *Journal of Economic Issues*, Vol. 22, No. 4, pp. 983-1003.

Hardin, G. (1968). "The Tragedy of the Commons." *Science*, No. 162, pp. 1243-8.

Haveman, R. M. (1976). *The Economics of the Public Sector*. 2nd edition. New York.

Hodgson, G. M. (1988). *Economics and Institutions*. Cambridge, MA.

Hoevenagel, R. and J. B. Opschoor (1990). "Economische Waardering van Milieuveranderingen" (Economic Values of Environmental Changes). *Milieu*, No. 3, pp. 65-73.

Hueting, R. (1980). *New Scarcity and Economic Growth*. Amsterdam.

James, D. E., H. M. A. Jansen, and J. B. Opschoor (1978). *Economic Approaches to Environmental Problems*. Amsterdam.

Kapp, K. W. (1969). "On the Nature and Significance of Social Costs." *Kyklos*, Vol. 22, No. 2, pp. 334-47.

Kapp, K. W. (1970). "Environmental Disruptions and Social Costs: a Challenge to Economists." *Kyklos*, Vol. 23, No. 4, pp. 833-47.

Kling, R. W. (1988). "An Institutionalist Theory of Regulation." *Journal of Economic Issues*, Vol. 22, No. 1, pp. 197-211.

Logeman, D. (1991). "De Achteruitgang van de Nederlandse natuur (The Deterioration of Dutch Nature)." *Natuur en Milieu*, March, pp. 12-5.

Mäler, K. G. 1990. "Sustainable Development." NAVF: *Sustainable Development, Science and Policy*. Bergen, May 8-12, 1990. Oslo, pp. 239-44.

Molle, W. (1990). *The Economics of European Integration*. Aldershot.

Opschoor, J. B. (1974). *Economische Waardering van Milieudegradatie (Economic Valuation of the Degradation of Nature)*. Assen.

—— (1987). *Duurzaamheid en Verandering (Sustainability and Change)*. Amsterdam.

—— (1990). "Economic Instruments for Sustainable Development." NAVF: *Sustainable Development, Science and Policy*. Bergen, May 8-12, 1990. Oslo, pp. 249-69.

—— and H. B. Vos (1989). *Economic Instruments for Environmental Protection*. Paris.

O'Riordan, T. (1981). *Environmentalism*. London.

Quiggin, J. (1988). "Private and Common Property Rights in the Economics on the Environment." *Journal of Economic Issues*, Vol. 22, No. 4, pp. 1071-87.

Ramstad, Y. (1989). "Reasonable Value versus Instrumental Value: Competing Paradigms in Institutional Economics." *Journal of Economic Issues*, Vol. 22, No. 3, pp. 761-77.

Reynolds, L. (1981). "Foundations of an Institutional Theory of Regulation." *Journal of Economic Issues*, Vol. XV, No. 3, pp. 641-56.

Swaney, J. A. (1987a). "Building Instrumental Environmental Control Institutions." *Journal of Economic Issues*, Vol. 21, No. 3, pp. 295-308.

—— (1987b). "Elements of a Neoinstitutional Environmental Economics." *Journal of Economic Issues*, Vol. 21, No. 4, pp. 1739-81.

—— and M. E. Evers (1989). "The Social Cost Concepts of K. W. Kapp and K. Polyani." *Journal of Economic Issues*, Vol. 23, No. 1, pp. 7-35.

Wiseman, J. D. (1989). "Economic Knowledge, Evolutionary Epistemology and Human Interests." *Journal of Economic Issues*, Vol. 2, No. 2, pp. 647-56.

World Commission on Environment and Development (WCED) (1987). *Our Common Future*. Oxford.

Sustainable Development and Stock Resources: Is There a Contradiction?

James Baines and John Peet

Introduction

The process we call "development" is a dynamic environment-society process. Social and economic development are possible as a result of managing the natural environment, but the environment itself is not under social control; its manipulation involves risks.

If we are to continue to benefit from exploitation of natural resources, we must appreciate better the environmental repercussions of our activities, and recognize ecological principles more forcefully in our institutions for resource management. This perspective provides the context for our interpretation of "ecological" relationships—*society as part of the biosphere, not apart from it.*

In this paper we propose an integrated conceptual framework that allows us to draw connections between the physical, social and political aspects of the development process. We then discuss the institutional requirements for making short-term, local objectives (more) consistent with long-term global goals.

Conceptual framework of sustainable development

Environment and society

We begin with the notion of *organizing concepts*. At the elementary level, an analysis from human ecology begins with a simple duality (see *Figure 1*): human society and its biophysical environment (Cronin, 1988). This duality has compelling precedents in many forms of scientific investigation, for example in the classical distinction in thermodynamics between "system" and "surroundings" (Sussman, 1982). It is also endorsed in the literature of major social sciences—sociology (e.g., Catton, 1982; Dunlap,

1983; Taylor, 1988); economics (e.g., Georgescu-Roegen, 1979; Daly, 1987; Dasmann, 1973; Goodland and Ledec, 1987); and geography (e.g., Burton, *et al.*, 1978; Garcia and Escudero, 1982).

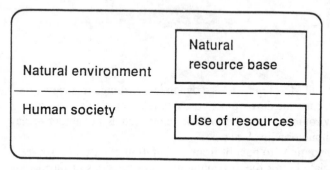

Figure 1:   Simple duality

This duality is, however, inadequate for our purpose, in that it does not enable us to make the distinction between features that distinguish humans from other species, and those we share in common with other species. It is therefore useful to go beyond the simple duality of *Figure 1* in describing the environment-society process. The conceptualization still recognizes the interdependence between the two, but, within this context, it also recognizes the importance of systems of societal control. Thus the simple duality is expanded to a three-part conceptual structure in *Figure 2*, where analysis of human society itself has two principal foci (i) the use of resources by people and the impacts of this on the environment; and (ii) the institutional arrangements that society adopts to control resource use.

The environment-society process must be seen not only in terms of individuals' actions, but also in relation to the aggregate behavior of communities and populations. Similarly, analysis of institutional arrangements must address interactions, not only between individuals and groups within society, but also between people and their natural environment.

We now discuss each of the organizing concepts in *Figure 2*, and the links between them, as they relate to sustainable development.

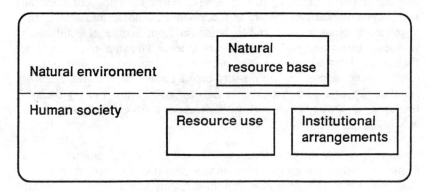

Figure 2:   *Three-part conceptual framework*

Organizing concepts

Natural resource base. The natural environment is the major source of economic opportunity, and the primary source of materials and services to which people ascribe value and add value in use. As with any such source, it has inherent limitations, imposed by its finite biophysical nature.

The natural environment comprises a variety of complex biophysical cycles, each using energy to develop and sustain a structure for matter. Many of these cycles are interlinked. Thus, what we choose to designate as "resources" are at the same time integral constituents of environmental systems. In the interests of sustainable development, we need to acknowledge that some of the most important ecological concepts are based upon ideas such as the laws of thermodynamics, resource stocks and flows, open systems, cybernetic feedback and dynamic steady state, carrying capacity, succession, and the existence of limiting factors.

Modern scientific understanding of the environment involves its description in "Systems Thermophysical" terms. The total environment of Planet Earth, and the ecological and other subsystems of which it is comprised, have a considerable ability to regulate their own functions, but they can also react to changing circumstances by rapidly altering their own internal structure and organization. The early (classical) idea that the world is in some sense, no matter how complex, at center a linear, reversible deterministic machine, has been replaced by the knowledge that all such large complex systems are in fact nonlinear, indeterminate; i.e., the systems are dynamically unstable, being far from a state of equilibrium with their surroundings. No matter how much is known about their past, their future behavior can never be predicted accurately, although in some cases it may be possible within very broad limits. Thus, exploitation of resources beyond a threshold point runs the risk of destabilizing the system(s) of which they are a part, with effects that are generally unpredictable.

Resource use. Use of the natural environment and of the resources within it can be either consumptive or nonconsumptive, in a physical sense. Resource use is ends-related, which immediately ties resource use to the social values that give rise to that use. These interrelated concepts— resources, uses, ends, values— can all be observed across a wide spectrum, ranging from the individual and particular to the collective and generic. Because not everyone holds identical values, conflicts over resource use are to be expected as an inherent part of everyday living. Such value conflicts can frequently be seen to occur between individuals and at the level of public policy. Mechanisms for resolving such conflicts are important to community and societal development.

We draw attention to the point that sustainable development only has significance in an integrative, collective context, since the life of an individual is not indefinitely sustainable. We would also make the point that, in a "systems" context, "reality" is fundamentally a reflection of emergent properties of the total system, not of the simple sum of its parts.

Institutional arrangements. Our interest here is in the institutional arrangements that influence the manner in which people use natural resources. Sustainable resource use (by a society) depends upon recognizing the integral "control functions" within natural (environmental) resource systems. Therefore it is logical to incorporate into the design of institutional arrangements, facts that humans have to accept about the workings of biophysical systems. While institutional arrangements for sustainable development should reflect essential attributes of the natural resource base, the actual need for them stems from the plurality of values held by individuals in society. People have different goals and priorities, leading to competing and perhaps conflicting styles of resource use.

Institutional arrangements legitimize resource-based activity, while at the same time attempting to minimize consequent harms, and share benefits and costs, in a manner that is deemed to be just. They also provide a legitimized basis for resolving potential conflicts among competing interests in society. Such arrangements are becoming increasingly formalized (e.g., taking the form of legislative guidelines, regulations, and public procedures) as the potential scale and frequency of interference between people increases.

Relationships between organizing concepts

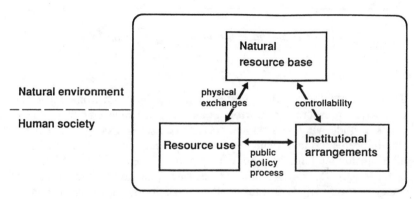

Figure 3: *Development as a dynamic environment-society process*

The conceptual framework that we present here is based on the three organizing concepts already discussed—the Natural Resource Base, Resource Use, and Institutional Arrangements. When seen as a coherent overall process, this framework describes the dynamic environment-society process of social and economic development in conjunction with management of aspects of the natural environment (*Figure 3*). It provides a basis for discussing sustainable development as concept, policy and practice.

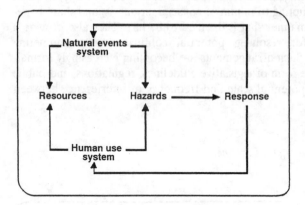

Figure 4:   Resources and hazards from nature and people

This conceptualization is supported by the model of environment-society interaction presented by Burton, *et al.*, (1978), which emphasizes feedbacks to underlying physical and social processes (*Figure 4*). Their depiction indicates the underlying duality, while including the concept of overall environmental and institutional "response." The conceptual framework in this paper has been structured so as to emphasize the integral parts of policy process and institutional arrangements, as components of "response."

The concept of environment-society interactions, as having the potential to create both resources and hazards, complements the conceptual framework presented here. The resource/hazard dichotomy is, as we would say, at the heart of sustainable development. The interaction of nature and people creates both useful resources and hazardous threats. Responding to hazards, society may seek to modify the natural events system, the array of wind, water and earth processes, and the human use system of locations, livelihoods, and social organization (Burton, *et al.*, 1978).

Principles and issues in sustainable development

We now summarize the main principles of sustainable development and highlight issues that seem to be important for future policy development.

The biosphere as physical context for development. The World Commission on Environment and Development devoted much attention to the concept of sustainable development. The major objective of development, it concluded, is the satisfaction of human needs and aspirations (WCED, 1987, p. 43).

> Perceived needs are socially and culturally determined, and sustainable development requires the promotion of values that encourage consumption standards that are *within the bounds of the ecological possible* and to which all can reasonably aspire. (WCED, 1987, p. 44)

The Commission emphasized that economy and natural environment are closely linked in the physical world, and urged far better integration of environmental considerations into all aspects of economic and development policy.

Society's dependence on ecological sustainability—a hierarchy for policy development. There is a Maori[1] proverb "Tukino ao tukino koe" "destroy nature; destroy yourself" (Palmer, 1989, p. 14).

> Putting sustainable development into practice, then, means recognizing the wider systems of which we are a part—locating human activities as a subsystem of the biosphere and constrained by the physical laws of the earth. (Cronin, 1989, p. 14)

This suggests the notion of a hierarchy built upon sustaining the integrity of the natural environment:

- ecological sustainability as an underlying principle for:
- sustainable resource use and waste management, which is, in turn, the basis for:
- sustainable society.

Ecological sustainability involves not deliberately interfering with major cycles in the biosphere, to an extent that makes them hazardous for life. It involves maintaining genetic diversity and diversity amongst ecosystems as the basis for biological resilience and adaptability.

Sustainable resource use involves harvesting resources within the carrying capacity of the renewable resource systems involved, and linking stock

---

1 Maori, a Polynesian people, are indigenous to Aotearoa - New Zealand.

depletion with resource conservation and recycling, to avoid fuelling unsustainable resource demands that would jeopardize an orderly transition to renewable substitutes.

Sustainable waste management involves minimizing waste production and managing waste disposal within the receiving capacities of environmental sinks, and includes avoiding the production of hazardous substances.

A sustainable society involves acceptance of the physical bounds of ecological sustainability, sustainable resource use, and waste management. It involves eliminating material poverty, integrating ecological, social, and economic considerations in resource management decision-making, and developing the "ecological" and integrative sciences.

Recognizing the "resource"/"hazard" dichotomy and developing approaches to risk avoidance. There are many sustainable futures. A policy of sustainable development is rather like one that seeks to promote efficiency. There is no single efficient use of resources, and there is no single, precisely optimal level of efficiency. Rather, we approach the objective of increasing efficiency in our use of resources by reducing the incidence and level of inefficiency in practice. Similarly, sustainable development is given practical effect by minimizing the incidence of unsustainable outcomes, by aiming to avoid such risks if possible. It is therefore both anticipatory (proactive) and adaptive.

In its proactive mode, sustainable development policy is built upon research to provide good base-line information. We need to know how ecosystems behave, and what makes them vulnerable to breakdown. We need to know about thresholds for irreversible damage, about critical limiting factors and indicators of environmental health, about the state of particular resources within these systems. We also need to understand how environmental costs impinge upon financial viability.

> Decision-making for resource management must be informed by an understanding of ecosystem process and management of resource demand in relation to carrying capacity. (Cronin, 1988)

Outcome-oriented policy development and the need for monitoring. Sustainable development also has an adaptive component to its implementation. To complement research and management activities, it is therefore essential to monitor the outcomes of resource use. Monitoring serves several purposes. Monitoring individual activities is important in the context of policy enforcement and compliance. It also underscores any government role in resolving conflicts over resource use. Its other main purpose is to provide information for assessing the effectiveness of policy measures and the need to adapt policy.

Ecological principles expressed in management institutions. The principles for sustainable development set out above indicate very strongly that environmental considerations should not be treated as "add-ons" in the resource management process, as has often been the case in the past. They should be integrated into the institutional arrangements and given the same sort of status as other social and economic development principles.

The idea that decision-making for resource management should be "informed" by ecological understanding is not simply a general call for people to be environmentally aware. It implies more formalized arrangements, covering specific institutions for "allocating" resources, and imposing practical conditions on resource use. These institutions can then be assessed in the light of subsequently observed environmental, social, and economic outcomes.

Application of the framework to energy policy

In order to ensure that, as far as is possible, sustainable development is not preempted by inappropriate policy prescriptions, we now examine some energy policy issues, in the context of the above conceptual framework. To develop energy policies that explicitly acknowledge the context of sustainable development, we need to address the aforementioned organizing concepts of sustainable development; natural resource base, resource use, and institutional arrangements.

Natural resource base

Stock energy resources. Over 90 percent of the world's commercially traded fuels currently come from stocks in the natural environment, and most of it from hydrocarbon stocks. The main concerns surround the emission of polluting gases to the atmosphere.

The management problem is made particularly difficult by several factors (*inter alia*): the persistent uncertainty; the physical problem is not contained within national boundaries; the atmosphere is a global commons; the beneficiaries of energy services are often not the same as those who endure the costs of its pollution; and the fact that fossil fuels account for such a high proportion of primary energy consumed.

Current policies for the use of stock resources rely heavily upon the (economic) theory of continuous substitution. This theory stands on the notion that, as a resource declines in quality and/or accessibility, its cost will rise until some other resource (currently more costly) becomes economic, whereupon substitution will occur (Beckerman, 1975). While this process may have taken place in the past, there is real doubt that it can continue for ever.

If the long-term question of substitutability of energy resources is addressed from the point of view of energy analysis, a different picture emerges. It is clear that the energy subsidy (embodied in capital and operating expenditures) needed to develop new, poorer quality resources has to come from current fuels. As they rise in cost, so will the energetic (and economic) cost of the putative substitute (see, for example, Slesser's [1982] discussion of the price of oil from shale). There is evidence from several countries (Hall, *et al.*, 1986; Peet, *et al.*, 1987) that this process may be already under way.

Over time, it can be taken for granted that the primary energy requirement of a given quantity of net energy will increase. In the long term this process can be expected to proceed at an accelerating rate (Gilliland, 1977; Penner, 1981), meaning that depletion rates (and, hence, emissions) would increase exponentially, even for a constant delivery of net energy to the economic system. Of course, we do not expect economies to ignore this process— when prices rise, as a result of cost pressures, demand will respond. Our point is that whereas energy analysis predicts the outcome in advance, conventional market economic processes wait until it happens before responding.

Environmental resources. Globally, the estimated recoverable reserves of coal are larger than for oil and gas (Ion, 1980). Any perceived scarcity of oil and natural gas will therefore be seen as opening the door to another era of coal development. However, the ratio of carbon released (to the atmosphere as carbon dioxide) to heat energy output doubles with a move from natural gas to coal. For many countries, where the major part of the stock resource endowment is in low grade lignite, the ratio could be even higher. A continuation of fossil fuel consumption will therefore pose even more challenges for pollution abatement, especially in the case of global problems such as accelerated climate change.

Renewable energy resources. If energy stock options have potential problems, do energy flow sources offer a way through? Proponents of substituting stock energy with renewable energy sources are the first to acknowledge that their increased use is not without its problems (Holdren, *et al.*, 1980). Increased harnessing of renewable energies has a corresponding impact on their materials requirements. Such sources are flow-limited and, with the exception of hydroelectric power, are relatively dilute and widely distributed in a pattern that does not necessarily match evolving distributional patterns of energy use.

Another characteristic that distinguishes renewable energy sources from their stock counterparts is competing use. Colonizing renewable resource streams implies diverting them from existing economic and environmental functions, thereby placing those functions under greater stress.

Resource use

Society cannot change its original endowment of stock resources, but it can exercise choice over the manner of its use (including the option of trading to import resources). Reflecting on trends in materials and energy use during the twentieth century, Page concluded that it is "time to make preservation of the resource base an explicit policy issue" (Page, 1977, p. 13). This is because material and energy flows involved in human consumption patterns have become so large in relation to the natural environment, and because the lead times for adaptive action have become correspondingly shorter and environmental and technological effects more pervasive.

Given the demand for physical goods and services that come from resource stocks, modifying depletion and pollution rates can involve several technical options— recycling, improved physical efficiency, and resource substitution.

- *At each extreme of the energy use spectrum* (e.g., mining at one end, and waste disposal at the other), the economy interacts directly with the natural environment. Policy is focused on depletion and pollution.
- *Within the economy itself* (e.g., resource processing, manufacture, and final consumption activities), cultural, institutional, and technical

factors combine to influence the ways in which individuals and communities use resources. Policy here is focused on physical efficiency, recycling, and substitution.

What happens at the boundary between the economy and the environment affects patterns of use within the economy, and *vice versa*. Increases in physical efficiency and rates of recycling will slow down depletion and pollution. If the existing institutional arrangements do not discourage pollution, however, economic efficiency and optimality will correspond to low efficiency of use and minimal recycling efforts (Bromley, 1988, pp. 20-1).

Institutional arrangements

In this subsection, we attempt to focus attention on recurring themes in the literature— the *ad-hoc* characteristic of much of stock resource management in the past; arguments over possible policy conflicts; present biases in institutional arrangements for managing stocks; the questions surrounding the generalizability of current levels of depletion; and whether stocks can be renewed. (The order in which we present these issues is not intended to signify ranking).

Ad-hoc decision-making of the past. For several decades, the focus of resource debates in many countries (our own included) has been either on mechanisms for promoting resource development (e.g., overcoming capital constraints or introducing market discipline through corporatization) or on other macroeconomic goals such as regional development or employment creation. The consequences for the future and for the environment, locally or globally, were not seen as issues. The perception of resource abundance often led to profligate levels of use of high quality stock resources, and excessive levels of pollution.

There was little evidence of any policy concept to balance investments in resource developments with investments in resource conservation and efficiency of use, or indeed in the systematic reduction of pollution. There was little indication that policy makers linked the health of the economy to the health of the environment; that resource protection and resource development could be seen as self-reinforcing; that public policy might be just as concerned for demand management as it always had been for supply management.

De-facto policy decisions were taken in an *ad-hoc* manner, insofar as they applied to the management of resource stocks and the environment. The energy sector in particular was characterized by supply-side planning that predominated until the 1980s.

Other examples of *ad-hoc* policy decisions include special tax provisions for mineral exploration; the privileged status accorded to mining over other land uses; and concessionary electricity tariffs for electricity-intensive activities such as aluminium smelting, etc.

Common to the experiences of many countries has been the influence of energy utilities. Their natural monopoly power, and (in all but a few) their insistence on monotonous increases in supply capacity rather than managing demand, all added up to a juggernaut which many governments appeared powerless to slow down. Now, billions of dollars of generating plant lie idle or half-used, throughout the world; evidence of mistakes with environmental, economic, and social consequences that will be with us for a generation or more.

In the context of sustainable development policy, we therefore see the need to formulate coherent policies for the management of energy (and material) stocks, so that policy options and their implications can be addressed together. Without a coherent policy framework, trade-offs between resource depletion and resource conservation will never be addressed specifically. Hence, key resource management options will remain beyond the reach—and often beyond the comprehension—of policy makers in pursuit of sustainable resource use.

Microeconomic and macroeconomic policy. Economic efficiency and sustainable development (and the policy goals that go with them) are both goals of economic management. Sustainable development is sometimes criticized because it does not maximize the net present value possible from resource extraction and use. Similar reasoning could be used to make the opposite assertion, that economic efficiency is invalid, simply because it does not ensure long-term sustainable development.

> The reasoning is surely wrong ... One cannot use one criterion to bludgeon another. They are on the same logical level. The most one can say is that the two criteria conflict; they imply different states of the world. (Page, 1977, p. 188)

A number of economists (Page, 1977; Daly, 1987; Goodland and Ledec, 1987; Pearce, 1987; Saeed, 1987;) have commented on the inconsistency between microeconomic goals applied in the microeconomic context and microeconomic goals applied in the macroeconomic context.

> In microeconomics, growth in production (or consumption) is possible or is
> considered desirable only to the point where the marginal benefit (e.g., rev-
> enue) equals the marginal cost. In macroeconomic theory, there is usually no
> concept of the optimum size of an economy over the long term; rather bigger
> is always better. This approach neglects the often severe environmental and
> other social costs associated with high and growing rates of per-capita natural
> resource consumption. (Goodland and Ledec, 1987, p. 39)

Society as a whole is thus encouraged to do what no firm would contem-
plate rationally; maximize resource throughput irrespective of the associated costs. The fact that environmental costs are usually nonmonetized, it
is argued, is responsible for this anomaly; public damage is not translated
into private cost. Economic efficiency is defined independently of the rate
of material and energy throughput in the economy. Yet, it is the level of
that throughput that correlates with environmental impacts.

In effect, however, the two goals are not in conflict. Economic efficiency is a microeconomic goal concerned with short-run individual
behavior, particularly with present-day allocation of economic resources.
Sustainable development goals are macroeconomic, and are concerned
with long-term aggregate behavior. In our opinion, clear establishment of
sustainable development policy objectives is the primary requirement, to
help set conditions within which markets will be able to do what they do
well.

> By modifying the flows across the boundary between the environment and the
> economy, myopic markets can be encouraged to be consistent with long-range
> social goals. (Page, 1977, p. 204)

As we see it, economic instruments are in most cases necessary, but not
normally sufficient components of the institutional arrangements which
we need to put in place to implement sustainable development policy.

Present biases. Resource markets are one major set of institutions for
implementing policies on the management of stock resources. While a lot
of ideological debate surrounds the use that is made of markets, one practical issue that is very important here is identification of the biases that
currently exist, and determination of what needs to be done at the policy
level to correct them.

Without policy influence, the behavior of markets will result in a certain level of material and energy through the economy—a certain balance
point, not itself predetermined by policy. But markets do not exist in a
policy and institutional vacuum. Two sorts of institutional factors can upset or alter the balance—deliberate, policy-motivated *distortions* and market *failures*.

Some people may argue, at the policy level, that resource exploitation should be further encouraged as the basis for future economic growth and development. Others urge the use of policy measures to encourage resource conservation as the basis for future economic security. The irony is that both policy arguments appeal to considerations of future benefits, yet they end up recommending diametrically opposed policies for the use of stocks, and hence will give rise to markedly different pollution outcomes (Page, 1977, p. 5).

Imposing some macroeconomic policy on the behavior of markets does not in itself invalidate the efficiency criterion. But it can change the resulting balance between depletion and conservation, disposal and durability, and so on. As an example, market failures due to exclusion of environmental and disposal costs from market processes have maintained a consistent (and, we would suggest, largely deliberate) bias against efficiency in use and materials recycling, in virtually all economies.

Among market distortions, taxation measures can influence the balance either way, as can regulatory measures. Preferential tax write-offs for mineral exploration, and preferential status for mining activities in land-use planning, will penalize both the search for more efficient extraction from existing operations and more efficient use of the product. Severance taxes, bounties for scrap materials, and more stringent standards for emissions to air and water will move the balance the other way.

Competitive market behavior has an inherent bias toward current beneficiaries. Hotelling's rule is a rule for today's markets, "and, by extension, cost-benefit analysis centered on present-value maximizations" (Goodland and Ledec, 1987, p. 21). The rule is ethically understandable, when couched in the form of the assumption that future generations will inevitably be better off than the present. However, its validity as a decision rule is immediately thrown into question by any acknowledgement that long-lived wastes and material depletion may—and probably will—impose a legacy of shared risk, rather than shared benefits.

Ultimately, the need for corrective policy action is influenced by unfolding outcomes. For example, if pollution is judged to be excessive, measures can be put in place to encourage increased efficiency of material and energy use or increased recycling effort. How stringent to make those measures is a judgment that only time will vindicate. Their effectiveness in altering the balance and reducing the perceived pollution problem will have to be monitored over time and further policy decisions taken at a later date.

Generalizability. The WCED has highlighted equity as a central issue: "Sustainable development requires meeting the basic needs of all and extending to all the opportunity to fulfil their aspirations for a better life" (WCED, 1987, p. 8).

If generalizability means "extending to all the opportunity," what are the physical implications of this for resources and the environment? As a guideline to the possible implications of generalizability, Daly (1988, p. 43) has done "some simple back-of-an-envelope calculations" to estimate that the annual extraction of nonrenewable resources "would have to increase by roughly a factor of 7" if the entire global population were to consume resources at current US per capita rates. An analysis by the US Geological Survey (Trainer, 1986, p. 23) comes to the similar conclusion, of about a tenfold increase in the rate of stock depletion.

Any such estimates are obviously highly speculative. However, even if they overstate the case by, say, 100 to 200 percent, the implications for global pollution are still substantial. In past discussions of generalizability, most attention has been given to what might be possible in terms of resource availability and technical innovation. The more pressing issue, in our opinion, is the global risk associated with "generalizing" current trends in environmental degradation.

Can stocks be renewed? "Keeping the resource base intact" is a useful slogan for those who acknowledge the potential anomaly that stock resource depletion might pose for sustainable development. How realistic is the assertion by some economists, that nonrenewable resources can, *in effect*, be renewed? (We ignore the processes of geological renewal, in the context of this particular discussion.)

The assertion appears to have two basic interpretations. One is that "renewal" of depleted stocks comes about through the development of improved methods for accessing lower grades (e. g., Beckerman, 1975). Thus extraction costs are prevented from rising. It sometimes employs the imagery of "sustained yield" from resource stocks. The other interpretation takes the line that liquidating resource capital provides opportunities to reproduce other future benefits (e. g., Solow, 1974)—the idea that future generations may not thank us for leaving resources in the ground.[2]

---

2 In both interpretations, it is implicit in the line of argument that "sustained growth" in the economy is not only desirable but necessary. The logical, biological, and sociological absurdity of this idea, in any context relating to material goods and services, is seldom acknowledged.

When all the arguments have been heard, they essentially come down to the fact that technological optimists and pessimists both acknowledge the importance of improving the efficiency of materials and energy extraction processes. The policy questions then become (i) should more be done by way of institutional incentives (particular policy instruments) to increase this effort? and (ii) why not apply the same logic right along the sequence, not just to resource extraction? Improvements can be achieved by end-use consumers, as well as by producers and manufacturers.

Having considered the questions that surround the proposition of stock renewability, it would seem that a more pertinent issue for policy-makers than "*can* stocks be renewed?" is "*are* stocks renewed by current patterns of development?" In response to this particular question, some countries have experimented with natural resource accounts so that they can, quite purposefully, try to reflect the net balance of capital accumulation and stock resource depletion (Wright, 1989). We see this as one very useful component of the overall monitoring effort.

Discussion

Stock resources and sustainable development—a contradiction?

On the surface, there would appear to be an unavoidable contradiction between growth in the use of nonrenewable or stock resources (a process which is, in the long term, obviously unsustainable) and the goal of sustainable development for society as a whole (which is implicitly concerned with the long term). However, we think there are arguments which make this not necessarily a foregone conclusion.

The first is that people are primarily concerned with sustaining a level of utility or service, rather than sustaining consumption rates of any particular stock resource. Utility can therefore be sustained while resource consumption shifts away from stocks. Sustainable development would only be compromised if the rates of resource consumption reached while using stocks were to lead to resource substitution demands which exceeded the carrying capacity of renewable resource systems (Baines, 1989, p. 8).

The second argument derives from giving policy priority to the avoidance of substantial or irreversible harms. These are exemplified in a general way by irreversible degradation of the natural environment (see pre-

vious section, and also Baines, 1989, pp. 19-20). By and large, we believe
the threat of ecological damage is now perceived with greater certainty
than the threat of scarcity of resources, although the two are obviously
related. Among such harms, those associated with global energy consumption patterns generate the most acute policy problems. The environment is
thus seen as central to the energy dilemma, not peripheral or external to
it. Ultimate limits on the use of energy are more likely to be imposed by
rising environmental and sociopolitical costs than by resource exhaustion
or production costs (Holdren, *et al.*, 1980, p. 241).

Establishing decision rules for sharing the once-only "goods" of
resource stocks across the many generations who might claim interests in
the resource base is an extremely difficult policy issue to resolve. By
contrast, establishing decision rules to try to avoid creating permanent
"bads" is already supported by current evidence and perceptions. This
approach, which is a cornerstone of sustainable development, has several
potential policy advantages:

- the policy initiatives are called for in terms of environmental protection
  anyway;
- it does not distinguish between stock and renewable resources;
- many of the policy initiatives would be as beneficial now as in the
  future.

Incentives for technological innovation arise if either resource scarcity or
environmental damage is seen as threatening. Both trends would encourage greater efforts at resource conservation and substitution. Whichever is
the cause hardly matters in the end, if unsustainable outcomes are
avoided. Thus, the use of stock resources *need* not lead to any contradiction or dilemma for policy prescription. However, this is not the same as
saying that it *will* not.

Energy and the future

> Will fusion energy or solar energy or conservation or some as yet unthought
> of energy source step in to save the day and keep economies growing? The
> technological optimists say yes and the technological pessimists say no. Ulti-
> mately, no one knows. Both sides argue as if they were certain, but the most
> insidious form of ignorance is misplaced certainty. (Costanza, 1989, p. 3)

What is the prudent path for public policy on the management of stock
resources? Because of uncertainty about future technological developments, we see the *general* thrust of sustainable development policy as

being the avoidance of unsustainable outcomes. The emphasis is thus on avoiding what are perceived as irreversible and costly impacts on environmental systems and the resource base (Baines, 1989, pp. 19-20). Three arguments have generally been advanced in support of this type of policy stance:

1. There is greater certainty about the impacts of "bads."
2. It gets away from the "language of sacrifice."
3. It is what might be termed a "reversible" policy stance.

The risks of unsustainable outcomes that are perceived with most certainty by people are: the risks to the environment of irreversible impacts from long-lived wastes; climatic instability; species and ecosystem extinction; contamination and disruption of conditionally renewable resource systems, e.g., fresh water aquifers and fertile soils. Some management of the use of nonrenewable stocks can thus be implemented by policy instruments aimed primarily at pollution abatement and reduction of ecological risk. These will affect the relative economics of stock use without necessarily prohibiting them outright.

Energy stocks, in the form of fossil fuels and fissionable uranium, are critical contributors of environmental bads. In this case, substitution by renewable energy sources and a concerted drive to improve energy efficiency provide prudent and strategic medium-term options. Compared with further advances in nuclear technology, these options have the advantage of virtually certain technical outcome and, in many cases, competitive economics as well (Lovins, 1981). Thus, it has been argued that they do not in fact involve any sacrifice on the part of the present generation; they simply make prudent economic sense, and also keep options open.

Making short-term objectives consistent with long-term goals

In order to put our sustainable development goals into practice, we need institutional arrangements to influence the ways in which people and societies use natural resources. These arrangements will, of necessity, be some type of "control procedures." In most Western societies it seems to be the preferred option, that such procedures take the form of microeconomic instruments, which, once set in place, encourage people to act in their individual best interests, to achieve the best interests of society as a whole.

We support the principle of using market methods, wherever they can be shown to be both socially and environmentally appropriate. However, we are also well aware that there are many situations in which markets have functioned in such a way as to create the very (macroenvironmental and macroeconomic) problems we are trying to overcome.

Regarding sustainable development and the use of stock resources, we therefore assert that microeconomic tools must always be subservient to the macro requirements of sustainability. That relationship, in turn, must be interpreted and mediated through moral and ethical imperatives. The imperatives that we see as dominant include *responsibility*—responsibility to future generations, and responsibility to those millions who, in this age of apparent abundance, have neither an adequate share of resources nor the power to avoid development paths that are clearly unsustainable.

If a contradiction does persist between the continued use of stock resources and sustainable development, it will most likely be because society, collectively, does not bother to "read the signs" of impending unsustainable outcomes soon enough and take adaptive actions.

References

Baines, J. T. *et al*. (1988). *The Sustainability of Natural and Physical Resources—Interpreting the Concept*. Studies in Resource Management, No. 5. Centre for Resource Management, University of Canterbury. Christchurch, New Zealand.

—— (1989). *An Integrated Framework for Interpreting Sustainable Development. Ecological Principles and Institutional Arrangements for the Sustainable Development of Natural and Physical Resources*. Report to the Ministry for the Environment. Centre for Resource Management, University of Canterbury. Christchurch, New Zealand.

—— (1989a). *Possible Roles for the Ministry for the Environment in Implementing Sustainable Development Policy*. Report to the Ministry for the Environment. Centre for Resource Management, University of Canterbury. Christchurch, New Zealand.

Beckerman, W. (1975). "The Fallacy of Finite Resources." *Bank of New South Wales Review*, Vol. 14, pp. 10-5, Australia.

Bromley, D. W. (1988). *Property Rights and the Environment; Natural Resource Policy in Transition*. Ministry for the Environment. Wellington, New Zealand.

Burton, I. *et al*. (1978). *The Environment as Hazard*. Oxford.

Catton, W. R. (1982). *Mines and Pitfalls in the Future of homo colossus*. Department of Mineral and Energy Resources, Colorado School of Mines.

Costanza, R. (1989). "What is Ecological Economics?" *Ecological Economics*, Vol. 1, pp. 1-7.

Cronin, K. (1988). *Ecological Principles for Resource Management*. Ministry for the Environment. Wellington, New Zealand.

—— (1989). "Entering the Mainstream—the Growing Importance of the Environment in Public Policy." Keynote paper at Third International Permaculture Conference, Kaiwaka, Northland, New Zealand, p. 18.

Daly, H. E. (1987). "The Economic Growth Debate. What some Economists have Learned but Many Have Not." *Journal of Environmental Economics and Management*, Vol. 14, pp. 323-36.

—— (1988). "On Sustainable Development and National Accounts." In Collard *et al.*, *Economics, Growth, and Sustainable Development*, chapter 4. New York.

Dasmann, R. F. *et al.* (1973). *Ecological Principles for Economic Development*. London.

Dunlap, R. E. (1983). "Ecological 'News' and Competing Paradigms." *Technological Forecasting and Social Change*, Vol. 23, pp. 203-306.

Garcia, R. and J. C. Escudero (1982). *Drought and Man. The 1972 Case History*. The Constant Catastrophe; Malnutrition, Famines and Drought, Vol. 2. New York.

Georgescu-Roegen, N. (1976). *Energy and Economic Myths*. Institutional and Economic Essays. New York

Gilliland, M. W. (1977). "Energy Analysis, a Tool for Evaluating the Impact of End Use Management Strategies on Economic Growth." In *Proc. Energy Use Management, International Conference*. Tucson, p. 613.

Goodland, R. and G. Ledec (1987). "Neoclassical Economics and Principles for Sustainable Development." *Ecological Modelling*, Vol. 38, pp. 19-46.

Hall, C. A. S., C. J. Cleveland, and R. Kaufmann (1986). *Energy and Resource Quality*. The Ecology of the Economic Process. London.

Holdren, J. *et al.* (1980). "Environmental Aspects of Renewable Energy Sources." *Annual Review of Energy*, Vol. 5, pp. 241-91.

Ion, D. C. (1980). *Availability of World Energy Resources*. London.

Lovins, A. B., L. H. Lovins, F. Krause, and W. Bach (1981). *Least-Cost Energy*. Solving the CO_2 Problem. Colorado (reprinted 1989).

Palmer, G. (1989). "Integrating Energy and Environmental Policies." Keynote Address to the Symposium on Energy and Environment organized by the Embassy of Sweden. Wellington, New Zealand.

Page, T. (1977). *Conservation and Economic Efficiency*. Published for Resources for the Future by the Johns Hopkins University Press, Baltimore.

Pearce, D. W. (1987). "Foundations of an Ecological Economics." *Ecological Modelling*, Vol. 38, pp 9-18.

Peet, N. J. *et al.* (1987). "Energy Supply and Net Energy in New Zealand." *Energy Policy*, Vol. 5, No. 3, pp. 239-48.

Penner, P. (1981). "A Dynamic Input-Output Analysis of Net Energy Effects in Single-Fuel Economics." *Energy Systems and Policy*, Vol. 5, No. 2, p. 89.

Saeed, K. (1985). "An Attempt to Determine Criteria for Sensible Rates of Use of Material Resources." *Technological Forecasting and Social Change*, Vol. 28, pp. 311-23.

Slesser, M. (1982). *A Thermodynamic Constraint on the Rate of Global Development*. Institute Chem. E. Symposium, Series No. 78. London, p. T1/37.

Solow, R. M. (1974). "The Economics of Resources or the Resources of Economics." *Journal of the American Economic Association*, Vol. 64, No. 2, pp. 1-14.

Sussman, M. V. (1982). *Elementary General Thermodynamics*. New York.

Taylor, C. N. and G. P. Fitzgerald (1988). *New Zealand Resource Communities*. Impact Assessment and Management in Response to Rapid Economic Change. 7th Annual Meeting of the International Association for Impact Assessment, Annual Conference. Griffith University, Brisbane, Australia.

Trainer, F. E. (1986). "A Critical Examination of The Ultimate Resource and The Resourceful Earth." *Technological Forecasting and Social Change*, Vol. 30, pp. 19-37.

World Commission on Environment and Development (WCED) (1987). *Our Common Future*. Oxford.

Wright, J. C. (1988). *Future Generations and the Environment*. Studies in Resource Management, No. 6. Centre for Resource Management, University of Canterbury. Christchurch, New Zealand.

if the economists propagating it do not make themselves better and more easily understood!

References

Ayres, R. U. (1992). *Industrial Metabolism*. Theory and Policy. Wissenschaftszentrum Berlin für Sozialforschung. Berlin.

Dolan, C. G. (1971). *TANSTAAFL*. The Economic Strategy for Environmental Crisis. New York.

Galtung, J. (1985). "Development Theory. Notes for An Alternative Approach." In U. E. Simonis (ed.), *Entwicklungstheorie - Entwicklungspraxis. Eine kritische Bilanzierung*. Berlin, pp. 73-89.

Jänicke, M., H. Mönch, Th. Ranneberg, and U. E. Simonis (1989). "Structural Change and Environmental Impact. Empirical Evidence on Thirty-Two Countries in East and West." *Environmental Monitoring and Assessment*, Vol. 12, No. 2, pp. 99-114.

Leipert, Ch. and U. E. Simonis (1990). "Environmental Damage—Environmental Expenditure 1. Statistical Evidence on the Federal Republic of Germany." *The Environmentalist*, Vol. 10, No. 4, pp. 301-9.

—— (1991). "Environmental Damage—Environmental Expenditure 2. Statistical Evidence on the Federal Republic of Germany." *The Environmentalist*, Vol. 11, No. 3, pp. 12-9.

Economic Council of Japan (1974). *Report of the NNW Measurement Committee: Measuring Net National Welfare of Japan*. Tokyo.

Uno, K. (1989). "Economic Growth and Environmental Change in Japan. Net National Welfare and Beyond." In F. Archibuyi and P. Nijkamp (eds.), *Economy and Ecology: Towards Sustainable Development*. Dordrecht, pp. 307-32.

Opschoor, J. B. and J. B. Vos (1989). *Economic Instruments for Environmental Protection*. Paris.

Repetto, R. and J. Pezzey (1990). Background Paper to the Workshop on "The Economics of Sustainable Development." Washington, D. C., January 23-25, 1990.

Speth, G. (1989). *The Greening of Technology*. Wissenschaftszentrum Berlin für Sozialforschung. Berlin.

World Commission on Environment and Development (1987). *Our Common Future*. Oxford.

Missing Links between Economic Theory and Environmental Policy

Frank J. Dietz and Jan van der Straaten

Introduction

This chapter deals with the discrepancy between environmental economics and environmental policy regarding the fight against environmental deterioration. In short, in mainstream economic textbooks environmental problems are seen as a market failure that, in the tradition of Pigou, can be corrected by imposing charges or taxes on activities that pollute the environment and deplete natural resources. In environmental policy, however, this recommendation is largely neglected, as in almost all countries only physical regulations (standards and requirements) are used to decrease pollution and depletion of natural resources. Section 1 describes this discrepancy more extensively.

This discrepancy can be explained as a cumulation of three circumstances. First, Pigovian internalization meets with fundamental obstacles, with which we already dealt with elsewhere in this volume. The same holds for the second circumstance, namely the insufficient ecological knowledge which hampers an optimum use of natural resources for human activities, as is the idea behind neoclassical analyses and policy recommendations. In this chapter we focus on the third circumstance, which is the pressure of vested economic interests to abuse the uncertainty of the environmental effects of human activity for weakening our retarding policy measures. In section 3 this is illustrated for the Dutch abatement policy of acid rain. Section 5 contains some concluding remarks.

Mainstream environmental economics versus policy practice

During the sixties it became clear in Western Europe and the United States that environmental problems belonged to normal life. Pollution of the air, water and soil, the presence of noise, monocultures, erosion and "asphalted zones," as well as the depletion of fossil fuels and minerals occupy a prominent place in the discussion. In this context, some economists realized that nature and the environment have become scarce factors, which implies that society has to choose for which ends the environment is used. Publications of economists such as Boulding (1966), Mishan (1967), Kneese, *et al.* (1970, 1972, 1975), Baumol and Oates (1975/1988), and in the Netherlands Hueting (1974) and Opschoor (1974), gave rise to a new subdiscipline: environmental economics.

Current environmental economics can roughly be characterized as an extension and application of neoclassical economic theory to environmental problems. Natural resources are an input for human production and consumption processes. In the same way as the scarcity of labor and capital forces choices, scarcity of natural resources forces economic agents to choose for which ends they are used. Consequently, given the ends of economic agents, the use of natural resources available is described as an optimization problem. Environmental deterioration, or, respectively, environmental quality is the result of the aggregated decisions of all individual economic agents, weighing the benefits derived from increasing production and consumption against the benefits enjoyed when environmental quality is improved.

A complicating factor is, however, that the preferences for environmental quality can only partly be expressed in exchange relations on the market, and this has to do with the problem of "external economies." Environmental problems have become outstanding examples of external diseconomies. External diseconomies prevent the natural resources available from being used in accordance with the preferences of economic agents. Since Pigou's *Economics of Welfare* (1920), an external diseconomy has been defined as the production of a negative by-product by one or more economic agents. This by-product, though unwanted and unasked for, is delivered unintentionally and "behind the back of the market." The loss experienced by the victim is not regarded as a cost-item by the originator of the external diseconomy. As a result, the costs of exploiting nature have been constantly underestimated. Consequently, nature is more harmed by production and consumption than the economic agents wish it to be.

In environmental economics, the central issue is how to reduce external diseconomies. Pigou's formula of internalization (1920/1952, p. 192) is often recommended, i.e., the state corrects the market failure by imposing a tax on the production of negative external economies (e.g., charging the emission of processing water) and/or by subsidizing the production of positive external economies (e.g., purification of processing water). The external economy, in this case the natural resource used, receives a shadow price which is included in the agents' private cost-benefit calculations. If the shadow prices are set at the right level, a Pareto optimum exploitation of nature—that is, pollution of the environment and depletion of natural resources according to the preferences of the economic agents—is considered to be possible.

In recent years, the Pigovian internalization method has been elaborated in several ways (Bohm and Russel, 1985; Opschoor and Vos, 1989). First, more or less considered as a price to be paid for pollution, various types of charges were developed, such as effluent charges, product charges, administrative charges, and tax differentiation. Second, various forms of financial assistance, such as grants, soft loans, and tax allowances, could be offered to firms as an incentive to alter their polluting behavior. Third, new incentive-generating instruments have been proposed, such as deposit-refund systems and marketable pollution rights. In a deposit-refund system a surcharge is put on the price of potentially polluting products; when returning these products or its residuals to a collection system, a refund of the surcharge follows. Pollution rights might be bought in artificially created markets, using them for actual or potential pollution; unused pollution rights might be sold to the highest bidder.

This theoretical picture strongly contrasts with actual environmental policy practice. The goals of environmental policy are seldom or never derived from individual preferences regarding the environment, that is, they are seldom or never based on cost-benefit analyses, showing which environmental quality offers society the highest benefits at the lowest costs. Instead, environmental policy goals are formulated in physical terms: rates for emission reduction, standards regarding emissions and discharges, product and process requirements.

Turning to the issue of policy instruments, hardly any of the instruments recommended in economic theory are used by current environmental policy. Traditionally, regulatory instruments have been used as the main equipment for carrying out environmental policy in most countries. The basis for such direct interventions is some form of legislation. Polluters' compliance is made mandatory, and often sanctions on noncompliance exist. The remaining pollution is frequently dealt with by public authorities. The tradition of applying this "command and control philosophy" has historical roots particularly in the urban sewerage and hygiene programs of the 19th century. So far as charges are applied, they only serve as a source for financing specific environmental policy expenditures. In addition to direct regulation, governments often enter into voluntary agreements with individual sectors, such as oil refinery and agriculture, concerning emission reductions.

When trying to explain this gap between economic theory and environmental policy, two reasons should be distinguished: the problems that arise when recommendations of economic theory are put into practice; and the influence of economic interest groups on the goals and instruments of environmental policy.

The impact of interest groups on environmental policy: the Dutch experience

In this section we discuss the influence of interest groups on the Dutch policy to reduce acidification. The reduction policy started in the seventies, although the name for the problem, "acid rain," was only introduced in the eighties.

In the sixties and seventies there was a general belief that sulphur dioxide (SO_2) was the main cause of acid rain. During the seventies, however, it became clear that nitrogen oxides (NO_x) were another important factor. In the eighties the emission of ammonia (NH_3) was discovered to be a further source of acid rain. Until 1980, acid rain had been seen as a problem of public health, and the aim of the measures taken in this period was to decrease the concentration of SO_2 in residential areas. Tall smokestacks were erected everywhere to achieve this goal. These measures were criticized by ecologists, who argued that tall chimneys only dilute the polluting substances (Baker and MacFarlane, 1961).

The same occurred in the Netherlands. The Dutch policy had focused on the reduction of the SO_2 emission, for which an emission ceiling of 500,000 tons per year was established. This ceiling was set as a compromise between the Ministry for Environmental Affairs and the refinery industry. From the viewpoint of public health considerably less would have allowed to be emitted. Pressure from the refinery industry, using the argument that the public health constraint would affect international competitiveness of the Netherlands, shifted the ceiling to 500,000 tons per year.

In the eighties, Dutch environmental policy concerning the reduction of acidification showed a remarkable change of philosophy. Initially, the basis for policy measures was sought in neoclassical economic theory. Attempts were made to calculate costs and benefits of reduction strategies in order to determine and to achieve an optimum use of the carrying capacity of the environment. Due to the fact that a substantial part of these costs and benefits cannot be calculated, the Ministry for Environmental Affairs was forced to look for another method.

In 1984, a standard was introduced based on the impacts of acidifying substances on ecosystems. Scientific research had made it clear that deposition of more than 1,800 acid equivalents per hectare per year would considerably damage ecosystems, while depositions below this figure would only cause marginal ecological damage (Ministry for Environmental Affairs, 1983-1984; Langeweg, 1988). So, the aim was no longer to optimize the use of the environment on the basis of (in the ideal case) individual preferences of economic agents or (more realistically) on the basis of the perceptions of policy-makers concerning the preferences for the environment in society. Instead, ecological knowledge, combined with the ethical view that irreversible changes in ecosystems were to be avoided, caused the Ministry for Environmental Affairs to opt for the standard of 1,800 acid equivalents.

The introduction of this standard, however, severed the relations between economic theory and environmental policy with respect to a vital element. Clearness about the standard that has to be met does not guarantee achieving it. Questioning the standard in good faith often proceeds from ignorance, followed by a reaction of alarm, or from disbelief and neglect ("it cannot be *so* terrible"). In the mid-eighties, deposition in the Netherlands amounted to approximately 5,500 acid equivalents per hectare per year. The emission from Dutch sources amounts to circa 8,000 acid equivalents per hectare per year.[1] To achieve 1,800 acid equivalents, emission reductions of 70 to 90 percent were required (Langeweg, 1988). Most people are suspicious when hearing this figure, expecting a dramatic change in their way of life. And this, indeed, could be necessary.

The standard of 1,800 acid equivalents, however, is also questioned in bad faith. Representatives of the ammonia-emitting intensive livestock sector time and again claimed that this standard was insufficiently substantiated. They expected that much smaller emission reductions were neces-

---

1 Hence, the Netherlands is a net exporter of acidifying substances.

sary, and requested further research to be done, what would lead measures to be postponed. Another example in which the deposition standard is questioned is the "contra-research" concerning the impacts of acidifying substances on Dutch forests undertaken by the joint producers of electricity and Shell Netherlands. Although official research of the Ministry of Agriculture yearly reported a decreasing vitality of the Dutch forests (60 percent of the forests being "less than vital"), the electricity producers and Shell downplayed the impact of acidifying substances on forests on the basis of their "contra-research."

Still, the pressing problem of acidification combined with the increasing pressure from public opinion is bringing about a consensus in society to ultimately reduce acidifying emissions by 70 to 90 percent. No consensus exists, however, concerning the pace at which such emission reductions have to be achieved. Emitting industries are very much interested in slowing down the pace for at least two reasons: their competitiveness on world markets (an argument which easily scores in the small and open Dutch economy) and sunk costs (firms seeking enough time to pay off their installed equipment before buying new, less emitting equipment). Furthermore, it is argued that production costs will inevitably increase due to reduction measures, ultimately jeopardizing employment, especially in emitting sectors such as oil refining, electricity, transportation, and agriculture.

Macroeconomic studies have shown that due to strict reduction measures employment will hardly decrease, and will even increase if similar measures are taken in other countries (Klaassen, *et al.*, 1985; Ministry of Housing, Physical Planning and Environment, 1988-1989). But macroeconomic figures do not dominate public debate. Instead, the need to restructure specific sectors and, subsequently, the threat of considerable loss of employment in these sectors are the hot issues. In the end, the short-term individual interests of those involved in the polluting industries may put the long-term collective goal of emission reduction out of sight.

Acidification and oil refineries

Oil refineries are of great economic importance in the Netherlands. Only a small part of the products of these refineries is delivered to the home market, while 70 percent or more is exported to other countries, particularly in Northwestern Europe. In these refineries crude oil is used as a fuel and as a raw material for petrochemical products. During the production processes the sulphur located in the crude oil is oxidized and emitted as sulphur dioxide. This sulphur dioxide, discharged in the air by tall smokestacks, is one of the causes of acid rain. Of the total emissions of acidifying substances, roughly 15 percent are from oil refineries.

A sound environmental policy cannot neglect these emissions. In 1985, parliament discussed the measures to be taken. In this discussion it became clear that the emission standards for oil refineries in Germany were stricter than those in the Netherlands. Still, the Minister for Environmental Affairs declared that the Dutch regulation was too strict, because Dutch refineries export the bulk of their production while the German refineries export only some 10 percent. So Dutch refineries, according to this type of reasoning, are more sensitive to strong regulations (Ministry of Housing, Physical Planning and Environment, 1984-1985, p. 59). Bowing to these arguments, the Dutch parliament decided to formulate weak restrictions for Dutch refineries.

On closer consideration, these arguments cut no ice. First, 30 percent of total production in the Netherlands is for the home market, for which the competition argument cannot be used, and about 50 percent of total export is delivered to Germany, where stricter regulations are applied. The conclusion is that 65 percent of total production is sold to countries where the competition argument is not valid.

But there is more. In publications by the Dutch government, reduction costs of $\pm$ Dfl 2,500 are mentioned for every ton of SO_2 which is suppressed in oil refineries. (These figures are in accordance with other publications; cf. Bains, 1980; van Oostvoorn and Tangena, 1985.) But these costs are related to outdated production methods, which are no longer used in modern refineries. At the beginning of the eighties, Esso and Shell had already built such modern refineries in the Rijnmond area. These refineries are better equipped to meet the increasing demand of lighter fractions such as gasoline and kerosine. In this type of refinery the reduction of SO_2 emissions is not as expensive, and the sulphur dioxide can be used for the production of sulfuric acid, in which case there are no actual reduction costs in these refineries. On the contrary, Pulles and Wiersma (1985) calculated that in these modern refineries a profit of Dfl 3,570 to Dfl 4,080 can be made for every ton of SO_2 suppressed in the production process.

The conclusion can be drawn that the Dutch government gave wrong information about the reduction costs of SO_2 emissions in oil refineries.

Moreover, in the light of the figures mentioned above, the argument of the weak position of the Dutch oil refineries melts into thin air. Actually, they make money with the reduction of their emissions.

To top it all, the Dutch government made substantial differences between oil companies. The limit of the emission in the permit for the old refinery had been 30,000 tons of SO_2 per year. The emission standard for the new refinery of Esso, the Flexicooker, had been reduced to 10,000 tons of SO_2 per year. Shell also constructed a new refinery, the Hycon installation. The total emission of the old Shell refineries amounted to 60,000 to 70,000 tons of SO_2 per year. For the new refinery, Shell requested an emission permit of 53,000 tons per year. This figure contrasts sharply with the figure of the Esso refinery. Fransen (1985, p. 25) calculated that the German standards for this Shell refinery would have amounted to 4,000 to 8,000 tons per year.

Initially, the regional authorities of Rijnmond and Shell had agreed on a rather strong standard for SO_2 emissions. However, the Minister for Environmental Affairs did not agree and overruled the deal (Barmentlo, 1988). The conclusion can be drawn that the Minister for Environmental Affairs protected one of the most polluting industries of the Netherlands, in particular the Shell refinery. The arguments serving traditional, vested economic interests proved to be stronger than the arguments based on environmental interests. Particularly, the connection between the Ministry of Economic Affairs and Shell is so strong that Shell continuously escapes from strict environmental regulations.

Acidification and power plants

Until the end of the seventies, natural gas was used as fuel in the majority of the Dutch power plants. Natural gas does not contain sulphur, and so the decrease of SO_2 emissions during the seventies had largely been realized by the increased use of this relatively clean fuel. But at the end of the seventies, coal became cheaper than natural gas and oil. Therefore, the Minister for Economic Affairs made proposals for an increased use of coal as fuel in power plants (Ministry for Economic Affairs, 1979-1980).

Using more coal, however, would also increase the emissions of SO_2. The Minister for Economic Affairs admitted that additional measures were needed to prevent the increase of SO_2 emissions. In his opinion, however, these additional reduction measures were not allowed to result in a higher price of electricity as this would affect the international competitiveness of national industries, while the very reason to use the cheaper coal was generated by the desire to maintain international competitiveness. So, conflicts between price and emission reduction measures were at hand.

The Minister for Economic Affairs made a proposal to desulphurize the fumes by 50 percent. In this case, the additional costs were thought to be acceptable for the exporting industries. But from an environmental point of view this percentage was far too low. A long quarrel started between the parties involved, i.e., the Minister for Economic Affairs, the Minister for Environmental Affairs, Parliament, the environmental movement, regional authorities, regional power plants, and the national cooperation of electricity producers. This dispute was mainly dominated by the Minister for Economic Affairs, to whose arguments the Minister for Environmental Affairs on the whole subscribed (van der Straaten, 1990).

After a long dispute the decision was made to desulphurize the fumes completely. This result was realized by the continuous efforts of the environmental movement. The Minister for Economic Affairs refused to accept a higher electricity price for industrial purposes, but succeeded in increasing the electricity price for households considerably. So the additional costs of SO_2 emission reduction in the Netherlands are ultimately paid by the small users of electricity, the ordinary consumers.

Acidification and transportation

The emission of NO_x by motorcars is an important source of acid rain. The reduction of these emissions can be realized by using an engine in which fuel is combusted with a low input of air. Such an engine is not yet generally available. Another solution is to add a catalytic converter to the existing engine types, with which NO_x emissions can be decreased by 90 percent. For the functioning of such a catalytic converter, unleaded gasoline must be used. This makes the introduction of a converter an international problem.

A decision had to be taken by the European Community because unleaded gasoline had to be available everywhere in Europe. The respective negotiations started in the early eighties. Germany and the Netherlands, suffering considerably from the effects of acid rain, tried to introduce strong restrictions concerning motorcar emissions. France, Italy, and the United Kingdom were against such restrictions, mainly because they feared that the competitiveness of their car industries would diminish. It took almost a decade to solve these problems. In 1989 finally, a decision was made that a catalytic converter had to be installed in all new cars from 1993 on. The ultimate decision came about by breaking of the unanimity rule in the EC Council. The upcoming European elections of June 1989 in which environmental issues gained the attention of the general public facilitated the decision.

The behavior of the Dutch government in this exercise of European environmental policy requires closer consideration. In many international publications a picture is given of Dutch authorities as the hard core of environmental progressiveness. But the real behavior does not fit this picture. During the period of the negotiations in the European Community, the Dutch government raised the speed limit on motorways from 100 kilometers per hour to 120 kilometers per hour; at a speed of 120 kilometers per hour the emissions of NO_x are 40 percent higher than at a speed of 100 kilometers per hour. The change of policy was forced by the motorcar lobby which has a strong position in one of the ruling political parties.

Another striking, or even perverse example of the strength of that lobby is the case of Volvo Car. This company was afraid that the introduction of the catalytic converter would negatively affect its position on the Dutch car market. In 1989, the Dutch government began to stimulate the use of catalytic converters by decreasing the consumer tax on "clean" cars and increasing the consumer tax on "dirty" cars. As a result, "clean" and "dirty" cars had more or less the same price. As potential buyers could easily be persuaded by the environmental advantages of a car with a converter, the intention of Volvo Car was to equip its cars with such a device within in two years. In order to maintain its market share until the catalytic car was introduced, Volvo Car succeeded in convincing national authorities to give a subsidy of Dfl 400 per produced car *without* a catalytic converter (Dietz, van der Straaten, and van der Velde, 1991).

Acidification and agriculture

After all the years of environmental policy, the emission of ammonia (NH_3) from the Dutch livestock sector is higher than ever. This sector succeeded in neutralizing every effort to reduce emissions. Initially, the Dutch government did not pay much attention to environmental problems in this sector. In the eighties, however, it became clear that the contribution of ammonia to acidification had increased to about 30 percent. Government developed a so-called manure policy to reduce, among other objectives, the emissions of ammonia from manure. However, legal regulations failed to stabilize livestock, and so the number of pigs and chickens has been increasing considerably (Dietz and Hoogervorst, 1991).

While national authorities often use the transboundary character of emissions like SO_2 and NO_x as an argument to take only weak measures or no measures at all, for NH_3 this argument does not hold. The fact that ammonia precipitates close to the emitting source offers an outstanding opportunity to reduce a substantial part of acidification locally and effectively. But it was precisely the intensive livestock sector that was the only sector in the Netherlands to increase its emissions during the last ten to fifteen years.

The main reason why the manure policy failed to materialize is to be found in the economic and social position of agriculture. The contribution of this sector to Dutch exports is high. Furthermore, this sector is well organized and takes a strong position in the state machinery. Under such conditions traditional economic interests will dominate over environmental interests (see Dietz and Termeer, 1991).

Missing links between economic theory and environmental policy

In general, economic theory provides a strong basis for policy measures. Without an idea about the causes of unemployment or inflation for example, state interventions to increase employment or decrease inflation, would be groping in the dark. In this sense, economic theory and policy are two sides of the same coin. Initially also, neoclassical environmental economic theory formed the basis for the Dutch policy on acidification. Since the mid-eighties, however, environmental policy and economic theory have been delinked regarding the objectives of the former.

Neoclassical theory recommends the optimum use of the natural resources available. But optimization is not possible if we are unable to determine the value natural resources have for society. Furthermore, optimization regarding natural resources often turns out to be meaningless because of the uncertainty about the impacts of economic activity on the environment. Regarding these fundamental problems, in the Netherlands no further attempts were made to determine the optimum level of acidification. Instead, an environmental standard of 1,800 acid equivalents was introduced, representing the limit above which the environment deteriorates as a result of the deposition of acidifying substances.

This change in policy has not been followed in the more traditional areas of economic policy. In fact, the Ministry for Environmental Affairs stood alone in its view that economic activities must be reassessed in the light of environmental standards. Hence, the forces supporting traditional views on economy and environment are dominantly represented in the government machinery. This has seriously hindered the reduction of acidification. To illustrate the point, the government is, directly or indirectly, involved with, and responsible for, both the *emission* of a large part of the acidifying substances (from electric power plants, transportation, intensive livestock sector, oil refineries, and the sole Dutch automobile plant) and the *reduction* of acidification. This duality also explains why large parts of the government machinery are influenced by well-organized industries (like oil refineries and agriculture), claiming that nature can bear far more than the standards set, arguing that international competitiveness prohibits large-scale emission reductions. In this arena of forces, the social objective to prevent severe environmental damage cannot be realized.

The neoclassical recommendation to internalize externalities disregards the existing imbalance of power in society. The above case study demonstrates that forces in society with interests in negative externalities are far more powerful than forces in favor of a sound environment. As a result, the aim of environmental policy deviates from the goal that is derived from, or is assumed in, neoclassical environmental economic theory.

Regarding the policy instruments used, the discrepancy between neoclassical recommendations (to use market instruments such as charges, subsidies, deposit-refund systems, and marketable pollution rights) and policy practice (almost exclusively using "command and control" instruments such as standards and requirements) is only partly explained in this chapter. In economic textbooks it is demonstrated that economic instruments are more efficient than direct interventions in economic processes. However, most politicians feel rather uneasy when changes in behavior of economic agents—and, consequently, changes in environmental quality—responding to particular policy measures cannot be exactly predicted, as is the case with economic instruments. The environmental effects of direct intervention are much clearer in advance.

Furthermore, polluting industries do not like taxes and charges. From the viewpoint of an individual firm, taxes and charges only cost money, without offering much opportunity to influence environmental policy, or, better, to use environmental policy to improve the competitiveness of the firm. By contrast, regulations in the form of emission standards do not cost money once the standard is achieved; and voluntary agreements to reduce the emission level are even more attractive, because both goals and instruments can be negotiated.

So, within the government as well as within polluting industries, many forces work into the same direction, that is, aiming at voluntary agreements and physical regulations while holding back economic instruments. Furthermore, due to the government's need for information and cooperation, industry is provided with amply rent-seeking opportunities (Buchanan and Tullock, 1975). Vested economic interests abuse environmental policy to hinder newcomers on the market ("the environment cannot bear more polluters"), and to improve their standing by negotiating for a large share of the legally allowed pollution (to be recorded in permits). Finally, individual firms and whole industries ask for subsidies to adapt their production processes to the imposed environmental standards and to maintain their international competitiveness.

To summarize this chapter briefly, the missing links between economic theory and environmental policy are partly due to the fundamental obstacles one encounters when attempting to follow the views and to execute the recommendations of neoclassical economics. The missing links are also due to the existing imbalance of power in society, offering vested economic interests the opportunity to put their individual and short-term interests before the collective and long-term interests of a sustainable society.

References

Bains, C. S. (1980). "Economics of Fuel Desulphurization." *Chemical Engineering Progress*, May, pp. 167-78.

Baker, K. and W. A. MacFarlane (1961). "Fuel Selection and Utilization." In World Health Organization, *Air Pollution*. New York, pp. 345-63.

Barmentlo, J. (1988). *Shell als succesvol lobbyist (Shell as a Successful Pressure Group)*. Rijksuniversiteit. Leiden.

Baumol, W. J. and W. E. Oates (1988). *The Theory of Environmental Policy*. 2nd edition. Cambridge, MA.

Bohm, P. and C. S. Russell (1985). "Comparative Analysis of Alternative Policy Instruments." In A. V. Kneese and F. L. Sweeney (eds.), *Handbook of Natural Resource and Energy Economics*. Vol. 1. Amsterdam, pp. 395-460.

Buchanan, J. M. and G. Tullock (1975). "Polluters' Profits and Political Response: Direct Controls versus Taxes. *American Economic Review*, Vol. 65, pp. 139-47.

Dietz, F. J. and N. J. P. Hoogervorst (1991). "Towards a Sustainable Use of Manure in Agriculture: The Dutch Case." *Environmental and Resource Economics*, Vol. 1, No. 3, pp. 313-32.

Dietz, F. J. and J. van der Straaten (1988). "The Problem of Optimal Exploitation of Natural Resources: The Need for Ecological Limiting Conditions." *International Journal of Social Economics*, Vol. 15, Nos. 3/4, pp. 71-9.

Dietz, F. J. and K. J. A. M. Termeer (1991). "Dutch Manure Policy: The Lack of Economic Instruments." In D. J. Kroon and R. J. in't Veld (eds.), *Environmental Public or Private Choice*. Dordrecht, pp. 124-47.

Dietz, F. J. and H. R. J. Vollebergh (1988). "Wishful Thinking about the Effects of Market Incentives in Environmental Policy." In F. J. Dietz and W. J. M. Heijman (eds.), *Environmental Policy in a Market Economy*. Wageningen, pp. 40-60.

Dietz, F. J., J. van der Straaten, and M. van der Velde (1991). "The European Common Market and the Environment: The Case of the Emission of NO_x by Motorcars." *Review of Political Economy*, Vol. 3, No. 1, pp. 62-78.

Downing, P. B. and K. Hanf (eds.) (1983). *International Comparisons in Implementing Pollution Laws*. Boston.

Fransen, J. (1985). "Bezwaren tegen vergunning voor luchtverontreiniging door Shell (Objections against Shell Permits on Air Pollution)." *Natuur en Milieu*, Nos. 7/8, pp. 25 ff.

Hueting, R. (1974/1980). *New Scarcity and Economic Growth*. Amsterdam.

International Energy Agency (1988). *Emission Controls in Electricity Generation and Industry*. Paris.

Klaassen, G. *et al.* (1985). *Werk maken van zure regen (Making Work of Acid Rain)*. Utrecht.

Kneese, A. V. (1970). "Economic Responsibility for the By-products of Production." *Annals of the American Academy of Political and Social Science*, Vol. 89, pp. 56-62.

Kneese, A. V. and C. L. Schultze (1975). *Pollution and the Public Policy*. Resources for the Future. Washington, D.C.

Langeweg, F. *et al.* (1988). *Zorgen voor morgen (Concerns for Tomorrow)*. Bilthoven.

Ministry of Economic Affairs (1979-1980). *Energiebeleid (Energy Policy)*. Handelingen 15802, Nos. 6-7, 's Gravenhage.

Ministry of Housing, Physical Planning and Environment (1983-1984). *De problematiek van de verzuring (The Problems of Acidification)*. Handelingen 18225, Nos. 1-2, 's Gravenhage.

—— (1984-1985). *Indicatief Meerjarenprogramma Lucht 1985-1989 (Indicative Long-Term Program Air 1985-1989)*. Handelingen 18605, Nos. 1, 2, 8, 's Gravenhage.

—— (1988-1989). *Nationaal Milieubeleidsplan (National Environmental Policy Plan)*. Handelingen 21137, No. 1, 's Gravenhage.

Mishan, E. J. (1967). *The Costs of Economic Growth*. London.

Oostvoorn, F. van and V. H. Tangena (1985). "Verzuring optimaal bestrijden (An Optimal Abatement of Acidification)." *Lucht en Omgeving*, April/May, pp. 40-5.

Opschoor, J. B. (1974). *Economische waardering van milieuverontreiniging (Economic Evaluation of Environmental Pollution)*. Assen.

Opschoor, J. B. and H. Vos (1989). *Economic Instruments for Environmental Protection*. Paris.

Pigou, A. C. (1920/1952). *The Economics of Welfare*. London.

Pulles, T. and D. Wiersma (1985). *Luchtverontreiniging door olieraffinaderijen in een veranderende markt (Air Pollution by Oil Refineries in a Changing Market)*. IVEM Report, No. 9. Groningen.

Straaten, J. van der (1990). *Zure regen, economische theorie en het Nederlandse beleid (Acid Rain, Economic Theory and the Dutch policy)*. Utrecht.

Environmental Movements and Sustainable Economic Systems

Michael D. Everett

A public choice model of political behavior

Creating environmentally sustainable economic systems involves a number of political questions. How do environmental movements develop or rejuvenate, and how do they motivate political actors to pass environmental regulations? And when these regulations impose substantial costs on key industries or threaten to slow economic growth, what kinds of counterforces develop? How can environmental movements deal with these counterforces to preserve and implement meaningful environmental regulations?

In the early 1970s Everett (1972) used a narrow, rationalistic public choice model of political behavior[1] to generate insights into the above questions as they applied to the newly emerging environmental movement in the United States. He predicted:

---

1 Public choice models start with the assumption that individuals make political, as well as economic, decisions based on their narrow self-interested, expected benefit-cost calculations. Anthony Downs' (1957) article, which still forms the basic paradigm (Mueller, 1979; Hardin, 1982; McLean, 1987), assumed that: 1. three ideal types of actors exist in the political economy-voters, organized pressure groups, and elected politicians; 2. the first two provide pressure for public goods; and 3. the latter respond so as to maximize expected votes.

Politicians and voters lack information about each others' attitudes and behaviors. Narrower, special interest groups find it relatively easy to organize and provide flows of information between politicians and voters. Broader, more general interest groups find it relatively difficult to organize and provide similar flows of information given the free-rider problem (Olson, 1965). Thus, special interest groups tend to control political systems within limits.

The news media often help set these limits. When an issue becomes of general enough interest the news media will devote space and time to it to increase long-run profitability. This tends to generate information flows more directly between voters and politicians. As a result, the special interest pressure groups tend to lose power and the general interest tends to reassert itself (Downs, 1957, p. 137; Downs, 1972 and Stigler, 1961; Tullock, 1967, pp. 57-61).

1. News media information on environmental deterioration could compensate for the organizational and financial weakness of general interest environmental groups relative to well organized special interest industry groups. Environmental groups also could leverage their limited resources through government bureaucracies and environmental regulations. These mechanisms would enable environmentalists to convince large numbers of voters and politicians that the expected benefits of environmental protection would exceed the expected costs.

2. Strong federal environmental regulations would impose costs on basic industries prompting their managers to form pressure groups to weaken the regulations. These counterforces would tend to win in the long run unless substantial media coverage and environmental education helped environmental groups keep strong information flows between voters and politicians.

3. Politicians caught between these two forces would look for compromises and technologies which would allow both rapid economic growth and reduced environmental deterioration. These technological escape routes, however, were likely to break down. Given imperfect information and uncertainty some of the new technologies and economic growth would lead to serious pollution. Scientific information would lag behind the actual damage, and public regulation would lag much further. Thus, continued environmental deterioration remained likely.[2]

In this paper we evaluate those predictions for the United States in terms of the historical record between 1970 and 1990 and seek new insights for the emerging global environmental movement. Our findings were somewhat mixed. In support of the model, we found that scientific and news media concerns did generate broad public concern about environmental problems and motivated political actors to pass significant environmental legislation. Contrary to the model, however, well organized industrial counterforce groups could not prevail over weaker environmental groups and could not roll back environmental legislation. Moreover, the laws appear to have achieved many of their stated objectives such as reducing most of the targeted air pollutants, particularly where the increased bene-

---

2 Similar paradigms of how lags in knowledge and regulation can lead to long-term environmental deterioration have become more common (Costanza, 1991; Meadows, *et al.*, 1992). In the 1970s, however, the mainstream economic view held that markets have and can continue to handle scarcity by rising prices and finding substitutes. Barnett and Morse (1963) provided a rigorous demonstration of this thesis for nonrenewable resources over the last hundred years or so.

fits to society seemed to have exceeded the increased costs of control. Finally, in support of the model, examples of technological breakdowns exist in the 1970-90 period.

From these findings several implications for the global environmental movement of the 1990s emerge. A *revised* public choice model suggests that the global environmental movement of the 1990s will be able to reduce targeted pollutants. This, however, may not lead to sustainable environments and economic systems. Rational political actors will still seek technological escape routes to allow rapid economic growth, and lags will still occur in the detection and regulation of serious environmental deterioration. To help offset these tendencies, the revised model places emphasis on environmental monitoring and free flows of information. Detailed support for this summary follows.

Historical evaluation of the 1972 model

The development of the environmental movement

The development of the environmental movement in the late 1960s and early 1970s tends to support the first prediction. Organized environmental pressure groups had small memberships and modest financing compared to industry groups. Increased information on environmental pollution through the mass media correlated with increased public concern as expressed in public opinion polls and increased memberships of environmental pressure groups. Most politicians began to support substantially stronger federal pollution control regulations, albeit with a lag of several years. Expenditures on pollution control equipment increased with a similar lag.

Table 1 provides some data for a more detailed analysis of this initial stage of the environmental movement. Column 1 suggests the weakness as well as the rapid growth of organized environmental pressure groups during the 1960s. These groups ranged from 60,000 to about 700,000 members with an estimated $1.2 to $14 million in revenues (at $20 per member) of which only a small portion could be devoted to lobbying. Organized pressure groups of such limited size and funding probably could not have directly contacted more than a small fraction of voters nor systematically lobbied more than a small group of political representatives.

Table 1: Indices of the environmental movement, United States

Year	Memberships of the main environment groups (1)	News Media % of three major news indexes (2)	Opinion Polls % who feel pollution is very serious (3)	(4)	Expenditures Capital (billions of 1982 dollars) (5)	Total (6)
1960	60,000	0.10			4	
1961		0.10			5	
1962		0.10			5	
1963		0.10			5	
1914		0.20			6	
1965	112,500	0.30	28		7	
1966	382,500	0.50	48		8	
1967	497,500	1.50	53		9	
1968	555,000	0.80	55		10	
1969	705,000	1.50			12	
1970	874,000	3.90	69		14	
1971	929,000	4.10			17	
1972	1,011,100	4.90		80	21	43
1973	1,098,500	4.20		71	25	49
1974	1,183,500	3.70		61	29	50
1975	1,248,500	2.70		62	34	54
1976	1,294,000	2.90		65	38	57
1977	1,455,000	2.60		62	42	59
1978		2.20		65	46	62
1979		2.10		57	50	63
1980		2.40		60	54	62
1981		1.80		60	57	60
1982		2.50				58
1983		3.30				60
1984		2.60				65
1985		2.50				68
1986		2.40				71
1987	3,400,000	2.60				71
1988		3.60				74
1989			72	63		
1990			64	58		74

Sources: *Memberships* from Robert C. Mitchell (1979) and Congressional Quarterly Weekly Report (January 20, 1990) for late 1980s; *News Media* used Readers' Guide, Public Affairs, and New York Times Indexes. Polls came from several similar public opinion polls:
1. 1965-70 Hazel Erskine (1972). "Compared to other parts of the country, how serious, in your opinion, do you think the problem of air/water pollution is in this area very serious . . .?"

2. 1972-81 John M. Gillroy and Robert Y. Shapiro (1986). "As for their effect on your
    way of life in the next few years, say within 10 years, how would you rate the impor-
    tance of each of the following topics . . . (air pollution) . . . very important . . .?"
3. 1989-90 Hueber (1991). ". . . pollution is very serious . . .?"
Expenditures: Capital stock data came from Kappler and Rutledge (1982). Total
capital and operating expenditures per year from (EQ, 1991, p. 220). These represent
rough estimates given variations in accounting procedures.

The news media may have compensated for this weakness by conveying
information on environmental problems directly to political representatives (column 2). Environmental crises such as killer smogs and oil spills,
books such as Rachel Carson's *Silent Spring* (1962) on DDT poisoning, and
political pronouncements such as President Johnson's Natural Beauty and
Conservation message in 1965 (CQ Almanac, 1965, p. 464) helped stimulate this media attention. By 1970 indexes of the news media increased
their citations to environment articles from one-tenth of a percent to
almost 4 percent of all articles or to 15 pages of citations (column 2).

The increase in media information correlated with increased public
awareness and concern about environmental problems. In column 3, we
have spliced together public opinion polls which suggest a substantial
increase in public concern about pollution from under 30 percent in the
mid-1960s to 80 percent in the early 1970s. Although such time series for
opinion polls on the environment remain imperfect, qualitative comments
from polling experts corroborated this increased concern in the late
1960s.[3]

By the early 1970s the growing news media information, public
opinion polls, and perhaps environmental group size and lobbying effort
theoretically increased the benefits which many national politicians
expected from supporting environmental protection. For example, President Nixon had shown no interest in environmental issues until 1969 when
he suddenly began to champion major environmental legislation (Hardin,
1982, p. 35). Congressional representatives introduced literally hundreds
of environmental laws—usually just for the record—to indicate their support for environmental protection (Congressional Index, 1968-69 and

---

3 Erskine (1972, p. 120) estimated that when polling on the environment started in
   1965, only about 10 percent of the public considered pollution important; but by
   1972 the majority held that opinion. Gillroy and Shapiro (1988) concluded that the
   environment had become a mid-level public concern by the late 1960s. Murch
   (1971, p. 101) postulated that the mass media had generated, or at least heavily
   influenced, the concern over environmental pollution.

1970-71). A few like Senator Edmund Muskie of Maine expended the time and energy necessary to push through laws which for the first time gave the federal government the power to set and enforce environmental standards.

These laws and a Supreme Court interpretation (Sierra Club versus Morton, 1971) gave private environmental organizations the right to sue private industry and government agencies to help set and enforce environmental standards (Jorgenson and Kimmel, 1988). As a result basic industries such as steel, coal, and automobiles began to spend heavily on pollution abatement. Capital for pollution abatement grew, in real terms, from a few billion dollars in the early 1960s, mainly for municipal waste water treatment, to nearly $40 billion by the mid-1970s (column 5). Hence, the public choice paradigm produces fruitful insights to the initial growth of the environmental movement of the 1970s.

Counterforces of the mid-1970s

The second prediction of the 1972 model on counterforces does not hold up as well. Although counterforces arose and news media attention to environmental concerns dropped substantially, counterforces were not able to roll back environmental laws and regulations even in the context of energy shortages, stagflation, and the severe recession of 1982.

For example, a few basic industries such as primary metal, paper mills, chemicals, petroleum, and electric utilities vigorously opposed most air quality regulations. They had to devote more than 10 percent of their investments to pollution control equipment by the mid-1970s (Council of Environmental Quality [CEQ], 1976, pp. 154-66). They, along with other affected industries such as coal and automobiles, modified their trade associations into stronger national coalitions to moderate and roll back the environmental laws. Although no hard data exist, Vietor (1980) estimates their funding in the hundred of millions of dollars per year.[4]

---

4 Their strategies included convincing the public through grass roots "educational" campaigns that private enterprise could take care of the problem without regulation, and that rigorous regulation would exacerbate the energy shortage and stagflation. These associations gave large campaign contributions to key politicians. They provided extensive technical information to agencies and congressional committees responsible for implementing the environmental regulations on a continual year-after-year basis. When advantageous they opposed rigorous environmental regulation through the court system (Wenner, 1982).

These industrial counterforces, in the context of the energy shortages and stagflation of the mid-1970s and with the support of the Nixon and Ford administrations, were able to delay the implementation of some pollution standards. Yet, in 1977 Congress voted to preserve most of the rigorous air pollution standards and added restraints on industrial location in and degradation of relatively clean areas (Vietor, 1980; CEQ, 1977, p. 22). Industry spending on pollution abatement increased throughout the 1970s. Under President Carter, Congress also passed other important environmental laws such as the 1977 Surface Mining Act.

Continued information flows on environmental problems may help explain this failure to roll back environmental regulations, in spite of the well organized counterforces and stagflation. Although news media attention to environmental problems dropped, it stayed well above preenvironmental movement levels (*Table 1*). Also, environmental educational material, presentations, and courses grew rapidly at least into the mid-1970s (Schoenfeld and Disinger, 1978). This helped provide a constant flow of information. Public concern dropped but still remained at moderate levels well above the preenvironmental movement period, even with the economic problems of the 1970s (*Table 1*). For example, on questions about the importance of the environment versus energy, respondents split about equally—roughly 40 percent for each during the 1970s (Gillroy and Shapiro, 1986).

Also, institutional changes lowered the cost of information to environmental groups. For example, environmental impact statements, which the National Environmental Policy Act of 1969 mandated for government projects, allowed environmental groups to quickly find out about programs they opposed (Andrews, 1976, Chapter 7). Congressional reforms which opened committee sessions, including the preparation of the final drafts of bills (markup sessions), reduced the cost of keeping up with legislation (Evans, 1982; Rieselbach, 1986, pp. 52-6, 136-7).

The Reagan counterforces of the 1980s

The Reagan administration and current economic conditions posed a greater counterforce to the environmental movement than did the energy crisis and stagflation of the 1970s. Inflation exceeded 10 percent in 1980. Then tight monetary policies to reduce it created a severe recession in 1982 and then a large drop of exports and a trade deficit of over $100 billion per year. Yet the Reagan administration also failed to roll back the environmental laws, regulations, and spending.

Reagan's election represented a mandate for, among other things, reducing inflation and stimulating economic growth through reduced government regulation. Reagan appointed administrators such as James Watt and Anne Gorsuch, who previously had represented business interests, to the Department of Interior and the Environmental Protection Agency (EPA), respectively. His administration also launched a major effort to "reform" the environmental laws by making the regulations more flexible and market oriented, returning more control to the states, and using stricter benefit-cost criteria, which in essence would reduce control standards (House and Shull, 1985).[5]

Nevertheless, Congress and the Reagan administration stalemated over environmental issues. The administration could not reform or roll back environmental legislation and Congress generally could not push it forward. The environmental movement did obtain some strengthening of hazardous waste laws, more wilderness areas, and more environmentally oriented administrators at EPA and Interior. Total expenditures on pollution abatement, capital plus operating costs, started to rise again after the 1982 recession (*Table 1*, column 6).

Moreover, most environmental indices continued to improve. Overall national indexes for most of the air pollutants which the environmental laws of the 1970s had targeted showed very substantial decreases of 20 to over 80 percent (*Table 2*). Although many large cities failed to meet the national air quality standards in some pollutants such as ozone, on the average the nation met the primary standards. The Council on Environmental Quality (1989, pp. 34-5, 140, 116-17) estimates that the nation's lakes, rivers, and streams generally maintained their quality inspite of rapid increases in use and actually improved their quality in some areas. Control over toxic wastes, particularly for surface mining and pesticide residuals, also improved. The government made substantial additions to national parks, wilderness areas, and wildlife preserves.

---

5 The issues, of course, were more complex than simply pro or con environmental regulation. For example, economists were pointing out that regulation through direct controls on industries, as opposed to pricing of effluents or sale of permits to pollute, increased the cost of abatement 30 to 50 percent (Baumol and Oates, 1988, pp. 171-2). Thus, market approaches might allow more pollution abatement. Also, some large firms might welcome environmental regulations to restrict competition (Buchanan and Tullock, 1975).

Table 2:   National ambient concentrations of targeted air pollutants

Year	Sulfur dioxide agm ppm	Carbon monoxide 8 hr ppm	Ozone 1 hr ppm	Nitrogen dioxide aam ppm	TSP ($\mu g/m^3$) agm	Lead ($\mu g/m^3$) quarter
1975	0.015	11.96	0.153	0.029	61.9	1.04
1976	0.016	11.32	0.153	0.029	62.8	1.05
1977	0.014	10.66	0.155	0.029	62.9	1.16
1978	0.013	10.07	0.156	0.029	62.4	1.04
1979	0.012	9.07	0.134	0.029	63.1	0.77
1980	0.011	8.52	0.136	0.025	64.2	0.61
1981	0.010	8.29	0.127	0.024	57.4	0.48
1982	0.010	7.95	0.125	0.024	48.7	0.48
1983	0.009	7.74	0.137	0.023	48.4	0.41
1984	0.009	6.99	0.124	0.024	49.9	0.38
1985	0.009	7.11	0.123	0.024	47.7	0.26
1986	0.009	6.67	0.118	0.024	47.6	0.15
1987	0.009	6.67	0.125	0.024	48.6	0.11
1988	0.009	6.42	0.136	0.024	49.7	0.09
1989	0.009	6.32	0.116	0.023	48.0	0.07
1990	0.008	5.89	0.114	0.022	47.3	0.07
Primary standard	0.030	9.00	0.120	0.050	75.0	1.50

agm = annual geometric mean; ppm = parts per million; aam = annual arithmetic mean; $\mu g/m^3$ = micrograms per meter cubed.

Source: CEQ, 1991, p. 276

Again the persistence of the environmental movement may fit the model in terms of continued or increased information flows. Congressional committees held many hearings open to the press on "mismanagement" at the Interior Department and EPA where Watt and Gorsuch became prime news media targets. Environmental articles in the news media indexes increased again in 1982-84 (*Table 1*). Although courses on the environment may have dropped off in the late 1970s, many remained in the curriculum and grew in other areas such as nature study and environmental ethics centers (Disinger, Schoenfeld, and Howe, 1988).

These information flows may help explain the continued high level public concern for the environment and growth of environmental groups. Public opinion polls continued to show a majority of the public felt that pollution was a serious problem in the early 1980s. Again observations from polling experts support these imperfect inter year comparisons.[6] These variables also may help explain the continued gain in environmental group membership and funding during the 1980s (*Table 1*).[7] Even industry groups restrained their lobbying efforts for fear of adverse publicity and loss of corporate good will (House and Shull, 1985).

Finally, many political actors may have continued to support environmental regulation not only for the direct vote getting appeal but also because the more indirect expected economic benefits exceeded the expected costs. Although pollution abatement expenditures equalled 1.5 to 2.0 percent of GNP by the 1980s and over 10 percent of investment for a few basic industries, these expenditures apparently had little negative impact on the larger economy. Econometric studies which the Council for Environmental Quality and EPA commissioned and others they reviewed over the years found that pollution control raised inflation slightly; lowered productivity and gross national product slightly; and had no net impact on foreign trade.[8] Moreover, measurable economic benefits, particularly reduced morbidity and mortality from air pollution, seemed to outweigh the increased pollution abatement costs by 1978 (CEQ, 1979, pp. 666-7).

---

6 Polling experts such as Gillroy and Shapiro (1986) observed a consistently high level of public support for environmental protection and a willingness to help pay to reduce it. The *Gallup Report* (1982) found a majority, during the severe recession of 1982, opposed reducing environmental regulation even if that would help business.

7 Hardin (1982) reviews related explanations for why public interest environmental groups continued to grow after the more intense public concern of the early 1970s and did not whither away as Olson's model (1965) would predict. For example, Mitchell (1979) suggests that the costs of membership remained very low with convenient mailings for dues and return envelops. In return members may have felt they were leveraging their dues through government regulations to obtain environmental goods, although their individual dues or contributions probably made little or no difference. Members also may have enjoyed a sense of belonging to a movement. Margolis (1982) draws on sociobiology to develop a rational model of human behavior based on altruism as well as narrow self-interest. After individuals have amassed a certain level of personal goods, they may have a higher marginal utility from helping produce social goods.

8 Abatement expenditures increased inflation by only two-tenths of a percent and had a "negligible" impact on gross national product (CEQ, 1976, pp. 147-154; CEQ, 1979, pp. 432, 435, 655). Environmental regulations had little negative impact on productivity (-.05 to -0.3 percent) and no overall impact on foreign trade (CEQ, 1979, p. 436; CEQ, 1980, pp. 387-9).

Breakdowns of technological escape routes: 1970-90

This pessimistic insight (that is, new, apparently safe technologies end up creating serious pollution) from the 1972 article seems to hold up. Substantial evidence exists that rational political actors attempted to use technological escape routes to maximize votes. For example, Presidents espoused both economic growth and environmental quality (CEQ's, 1972-86-88, "the President's message"). They and the Council of Environmental Quality stated that environmental quality could coexist with economic growth (e.g., CEQ 1990, p. x and 9). According to many economists the solution lay in developing and substituting environmentally safe technologies for dangerous ones.[9] The imposition of environmental regulations and improvement of a number of environmental indices along with continued economic growth from 1970 to 1990 seemed to support this position.

Nevertheless, during those years, breakdowns in some of the technological escape routes led to unexpected long-term environmental damage. Well established examples include ozone build-ups in large cities and acid rain. Pollution control devices on cars theoretically would allow their continued and growing high level of use in congested urban areas while still reducing air pollution. In fact, increased car usage swamped the control devices and generated higher levels of some pollutants such as nitrogen oxides and ozone in the large cities. *Table 2* shows that nationally, on the average, ozone finally dropped below the national primary standard of the 1970s; it, however, stayed well above that standard in many cities. The 1990 amendments to the Clean Air Act may finally reduce these ozone levels but not until the late 1990s (CQ Almanac, 1990, p. 231).

Acid rain provides another example of the breakdown in a technological escape route. Scrubbers and tall stacks on coal-burning electric power plants would reduce sulphur oxides and transport residuals away from populated areas. This theoretically would allow continued growth of these plants and improved environmental quality. In fact, however, substantial evidence emerged that this technological fix created acid rain (CQ Almanac, 1990, p. 237) which could deteriorate forest resources and other vegetation. Scientists are still trying to assess the actual and potential damage. The 1990 amendments to the Clean Air Act seek to reduce sulphur oxide emissions but not for five to ten years. In the meantime, long-term changes in the acidity of soils will continue.

---

9 Barnett and Morse (1963), for example, provide a rigorous development of this idea as it applies to natural resource scarcity and economic development.

Implications for the global environmental movement of the 1990s

A revised, but still abstract and rationalistic, public choice model with greater emphasis on the role of information flows may provide some insights for the current global environmental and sustainability movement. Such a model would predict that scientific information on serious pollutants should result in at least moderate levels of news media information, public concern, and continued existence and funding of environmental pressure groups. These forces in turn would increase the perceived benefits (votes or public support)[10] to political actors for sponsoring environmental regulations. Whether or not these benefits exceeded the expected costs would depend on what the information flows revealed about current support and more delayed economic impacts.

Chlorofluorocarbons (CFCs) provide an example where such a model would tend to predict effective control of the targeted pollutants and probable stabilization of the outer ozone layers. The model would also predict that further irreversible damage will have occurred before effective control. Global releases of CFCs have grown rapidly from their introduction in the 1930s to 700 million kilograms a year by the late 1980s. Atmospheric concentrations nearly doubled from 1975 to 1985 (CEQ, 1990, pp. 468-9). By the late 1980s scientists had definitive evidence that CFCs were contributing to a hole in the outer ozone layer. Theoretically, this fact, along with available substitutes for CFCs, motivated political actors to mandate their phasing out, but over a ten-year period (CQ Almanac, p. 269).

On the other hand, when the expected present costs seem high and the benefits remain uncertain and well into the future, the model would predict much less probability of effective control. Significant reductions in atmospheric greenhouse gases such as CO_2[11] and slowing of traditional industrial growth may provide examples. Presently many political actors, particularly those in the United States and less developed countries, prob-

---

10 Although the public choice model assumed democratic voting, it should also apply to nondemocratic systems where the leader depends, at least partly, on broad public support to retain power. Thus, in the last section of the paper "votes" or "voters" will also mean public support or supporters.

11 Global emissions of carbon dioxide increased about 25 percent from the mid-1970s to the mid-1980s, and concentrations in the atmosphere increased roughly 10 percent (CEQ, 1990, pp. 466-7). Although evidence of temperature rises exist, scientific controversy over their accuracy and causes remains.

ably would find the present costs, in terms of economics and lost votes, too high to support substantial reductions of CO_2 emissions, regardless of the uncertain future costs of not reducing them.[12] Thus, the model would predict a continued build-up of atmospheric CO_2 and probable global warming before political actors would vote to control CO_2 adequately, unless they could find a technological escape route.

The model would predict, however, that technological escape routes often break down with lags in scientific understanding, social regulation, and pollution abatement. For example, a substantially increased reliance on nuclear energy provides a possible escape route to some pressure groups and politicians in the CO_2 controversy. Evidence of potential breakdowns, such as nuclear accidents and waste disposal problems, however, already exist.

In the United States nuclear reactors increased in number from 20 in 1970 to over 100 in 1990. Concomitantly, US nuclear waste increased from less than one tenth of a metric ton to over 20 metric tons (CQ, 1990, pp. 447-8). Given lags in understanding and weighing the potential hazards of storing this waste, and subsequent lags in regulation, nuclear energy could leave a legacy of pervasive toxic wastes. These could last for hundreds to thousands of years and create their own form of serious environmental deterioration.

In conclusion, a narrow rationalistic public choice model indicates that moving toward environmental and economic sustainability depends on the benefit-cost calculations of voters and political actors. Methods to increase the perceived benefits of environmental regulation include increased information on potential environmental problems and their health, economic, and amenity costs. Methods to decrease perceived costs include: use of market systems for implementing regulations (Baumol and Oates, 1988); incorporation of environmental capital and subtracting out its deterioration in national accounting systems (Costanza, 1992); and providing for voters' income security, status, and other basic material and

---

12 The line up on global warming treaties seems to fit the model fairly well. The less developed countries, which remain more dependent on traditional industries based on coal and oil, and the United States, with its abundant coal reserves, resist restrictions on CO_2 emissions. Western Europe and Japan with little fossil fuel and high fuel efficiency, and particularly the Netherlands with a great deal to lose from global warming and rising sea levels, push for restrictions.

psychological needs by means other than continued rapid economic growth (Meadows, Meadows, and Randers, 1992).[13]

References

Andrews, R. N. L. (1976). *Environmental Policy and Administrative Change*. Lexington, MA.

Barnett, H. J. and C. Morse (1963). *Scarcity and Growth*. Baltimore.

Baumol, W. J. and W. E. Oates (1988). *The Theory of Environmental Policy*. 2nd edition. Cambridge, MA.

Buchanan, J. M. and G. Tullock (1962). *The Calculus of Consent*. Ann Arbor.

—— (1975). "Polluters' Profits and Political Response: Direct Control Versus Taxes." *American Economic Review*, Vol. 65, pp. 139-47.

Carson, R. (1972). *Silent Spring*. Boston.

Congressional Index (1968-69; 1970-71). New York.

Congressional Quarterly (CQ) (various years). *Almanac*. Washington, D.C.

Congressional Quarterly (CQ) (various dates). *Weekly Report*. Washington, D.C.

Costanza, R. (ed.) (1991). *Ecological Economics: The Science and Management of Sustainability*. New York.

Council on Environmental Quality (CEQ) (1970-91). *Environmental Quality: Annual Reports of the Council on Environmental Quality*. Washington, D.C.

Council on Environmental Quality (CEQ) (1989). *Environmental Trends*. Washington, D.C.

Disinger, J. F., C. Schoenfeld, and R. Howe (1988). "Recent Developments in College Level Environmental Studies Courses and Programs."

Downs, A. (1957). "An Economic Theory of Political Action in a Democracy." *Journal of Political Economy*, Vol. 65, pp. 135-15.

---

13 This last, important method of reducing the perceived costs of environmental sustainability falls partly outside the range of narrow rationalistic economic and public choice models. Psychology and sociobiology may provide valuable insights on how masses of people might satisfy their basic material and psychological needs through non material growth systems (Margolis, 1982). These would help predict how voters might trade off narrow self interest versus altruism in the face of convincing information that continued rapid economic growth had a high probability of creating very serious environmental collapses. Future public choice models may be able to incorporate these insights and develop more accurate predictions about future environmental movements.

—— (1972). "Up and Down with Ecology—The Issue-Attention Cycle." *The Public Interest*, Vol. 28, pp. 38-50.

Evans, B. (1982). "People Power." *Audoban*, Vol. 5, No. 84, pp. 12-5.

Everett, M. D. (1972). "The Role of Formal Education in Environmental Movements." *Journal of Economic Issues*, Vol. 6, Nos. 2-3, pp. 87-95.

Erskine, H. (1972). "The Polls: Pollution and Its Costs." *Public Opinion Quarterly*, Vol. 26, pp. 120-35.

Gallup Poll Report (1982), November, p. 14.

Gillroy, J. M. and R. Y. Shapiro (1986). "The Polls: Environmental Protection." *Public Opinion Quarterly*, Vol. 50, pp. 270-9.

Hardin, R. (1982). *Collective Action*. Baltimore.

House, P. W. and R. D. Shull (1985). *Regulatory Reform: Politics and the Environment*. Lanham, MD.

Hueber, G. (1991). "Americans Report High Levels of Environmental Concern, Activity." *The Gallup Poll Monthly*, No. 307, pp. 6-12.

Kappler, F. G. and G. L. Rutledge (1982). "Stock of Plant and Equipment for Air and Water Pollution Abatement in the United States, 1960-81." *Survey of Current Business*, Vol. 62, No. 11, pp. 18-25.

Margolis, H. (1982). *Selfishness, Altruism, and Rationality: A Theory of Social Choice*. Cambridge, MA.

McLean, Ian (1987). *Public Choice: An Introduction*. Oxford.

Meadows, D. L., D. H. Meadows, and J. Randers (1992). *Beyond the Limits*. Post Mills, Vermont.

Mitchell, R. C. (1979). "National Environmental Lobbies and the Apparent Illogic of Collective Action." In C. S. Russell (ed.), *Collective Decision Making: Applications from Public Choice Theory*. Baltimore, pp. 87-121.

Murch, A. W. (1971). "Public Concern for Environmental Pollution." *Public Opinion Quarterly*, Vol. 25, pp. 99-108.

Mueller, D. C. (1979). *Public Choice*. Cambridge, MA.

Olson, M. (1965). *The Logic of Collective Action*. Cambridge, MA.

Rieselbach, L. N. (1986). *Congressional Reform*. Washington, D.C.

Schoenfeld, C. and J. Disinger (eds.), (1978). "Environmental Education in Action—II: Case Studies of Environmental Studies Programs in Colleges and Universities Today." Educational Resources Information Center (ERIC). Washington, D.C.

Stigler, G. J. (1961). "The Economics of Information." *Journal of Political Economy*, Vol. 69, pp. 213-25.

Tullock, G. (1967). *Toward a Mathematics of Politics*. Ann Arbor.

Vietor, R. H. K. (1980). *Environmental Politics and the Coal Coalition*. College Station, Texas.

Wenner, L. M. (1982). *The Environmental Decade in the Court*. Bloomington.

Human Sustainable Development

Paul P. Streeten

Policy issues

There is some overlap with, but there are also important differences between, the environmental problems of poor and rich countries. Poverty has been one of the most important enemies of sustainable environment, and environmental degradation has reinforced poverty. The poor are both the cause and the principal victims of environmental degradation. To be freed from this vicious circle not only helps sustain the environment, but is above all beneficial for the human beings who live in it. The fundamental concern of the development effort is not with enlarging the choices of trees, but of humans. Deforestation and soil erosion as a result of the growing need for fuel wood; the spread of schistosomiasis or bilharzia from stagnant water reservoirs; the spread of onchocerciasis or river blindness from running mountain streams; these are the environmental problems of poor rural people, caused by them and imposing suffering on them. The eradication of poverty will also remove these environmental threats, and their removal will contribute to the reduction of poverty.

1. The first lesson is that latecomers can learn from the mistakes of fore-runners. It is possible to avoid in the beginning the creation of the environmental damage that the advanced industrial countries have inflicted upon themselves, and the wasteful uses of energy that the Western style of industrialization has involved. Heavy dependence on oil supplies and being hooked on the motor car, can be avoided by more energy conservation and greater use of indigenous sources of energy. These would also contribute to greater self-reliance.

2. A second set of policy questions relates to the international location of dirty processes. Just as differences in factor endowments guide the allocation of resources according to comparative advantage, so differences in pollution costs guide international specialization of industry. The costs of pollution will tend to be lower in many developing countries, and the benefits to be derived from industrial production will tend to be higher, because incomes are lower. For both these reasons,

a shift of some polluting activities from the industrial countries to the developing countries can be envisaged. The rule might be summed up by saying, what some find grubby, others find groovy. But, this has to be qualified to protect the poor in the developing countries, who are liable to be the chief victims of uncontrolled pollution.

A distinction must be drawn between *local, regional and global* pollution. *Global pollution* includes the spread of persistent pesticide residues that can be carried far beyond national frontiers; acid rain that ruins forests; the burning of fossil fuels, and the release of carbon dioxide, methane, nitrous oxides and chlorofluorocarbons (CFCs) into the atmosphere that may lead to global warming; deforestation, especially in the tropical rain forests, which may upset the ecological balance and deplete genetic resources; the pollution of the oceans through oil spillage or dumping from ships; the pollution of air streams by jets; the destruction of the ozone layer through chlorofluorocarbons, which causes skin cancer, cataract and other health problems; ultraviolet radiation that may lower the harvest of soybeans, the world's leading protein crop; chemical wastes that seep downwards to poison ground water and upwards to destroy the atmosphere's delicate balance; and others.

Regional pollution arises from the geophysical linkages between several countries, such as river pollution, desertification and regional air pollution. Deforestation in the Himalayas causes flooding in Bangladesh. DDT is banned in the United States, yet it is found in the mud of Lake Siskiwit near Lake Superior, carried by the wind. Acid rain, sulfur dioxide emitted from US coal-fired power plants, is carried to Canadian forests, etc.

Local pollution is confined within national boundaries, such as the eutrophication of a lake from fertilizer of sewage discharge. It would be legitimate for a country to restrict activities and products that would affect it and that result from another country's activities, but such restrictions must not be used as a pretext for protectionism by the industrial countries, where the pollution is purely local and remains confined to the area of production in the developing country. Taxes imposed by industrial countries on their pollution-intensive activities can be used by them as an excuse to exclude imports form countries that can conduct these activities at lower social costs without harm to the importing country. The "sweated environment" argument for protection is as fallacious as the "sweated labor" argument. The international free trade unions are misguided (or act in the interest of rich country trade unions) in advocating a clause in GATT that would insist on the same environmental standards for all countries, so as not to give an "unfair" advantage to poor countries. Local environmental problems are also presented by traffic congestion in cities, pollution of beaches and along coast lines, and suburban sprawl.

3. A third set of policy questions relates to the return of the use of some natural products that had been hit by the invention of synthetics, but in the production of which the costs of pollution had not been allowed for. Pyrethrum against DDT is one example; natural fibres against synthetic fibres, another. Some of these natural products have the advantage not only of being free from pollution, but also of being efficiently labor intensive (often female labor intensive) and contributing to rural development, and therefore to employment and reduced rural-urban migration.

4. A fourth set of policy questions concerns the actions developing countries should take in the face of growing scarcity of nonrenewable natural resources. Many of these have not been priced according to their scarcity, taking into account a proper social discount rate and risk premium. A correct pricing policy would provide incentives for more economical use of these products, for switching to products that use less of these materials or none, for a search for new sources of these materials, and for the development of substitutes. Meanwhile the higher revenue earned by the material-exporting developing countries should be used for diversification and development, while developing countries dependent on their imports but without corresponding high-priced exports should be insured against damage from higher prices.

Economists have a bias in favor of using prices to reduce pollution and raw material exhaustion. Noneconomists object to using taxes to discourage damaging activities and to granting "licences to pollute" and licences to despoil. The differences rest upon attaching different moral evaluations to different things. People value the opportunity to express *disapproval*, which would not be reflected in a fine balance of benefits and costs. Licences are normally not given for activities that should be stamped as illegitimate. (But licences are given to carry guns in the United States.) Putting a price tag on a highly valued item demeans it. The opponents of price policies may also think that the motive makes a difference, whereas taxes are indifferent to motives.

But it is not enough to estimate the possibility of exhaustion and to attach a price to these materials, allowing for time and uncertainty; what is also needed is coordinated action between the developing countries in which these nonrenewable materials are to be found. Incentives, both rewards and penalties, are required to secure joint action, and agreement on rules about how increases in revenue derived from joint scarcity pricing should be shared and used for development. In particular, ways should be found to mitigate or prevent harm being done to developing countries that depend on the imports of these materials.

5. A fifth set of policy questions concerns the role of transnational companies for environmental policy. In the new international division of labor, which would be guided by differential pollution costs in different countries, the location of certain "dirty" processes in developing countries could be one of the functions of the transnational corporation. This could be done either by the firm locating certain "dirty" processes within its vertically integrated system of operations in a developing country where the social costs of pollution are lower and the benefits from industrialization higher, or by transferring the whole integrated operation to such a country. The argument would be analogous to that of locating unskilled or semi-skilled labor-intensive processes and products in developing countries. One important advantage, however, is that the transnational corporation will act as a pressure group to ensure access for the products to the markets of the developed countries, which might otherwise put up protectionist barriers under the pretext of environmental protection.

Institutions for sustainable development

The problems of the local environment are different from those of the global environment. Common property rights to a local pond or grazing area are often respected, and behavior has evolved that presents their destruction. Not so for the global commons. Our present interdependent, pluralistic, multi-polar world is less stable, and more in need of the promotion of peace, prosperity, conservation and global leadership than past orders, in which a single dominant power has assumed these responsibilities. No single power is both able and willing to assume these functions today. Although this can be a danger, it also presents us for the first time in history with the opportunity to create a world order based not on dominance and dependence, but on equality, pluralism and cooperation. This calls for the exercise of our creative institutional imagination *and* for sacrifices of national sovereignty.

We are suffering from a lag of institutions behind technology. The revolutions in the technologies of transport, travel, communications and information have unified and shrunk the globe, but the organization of the world into nation states dates back to the Peace of Westphalia in 1648, to the 19th century unifications of Germany and Italy, and the post-world war I creation of new nation states. When the nation states were founded, the city states and the feudalism that preceded them had become too small for the scale of operations required by the *Industrial Revolution*. The political institution therefore was adapted to the industrial technology, to the roads, railways and canals. The nation state was then a progressive institution. But technological determinism is not plausible. The adaptation of institutions to technology is not an inevitable process. The *Middle Ages* had, for example, lost the Roman technology about roads, baths, aqueducts and amphitheaters, and these were allowed to fall into disrepair. But now the nation state, with its insistence on full sovereignty, has become an obstacle to further progress. It has landed us in several *prisoners' dilemmas*: each nation acts in its rational self-interest, and the result is that every country is worse off. It pays each nation to pursue this mutually destructive course, whether others to likewise or not.

Common interests and conflicts are running nowadays across national boundaries. The European farmers are in conflict with the European industrialists and the public that has to pay for the Common Agricultural Policy. The advanced countries' textile manufacturers are aligned in the Multifiber Arrangement against Third World textile exporters and the consumers in industrial countries. U.S. industrial interests are aligned with Third World debtors in wishing interest rates to be low, against its financial interests, who like high interest rates. Industrial countries' bankers are aligned with developing countries' exporters, against the protectionist lobbies of those who fear imports. The nation state may become the inappropriate level at which such issues can be resolved.

Clearly, *prisoners' dilemma* outcomes move the world economy away from a more to a less efficient allocation of resources. There exist, therefore potential gains by moving back to more efficient allocations. According to *Coase's theorem*, in the absence of transaction costs and in the pre-

sence of well specified property rights, a legal framework, and full information, if one country inflicts damages on another which are greater than
the benefits to the first country, the injured country will enter into a contract with the injuring country and compensate it for not inflicting the
injury, and still be better off. Or, if the benefits are greater than the damage, the injuring country can compensate the injured country for accepting
the damage, and still be better off than it would have been, had it been
prevented from inflicting the damage.

For example, the United States emits acid rain to Canada. Canada
could then offer compensation to the United States for relinquishing the
emission of sulfur dioxide, the chief component in acid rain, and still be
better off than it would be in accepting the acid rain; or the United States
could offer compensation to the mess and stop the emission.

But as we all know to our regret, we are far away from outcomes
according to Coase's theorem, although we are not always at the other end
of the spectrum, the prisoners' dilemma. Coase's theorem remains useful,
in spite of its strict assumptions, in drawing our attention to the fact that
there are unexploited mutual profit opportunities from restraint. Obviously compensation ought not always, or even often, to be paid. The
losers, such as the English landlords after the repeal of the Corn Laws in
1846, may not deserve to be compensated; or, even if they do deserve it,
the costs of imposing taxes to finance the compensation may be so large as
to make the compensation uneconomic. But the fact that it *could* be paid
draws our attention to potential unexploited gains.

Add to the prisoners' dilemma the *free rider problem*, according to
which each country relies on others to bear the costs of arrangements that
benefit everybody. As a result, public goods, such as peace, an open trading system, well defined property rights, a working monetary system, or
conservation of the global environment, are *under*supplied, while public
bads, such as wars, pollution, raw material exhaustion, and poverty, are
*over*supplied. The situation has been described in parables and similes
such as the *Tragedy of the Commons, Social Traps*, the *Isolation Paradox*,
etc. Everybody free rides, and thereby ensures that there is no horse.
These parables contradict the parable of the *Invisible Hand*, according to
which the pursuit of self-interest by each individual promotes the good of
all.

The ranking of preferences by each country is the following:
1. My country does not contribute while others do (*free rider, defection of
   one*).

2. My country contributes together with others (*cooperation*).
3. No country contributes (*prisoners' dilemma outcome*).
4. My country contributes while no other country does (*sucker*).

Behavior by each according to 1, or fear of 4, leads to outcome 3. Although 2 is preferred to 3, we end up with 3, unless either rewards and penalties, or autonomous cooperative motivations, lead to 2. Incentives and expectations must be such as to rule out outcomes 4 and 1, so that if I (or you) contribute, I will not end up a sucker. In the absence of such motivations, the result is that peace, monetary stability, an open world economy, environmental protection, debt relief, raw material conservation, poverty reduction and world development will be undersupplied.

It has been shown that iterative games of the prisoners' dilemma type lead to nondestructive outcomes. The partners learn and adopt mutually beneficial strategies. It has also been shown that we often find ourselves between the two extremes of prisoners' dilemma and Coase's outcomes. For several reasons it is harder to reach cooperative agreements. Change is rapid, which undermines the basis of stability on which agreements are based. The absence of a hegemonic power also removes the sanctions against breaking the agreement. And all these factors prevent the trust from being built up, which is an essential prerequisite for international agreements.

Examples of prisoners' dilemma on the global scale are ubiquitous. Above all there is the arms race, which, though we have so far avoided a major nuclear war, has contributed to hundreds of minor wars, mostly in the Third World; then there is competitive protectionism, through which each country casts its employment problem onto others; competitive exchange rate movements; research and development wars; investment wars; environmental pollution; the killing of whales and the debt crisis are only some of the areas in which these battles are fought.

To avoid these traps, coordination and enforcement of policies are needed. But coordination means that each country has to do things it does not want to do. The United States has to balance its budget in order to lower world interest rates; Germany has to grow faster, but she does not want to suck in guest workers from Turkey and Yugoslavia; many say Japan should import more, but she does not want to hurt her domestic industries. And so on.

Even Mrs. Thatcher, a powerful advocate of free markets and state minimalism, in a speech to the United Nations in New York on the 8th of November 1989, has come to recognize that in order to avoid global warming and costal flooding, countries that emit carbon dioxide and other gases that trap heat in the atmosphere would have to act together, that restrictions would have to be obligatory, and their application would have to be carefully monitored. Any one country acting by itself would be at a competitive disadvantage by having to incur the higher costs of protecting the environment.

A Global Environmental Protection Agency

Just as in an uncoordinated world each country has an incentive to pour its problem of unemployment, metaphorically, into the yards of others, so does it, literally, cast its muck into the neighboring fields or into the oceans, the lakes, the atmosphere, the land, or the food chains which are the global commons. Acid rain that kills forests, the emission of chloro-fluorocarbons that destroy the ozone layer, the global warming resulting from the burning of fossil fuels, overfishing in common waters are examples of global abuse that can be stopped by global agreements that limit national sovereignty.

The domestic environmental problems of rich countries are often in conflict with poverty reduction in developing countries, while the domestic environmental problems of poor countries both arise from, and contribute to, poverty. But the global environmental problems are shared by the whole of humanity and call for global solutions.

The solution to mutually destructive actions pursued by each country separately is the establishment of a Global Environmental Protection Agency, with powers of enforcement. Each country, by sacrificing some of its national sovereignty, gains more in the pursuit of its national interests than it would have done, had it continued to act independently.

Such an agency would be require substantial finance and powers. A tiny step in this direction was taken in November 1990. 25 industrial and developing countries agreed to establish a Global Environmental Facility (GEF), run jointly by the World Bank, the United Nations Development Programme (UNDP), and the United Nations Environment Programme (UNEP). It started off with a fund of about $1.3 billion. A little progress was made at the United Nations Conference on Environment and Development in Rio de Janeiro, which gave strong verbal support to the Facility. Pledges of about $2.5 billion a year were made. This compares with

$70 billion which the UN said was needed for sustainable development, and about $5 billion which had been predicted. For the time being, therefore, only modest resources will be devoted to providing help in financing programs and projects that affect the global environment. Four areas have been selected for the operations of the Facility:

1. *Protecting the ozon layer.* The work will be coordinated with the implementation of Montreal Protocol to phase out the use of CFCs, halons, and other harmful gases.
2. *Limiting greenhouse gas emissions.* The emission of carbon dioxide, CFCs, and methane will be limited, the adoption of cleaner technologies and fuels will be encouraged, as well as reforestation and forestry conservation.
3. *Protecting biodiversity.* The diversity of species contributes to materials for medicines and industrial products, genetic resources for food production, and the regulation of climatic and rainfall patterns.
4. *Protecting global water resources.* The Facility will support programs that encourage planning against oil spills; to abate water pollution, to prevent and clean up toxic waste pollution along major rivers and to conserve water bodies.

Developing countries with a GNP per head of less than $4,000 a year will be eligible for GEF funding for investment projects and supporting services.

The initial steps towards a Global Environmental Protection Agency (GEPA) should be on very specific issues, such as the Montreal Protocol or the International Whaling Commission. A sharp and narrow focus in the early stages will prevent endless discussion, frustration, and acrimony. But the problems of primary concern to the poor people in the developing countries—clean air in the cities, access to safe water and sanitation, the prevention of soil erosion, and population control—are not touched by the Facility. From the point of view of these concerns, the Rio conference was a failure.

Sustainable Development against Vested Interests

Johanna M. Kasperkovitz

Introduction

In 1987 the World Commission on Environment and Development formulated the concept of "sustainable development," which was given massive support from many writers, countries, and organizations. Presumably the market process will not bring forth a sound environmental situation without the implementation of the concept of sustainable development in environmental policy in particular, and in economic policy in general. This process of implementation is far from easy, both for national and international authorities. A significant factor will be the influence of vested economic interests, which have reached a strong position by using nature and the environment in one way or another without paying a price for it.

Any policy of sustainable development will definitely be weakened by these vested interests. Given the general dominance of neoclassical economic theory, they are in a strong position to stress their influence on strategic economic variables such as per capita income, employment, and export performance, while other variables such as the occurrence of acid rain, the greenhouse effect, and the pollution of rivers and seas are neglected. Their use of a narrow pattern of perception and valuation, which credits only short-term economic values, forms an obstacle for any effective environmental policy.

In the present paper, we shall investigate the role of the government in counteracting the influence of vested economic interests. This is an important issue as only the government is in the position to implement an effective environmental policy. We investigate the relationship between government and vested interests in a case study on the use of pesticides in the Netherlands in the last decades. The situation in the Netherlands is interesting as the government proclaimed in 1976 that the Dutch economy should integrate environmental standards, and as in 1989 the government accepted "sustainable development" as a guideline for all economic activities (Minister van Volkshuisvesting, Ruimtelijke Ordening en Milieubeheer, 1989a). So, it should be illustrative to examine what the Dutch government actually did in a situation where vested economic interests are significant.

The Dutch policy on the use of pesticides: an overview

In the Netherlands the use of pesticides is regulated by the Pesticide Law (Bestrijdingsmiddelenwet) of 1962. This law prohibits the use of all pesticides which are not allowed by a special governmental commission. This commission uses several criteria to test pesticides. Until 1975 these criteria mainly concerned the effectiveness of the pesticides and the protection of health. Since 1975 potential environmental damage caused by pesticides has also to be taken into account. In the early eighties the growing concern about environmental pollution gave rise to the need for a new policy. Since 1983 the existing legislation was extended several times by additional regulations. This new policy focuses on a substantial *reduction* in the use of pesticides.

So far, however, the Dutch policy on the use of pesticides was not effective in protecting the environment. Its legislative framework has proved to be inadequate. Although the toxicity of several pesticides has been known for more than twenty years, the legislation did not enforce prohibition of these chemicals. Despite the proclaimed objectives of the new policy, namely a 50-percent reduction in the use an a 90-percent reduction in the emissions, the use of pesticides has remained more or less the same, whereas the detected pollution has been increasing continually.

The ineffectiveness of this policy is strongly related with the dominant position of certain vested economic interests, particularly those represented by agriculture and the pesticide industry. Their influence can first be shown by an analysis of the *formation* of the Dutch pesticides policy.

Various actors with different backgrounds participated in the policy formation. Special attention should be given to the fact that in the Netherlands there is a long tradition to engage in a lengthy public discussion before a decision on the implementation of a policy is taken. In this process of discussion and public debate, all parties possibly involved in the implementation of the policy are invited by the government to enter the debate. This neocorporatistic approach became a tradition in Dutch labor policies (van der Straaten, 1992).

Formally, four ministers, the Minister of Agriculture, the Minister of Environmental Affairs, the Minister of Health, and the Minister of Social Affairs, are responsible for the formation of the pesticides policy. Besides these formal policy makers, several external interest groups are involved. The most important of them are organizations that represent agriculture, the pesticide industry, and the environment. The participation of so many different actors turns policy formation into a bargaining process. Each actor tries to push the outcome of this process in the direction of political, industrial, agricultural, or environment-oriented values. The predominance of economic values can be illustrated by a closer look at the objectives of the policy and the choice or means to implement the stated objectives.

Policy objectives

Since 1983 the main objective of the Dutch policy on the use of pesticides has been a *reduction in the use* of pesticides. The extent of pesticide use can be expressed in several ways, for example, by the volume of the active substance of pesticides, the frequency of application, the pesticidal effects, or harmful effects on the environment. The intended reduction, which was set at 50 percent in 1990, was expressed in kilograms active substance.

This way of expressing the reduction objective is very convenient for agriculture and the pesticide industry, but very ineffective for the environment. By developing new, and more expensive, pesticides, with less volume of the active substance but with the same (or even stronger) pesticidal and harmful effects, the pesticide industry can undermine environmental policy. By creating a situation, in which neither industry nor agriculture suffered, the policy makers made it possible for their stated objective to be realized while environmental damage remained the same or even increased.

Since 1990 another objective of the policy is a 90-percent *reduction in emissions* of pesticides. However, a close examination of the development of standards for groundwater leads to the conclusion that even more emissions are being tolerated in the course of time. Since 1983 the policy concerning residues of pesticides in drinking water has been based on the principle that no pesticides at all are to be allowed in the groundwater that is to be used as drinking water. When this principle was formulated, the smallest amount of pesticides that could be detected in water was 0.1 μg per liter. Therefore the standard for residues of pesticides in groundwater was set at 0.1 μg/l. Meanwhile the methods for detection have been improved, which makes it possible to detect much smaller concentrations. The principle of "no pesticides in groundwater" still holds, but the amount of residues tolerated has not been decreased. In actual fact, several kinds of restrictive measures have been relaxed or were delayed, so that even larger concentrations of pesticides are tolerated now. Relevant information in this respect has been known for years, but the use of research findings during the formation of the policy was consequently obstructed by the struggle for power between the conflicting interests. A chronology of some scientific and political facts shows that the decisions made have little relation to well-known information about environmental effects of pesticides:

1984: Research

In groundwater, destined for the use as drinking water, pollution caused by pesticides was detected in concentrations up to 15 μg per liter. Researchers predicted that even after immediate prohibition of the pesticide the concentrations in the groundwater would exceed the standards for another 250 years (KIWA, 1987).

Since 1987: Policy

The Minister of Agriculture tried to realize a relaxation of the restrictive measures, by proposing the use of different standards based on a distinction between high and low groundwater. Based on the assumption that the concentration of pesticides decreases while travelling from high to low groundwater, the Minister suggested allowing higher concentrations in the upper groundwater. By contrast, the Minister of Environmental Affairs supported the maintenance of the current standard of 0.1 μg/l for every level of groundwater.

1988: Research

National and international research showed that some 43 pesticides, though applied in a normal way, could lead to exceeding the allowed concentration of 0.1 μg/l. Only five of these pesticides were nominated for prohibition (Stichting Natuur en Milieu, October 10, 1988).

1989: Policy

The Minister of Environmental Affairs presented a paper concerning a number of standards for the allowance of pesticides, with which several interests of the Minister of Agriculture were met (Ministerie van VROM, Notitie "Milieucriteria t.a.v. stoffen ter bescherming van bodem en grondwater," 1989b). In accordance with a request of the Minister of Agriculture, the decision about maintenance or alteration of the 0.1 μg/l standard was postponed by arguing that further research was needed. The research was meant to verify the assumption about the dilution of pesticides on their way from high to low groundwater.

1990: Research

The requested research showed that no significant dilution of pesticides on their way down from high to low groundwater takes place. Meanwhile researchers found out that some 67 pesticides could lead to concentrations higher than 0.1 μg/l. 30 of these chemicals were actually detected in the upper groundwater, while 10 of them were also found in deep groundwater (Ministerie van LNV, "Beleidsvoornemen Gewasbescherming," 1990).

1990: Policy

Despite the rejection of the assumption about the dilution of pesticides, the Minister of Agriculture presented a policy in which larger concentrations of pesticides in the upper groundwater were tolerated (LNV, Beleidsvoornemen "Meerjarenplan Gewasbescherming," 1990). The policy included a list of 111 pesticides, that "in principle" were nominated for prohibition. One of the criteria for prohibition was the potential pollution of the groundwater caused by these chemicals. The pesticide industry replied that prohibition of these 111 pesticides would lead to an 80-percent loss of turnover.

1991: Policy

The number of pesticides on the list was extended to 158. On the other hand, a possibility for exemption was added to the policy: The pesticides on the list were not to be prohibited as long as there were no alternatives. The phrase "no alternative" also included a more expensive alternative.

1992: Policy

Some 1,600 applications of the pesticides on the list are considered to be too harmful for the environment. Only 500 of them will be prohibited. The remaining 1,100 applications will be tolerated as long as there are "no alternatives" that are equally or less expensive.

This description of several decisions in the Netherlands about the standards for drinking water shows that—despite the general objective "reduction in emission"—agriculture and the pesticide industry succeeded to put through a relaxation of operational regulations.

Policy instruments

The fact that the general objectives of Dutch environmental policy were undermined so easily by agriculture and industry is highly related to the choice of the means to implement the stated objectives. The most important means is a *legislative framework*, consisting mainly of the previously mentioned "Pesticide Law" (Bestrijdingsmiddelenwet), dating from 1962. The formulation of this law created a situation in which prohibition of harmful pesticides could be obstructed for many years by agriculture or the pesticide industry. The procedure that led to prohibition of the herbicide *dinoseb*, for instance, took eighteen years.

The negative effects of dinoseb on human reproduction were already known at the latest in 1972. However, this knowledge was not verified of additional research until 1986. These research data led to an immediate prohibition of dinoseb in the United States. By this time, prohibition of the use of dinoseb in the Netherlands was proposed by the Minister of Environmental Affairs. Meanwhile, residues of dinoseb were found in concentrations that exceeded the standard one hundred times. The governmental "Commission for the Allowance of Pesticides" discussed the proposal for prohibition with agriculture and the pesticide industry. During this discussion arguments such as the export of potatoes and employment in the pesticide industry came up, and after the discussion the prohibition of dinoseb was postponed until 1990, which is one year later than the official prohibition by the European Community.

A situation like this is facilitated by the Pesticide Law. This law actually gives agriculture and the pesticide industry the possibility to overrule environmental considerations. The criterion for environmental damage in this law is not binding because of its formulation: "Environmental damage is not allowed in an amount that is not acceptable." Acceptable by whom? Moreover, once a decision is made about allowance or prohibition of a certain chemical, only agriculture and the pesticide industry are permitted to object. No organization that represents environmental values can object to a decision of the "Commission for the Allowance of Pesticides."

Vested interests and their influence on policy

The examples mentioned above are an illustration of the fact that the Dutch policy on the use of pesticides is quite consequently formulated in a way that makes it possible for agriculture and the pesticide industry to overrule environmental considerations. One may conclude that the same vested interests that dominate the market process, the traditional, short-term economic interests, also dominate the environmental policy which basically is meant to guide the market process toward sustainable development.

The Dutch policy consists of a large number of decisions on different items in regard to the use of pesticides. The standards for drinking water and the formulation of the Pesticide Law are just some of them. Based on a in-depth investigation of a larger number of decisions about seven items related to the use of pesticides, an attempt was made by the author to quantify the influence of the different actors on this environmental policy (Kasperkovitz, 1991). The seven items in this investigation concerned the problem statement of the policy (in *Table 1* these items are referred at as items A and B), the objectives (the items C, D, and E), and the choice of means (the items F and G). In regard to these items 36 decisions were analyzed (Kasperkovitz, 1991, pp. 94-101). The influence of five actors on these decisions was measured. The actors involved were the Minister of Agriculture (LNV), the Minister of Environmental Affairs (VROM), the national organization representing agricultural interests (LBS), the pesticide industry (NEF), and the environmental movement (SNM).

For every decision each actor was given a percentage of influence, expressing the extent to which the decision was in favor of the interests of the actor. If the interests of an actor concerning a specific decision were not known, the percentage for that decision was set at 50 percent $^{+/-\,50\,percent}$. The results of this analysis are shown in *Table 1*.

Table 1:   *Extent to which the Dutch pesticides policy meets the interests of different actors*

Items/ (Decisions)	LNV	VROM	LBS	NEF	SNM
A / (5)	80	40	80	80	40
B / (9)	66	$38.5^{\pm5.5}$	$60.5^{\pm5.5}$	$60.5^{\pm5.5}$	
C / (6)	66	33	66	66	33
D / (3)	99	$50^{\pm50}$	66	$66^{\pm33}$	66
E / (5)	80	20	80	80	20
F / (6)	66	33	66	66	33
G / (2)	100	0	100	$100^{\pm50}$	0
Average	80%	$31\%^{\pm8\%}$	$74\%^{\pm1\%}$	$74\%^{\pm13\%}$	$36\%^{+1\%}$

The table shows that in 74 to 80 percent of all decisions the interests of agriculture and industry were (partially) met while only about 31 to 36 percent of the decisions seem to have partially met environmental interests.

Why is it that agriculture and industry have had so much influence, while environmental organizations were overruled so often? The impact of an actor on environmental policy seems to be related to the extent to which the actor makes use of the established pattern of perception and valuation during stage of policy formation. A pattern of perception and valuation is a set of beliefs and values that determine which action can be seen as rational or valuable. Several patterns of perception and valuation can be used. The same action can be seen as rational through the perspective of one pattern of perception and valuation, and irrational through the perspective of another pattern.

During the formation of the Dutch policy on the use of pesticides, two different patterns of perception and valuation were used frequently. The pattern used by actors who were concerned about the effects of pesticides on the environment was based on environmental values and the conviction that protection of the environment is necessary and desirable. Actors who represented agriculture or industry used a pattern of perception and valuation that was based on short-term economic interests. These actors focused on agricultural and industrial production and employment. This second pattern had a much stronger impact on the environmental policy than the environmental one. Traditional short-term economic or agricultural values have been shown to be the cornerstones on which this policy is built. Critical arguments related to human health or environmental considerations were overruled by arguments concerning employment or export figures.

Relevant theoretical arguments

In Pigovian approaches to environmental policy, the "polluter-pays principle" is promulgated, i.e., the external costs generated by polluting industries should be made the burden of those industries. The government, in this view, is the sole economic agent standing above the other economic agents, the polluting industry and the victim threatened by environmental pollution. Most economists support this concept of internalizing externalities when confronted with environmental problems.

However, it has become clear that there are many obstacles to the implementation of this principle. For instance, it may be difficult or even impossible to evaluate the environmental costs due to the lack of a market for environmental goods and services. But the inability to calculate this environmental costs does not imply that the economic value of environmental goods is low or nonexistent. The contrary is true in cases such as acid rain, the greenhouse effect, and the pollution of rivers and groundwater. Another obstacle to the calculation of environmental costs is found in the complicated relations between the economic and the ecological systems. In many cases environmental damage can not be foreseen, or one may not imagine that the damage is so dramatic.

These arguments imply that a traditional neoclassical cost-benefit analysis may not give sufficient ground for the implementation of an effective environmental policy. This may lead to the conclusion that the only way out is the use of standards in environmental policy (Baumol and Oates, 1971). But introducing environmental standards cannot be the solution as long as natural resources are not seen as belonging to "real" economic theories. Therefore, Dietz and van der Straaten (1988 and 1992) argue that only with the inclusion of environmental standards in economic theory itself a solution can be found.

Conclusions

From the case study presented above some general conclusions can be drawn:

1. The environmental movement has used arguments other than those used by the industry and agriculture. It used arguments like sustainable society and stressed the negative effects of pesticides on the environment, for instance on the quality of groundwater used as drinking water. The pesticide industry and agriculture used traditional economic arguments like income, generation, export position, and employment. By doing so, the environmental movement was the loser in the debate. The decisions of the government were more in favor of agriculture or the pesticide industry than in favor of public health and the environment.

2. The concept of "sustainable development" did not function, even when it had been accepted as a starting point for all economic policies. The ministers of agriculture and of economic affairs were able to marginalize the importance of sustainable development. Policy thus is subject to the same pattern of perception and valuation as the market process itself, resulting in insufficient measures to correct the misallocation of natural resources caused by the disfunctioning of the market process. This paradox is mainly due to the neglect of the peculiarities of collective decision-making.

3. The position of the minister of environmental affairs in general is a difficult one. He cannot take decisions without considering the opinions of the minister of economic affairs and of agriculture. The neocorporative approach will have a negative effect upon the interests of nature and the environment.

4. One may conclude that environmental policy will not succeed in guiding the market process toward "sustainable development" as long as the mechanisms discussed are not recognized and taken into account. In particular this will be the case when the success of a government is measured in terms of employment or budget achievements only, instead of sustainability. So far, there is no national authority on sustainable development. By contrast, there are influential international institutions on economic performance such as the European Community, the OECD, and the World Bank. This implies that there are hardly any international correction mechanisms aiming at an increase in the quality of the environment.

5. The environmental movement has tried to influence the perceptions and values of people and society into the direction of sustainability. In many cases of local significance the environmental movement has been rather successful in this respect. However, implementing sustainable development on a broader scale is a far from easy task. This is so because there is hardly any difference between the perceptions and valuations in the state machinery and the vested economic interests in agriculture and industry. One may argue that the environmental movement therefore has to pay still more attention to the concept of sustainable development in the public debate, and try to change the perceptions and valuation of society in the desired direction. On the other hand, one could argue that the environmental movement made a mistake not using arguments in the field of traditional cost-benefit analysis. The difficulty is that in many cases the benefits are apparent only in the future, while the costs of cleaning up the environment are a burden to present economic agents. In addition, the benefits may be quite diffuse while the costs are more concrete and focused on powerful polluters, who can stress the disadvantages with which they will be confronted in the very near future. This may lead to a general perception in society that severe norms in environmental policy are always accompanied by high costs, what is actually not the case. All this places "sustainable development" in a difficult position—and probably so for some time to come.

References

Baumol, W. J. and W. E. Oates (1971). "The Use of Standards and Prices for Protection of the Environment." *Swedish Journal of Economics*, Vol. 73, No. 1, pp. 42-54.

Bestrijdingsmiddelenwet (Stb 288), Maart 1970, Toelichting.

Dietz, F. J. and J. van der Straaten (1988). "The Problem of Optimal Exploitation of Natural Resources: the Need for Ecological Limiting Conditions." *International Journal of Social Economics*, Vol. 15, No. 3, pp. 71-9.

—— (1992). "Rethinking Environmental Economics: Missing Links between Economic Theory and Environmental Policy." *Journal of Economic Issues*, March, pp. 27-51.

Kasperkovitz, J. M. (1991). "Beleidsvorming en belangenafweging: de totstandkoming van het bestrijdingsmiddelenbeleid in Nederland." *Stichting Natuur en Milieu.* Utrecht.

KIWA NV (1987). *Dichloorpropaan in grondwater*. Nieuwegein.

Minister van Landbouw, Natuurbeheer en Visserij (1990). *Beleidsvoornemen "Meer-jarenplan Gewasbescherming*." Den Haag.

Minister van Volkshuisvesting, Ruimtelijke Ordening en Milieubeheer (1989a). "National Environmental Policy Plan," Session 1988-1989, Nr. 21137-1, Den Haag.

Minister van Volkshuisvesting, Ruimtelijke Ordening en Milieubeheer (1989b). Notitie "Milieucriteria ten aanzien van stoffen ter bescherming van bodem en grondwater." Januari 1989, Tweede Kamer, Vergaderjaar 1988-1989, 21137, nrs. 1-2.

Pigou, A. C. (1920/1952). *The Economics of Welfare*. London.

Stichting Natuur en Milieu (1988). Brief aan de Minister van Landbouw, Natuurbeheer en Visserij, 31.10.1988.

Straaten, J. van der (1991), "Acid Rain and the Single Internal Market: Policies from the Netherlands." *European Environment*, Vol. 1, No. 1, pp. 20-4.

Straaten, J. van der (1992). "The Dutch National Environmental Policy Plan: To Choose or to Lose." *Environmental Politics*, Vol. 1, No. 1, pp. 45-71.

World Commission on Economic and Development (1987). *Our Common Future*. Oxford.

Sustainable Use of Nutrients in Agriculture: The Manure Problem in the Netherlands

Frank J. Dietz

Introduction

In the Netherlands agricultural production per hectare has increased considerably since World War II due to a rapid intensification of the production processes. As a result the Netherlands has become the fourth largest net exporter of agricultural products (after the United States, Australia, and Brazil), despite its being one of the world's smallest, most densely populated and most highly industrialized countries. Poultry, pork, cheese, eggs, and butter are among the most exported products. The "self-sufficiency" rates of these products vary between 200 and over 400 percent. The relative importance of the dairy sector and the intensive livestock sector in Dutch agriculture is indicated by the fact that these two sectors produce 60 percent of the total agricultural production value (Ministerie van Landbouw, Natuurbeheer en Visserij, 1990a).

The Netherlands have more cattle, pigs, and chickens per hectare than any other country in the world (Langeweg, 1988). However, large numbers of animals per hectare inevitably result in large quantities of manure per hectare. Most dairy farmers can use the slurry from their cattle on their own grassland. By contrast, specialized pig and poultry farmers have little land available for the disposal of their manure, so they are strongly dependent on the manure demand of arable farmers. But arable farmers usually prefer chemical fertilizers for providing the required nutrients, such as phosphate and nitrogen. Consequently, manure from the intensive livestock sector has become a waste product, being dumped on farmland rather than being utilized. Especially in the South and the East of the country where the intensive livestock farms are concentrated, manure is dumped in such large quantities that huge amounts of nutrients have leached into the environment, causing serious environmental effects. This *manure problem* will be discussed in section 2.

In an attempt to abate the environmental effects caused by nutrient leakages, the Dutch government has developed a *manure policy*. Section 3 describes the main goals of this policy as well as the instruments used. In section 4 the manure policy is criticized for being extremely ineffective and inefficient. Taking the nature of the manure problem as the starting point, an alternative abatement strategy, the *nutrient policy*, is developed in section 5.

Finally, in section 6, some observations are made concerning the European context of the Dutch initiatives for abating nutrient emissions. The European Community will critically evaluate the policy instruments used, especially from the perspective of the completion of the Internal Market. Section 7 contains the concluding remarks.

The manure problem in the Netherlands

Over the past 40 years Dutch agriculture has witnessed an unprecedented development in its livestock production. This is most clearly illustrated by the growth of animal numbers (*Table 1*). Between 1950 and 1990, cattle numbers have doubled, the number of chickens has quadrupled and—most dramatically—the number of pigs is almost seven times higher now than in 1950.

Table 1:   *Dutch livestock in million*

Year	Cattle	Pigs	Poultry
1950	2.5	1.9	23.5
1955	3.0	2.4	30.7
1960	3.5	3.0	42.4
1965	3.8	3.8	42.3
1970	4.4	5.7	55.4
1975	5.0	7.2	68.1
1980	5.2	10.1	81.2
1985	5.2	12.4	89.9
1990	4.9	13.9	92.8

Source: Wijnands, Luesink, and van der Veen, 1988, p. 242; Centraal Bureau voor de Statistiek, 1991

This development should be understood as a response to at least three circumstances (cf. van der Stee, *et al.*, 1989; Mansholt, 1990). Firstly, the growing international demand for animal products offered a sound economic basis for an expansion of the livestock sector. Secondly, the Common Agricultural Policy of the EC offers several favorable arrangements. The price support for milk, for instance, considerably decreases producers' risks, which stimulated the expansion of the dairy sector. Dutch intensive livestock farmers took advantage of the absence of an EC levy on feedstuffs imported from developing countries (tapioca and soy beans) and the United States (maize gluten), combined with the substantial price support for cereals produced in the European Community. Being situated near the port of Rotterdam, offers the opportunity of importing large amounts of cheap feedstuffs, which provides competitive advantages over inland EC farmers using cereals.[1] A third circumstance which stimulated the expansion of the intensive livestock sector in the Netherlands was the excessive labor supply in agriculture, especially in the sandy soil areas of the country. In these rural areas hardly any alternative employment was available. The best chance for survival as a farmer on the poor sandy soils was by raising pigs and chickens.

The production growth in the Dutch dairy and intensive livestock sectors was a success story that many EC farmers and ministers were envious of. However, the rapid increase in livestock production also means a tremendous increase in manure production. In the old days manure was highly valued for its ability to increase crop production levels. However, with the invention of chemical fertilizers, and with the segregation of the traditional mixed farms into specialized arable farming and specialized livestock production, manure lost its prominent role. On the specialized pig and poultry farms in particular, manure is now often treated as mere waste that needs to be disposed of in the cheapest possible way. As these farms are generally very small in area, manure has been applied to the land in such large quantities that serious environmental problems have resulted. These environmental problems are the result of nutrient leakages. Far more phosphate and nitrogen (in the form of manure or chemical fertilizers) is applied to the land than plants need for their growing

---

1 The intensive livestock of the Netherlands is mainly fed with tapioca from Thailand and soy from Brazil, which requires an area of arable land that covers approximately five times the available acreage of 2 million hectares in the Netherlands (Hoogervorst, 1991, p. 111). These nutrient extractions deplete the soil of large rural areas, implying erosion in the long run.

process. This has resulted in at least three categories of environmental problems.[2]

The first category is the *eutrophication of surface water* due to nitrogen and phosphate emissions, leading to the excessive growth of algal and aquatic plants. In freshwaters, such as lakes, slow-flowing rivers and canals, algal growth is mainly controlled by the concentration of phosphorus. Phosphate application from both fertilizers and manure can be technically attuned to crop needs. Excessive phosphate which is not taken up by plants is largely absorbed by the soil, which acts as a buffer. Presently, only 1 to 3 percent of the excessively applied phosphate reach the surface water. Hence, agriculture is by no means the most important contributor of phosphate to surface waters at the moment, being responsible for only 9 percent of the total annual emissions of 43,000 tons per year. However, by continuing to fill up the buffering capacity of soils, more and more land will become saturated with phosphate, producing a breakthrough of phosphate. Ultimately, the resulting algal blooms will destroy plant and fish life. Phosphate saturation is a threat especially in the sandy soil areas with manure surpluses from intensive livestock farms. In 1990, 50 percent of the sandy soils (293,000 hectare) were already found to be saturated with phosphate (Willems and Hoogervorst, 1991, pp. 290-1).

In contrast to freshwater, algae growth due to eutrophication of estuarial, coastal and marine waters is mainly controlled by the amount of nitrogen. However, the control of nitrogen leaching from agricultural production is technically complicated. In addition to the uptake by crops, applied nitrogen disappears from the top soil through processes like denitrification and volatilization. How much of the nitrogen applied will be utilized depends on local conditions, such as soil processes and rainfall. Since farmers aim for a maximum output, the uncertain efficiency of nitrogen applications have stimulated them to apply it in large quantity. The relatively low price of nitrogen probably encouraged farmers to consider inefficiently used nitrogen as a cheap insurance against disappointing yields (Hoogervorst, 1990). As a result, some 80 percent of the nitrogen applied, originating from both fertilizers and manure, is lossed, being

---

2 Manure also contains heavy metals, such as cadmium, copper, mercury, lead, and zinc, originating from concentrated feedstuffs. The application of manure to land substantially contributes to the accumulation of heavy metals in soils and food. In this paper we leave out this specific environmental problem, since we focus on the environmental effects of nutrient leakages from manure application.

a potential threat to the environment (Olsthoorn, 1989; Centraal Bureau voor de Statitiek, 1989).

The second category of environmental problems due to nutrient leakages is *nitrate pollution of groundwater*. This is primarily perceived as a health problem. Roughly 70 percent of the drinking water in the Netherlands is produced from groundwater. Moreover, the continuous deterioration of the quality of surface water increases the importance of groundwater as a source for drinking water. Due to high levels of nitrogen use in agriculture, nitrate concentrations in groundwater continue to rise. In some instances extraction points (water wells) have already been closed. Projections indicate that about 60 extraction points, which is nearly a quarter of the total, are threatened with closure in the foreseeable future due to increasing nitrate concentrations (Ministerie van Verkeer en Waterstaat, 1989).

The third category of environmental problems is the *acidification* caused by the volatilization of ammonia originating from manure. Ammonia emissions account for 60 percent of the deposition of acidifying substances that originate from Dutch sources, while ammonia from manure contributes more than 30 percent to the total acid deposition in the Netherlands (Erisman and Hey, 1991). It would therefore seem most effective for the Netherlands to focus on reducing ammonia emissions (instead of NO_x and SO_2 emissions) in order to reduce the acid deposition on Dutch territory.

Although these environmental problems occur throughout the country, certain regions are the worst affected. This is not only due to the regional differences in agricultural production, but also to the specific characteristics of the environment. Unfortunately, the activities in agriculture that pollute the most are located in the most vulnerable regions of the country, that is on the sandy soils in the South and the East. These sandy soils house the highest concentrations of pigs and poultry, which is reflected in the regional concentration of phosphate production in the intensive livestock sector (see *Figure 1*).

Water drains through sandy soils relatively rapidly, which explains why the leaching of nutrients into the groundwater occurs most prominently in these regions. The map in *Figure 2* shows the areas with the highest concentrations of nitrogen in percolation water. These areas generally correspond to the location of the sandy soils, as well as to the regional concentration of Dutch intensive livestock farms.

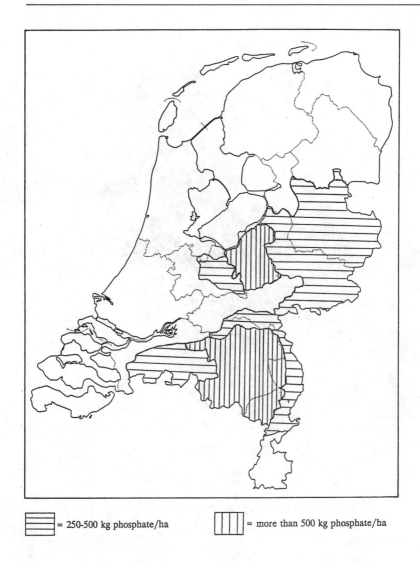

= 250-500 kg phosphate/ha   = more than 500 kg phosphate/ha

*Figure 1:   Phosphate production from livestock above 250 kilogram per
              hectare per agriculture area*

Source: Centraal Bureau voor de Statistiek, 1986, p. 22

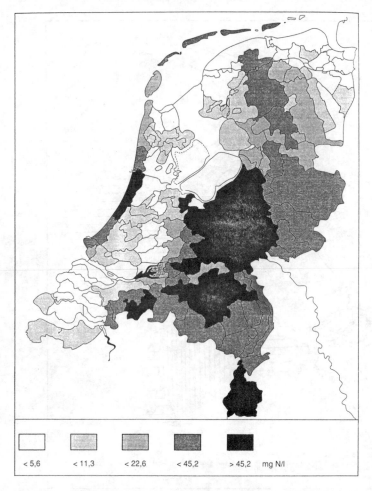

*Figure 2:   Average concentration of nitrogen in percolation water per agri-
            culture area*

Source: Langeweg, 1988, p. 208

Only 7 percent of the country is forested. Unfortunately, by far the greatest part of the Dutch forests is located on the sandy soils, which have been
shown to be highly sensitive to ammonia concentrations in the air. Over

50 percent of all Dutch forests are reported to be "less than vital," which is an euphemism for "dying."

Main features of the Dutch manure policy

In order to curb the adverse environmental effects of the livestock sector, the Dutch government has developed a "manure policy." The policy aims at a gradual reduction in the use of manure on agricultural land, without reducing the size of the national herds. In the government's view, farmers should be given enough time to make the necessary adjustments. The manure policy is designed to regulate the application of *phosphate* contained in manure. It is acknowledged that *nitrogen* in manure also causes environmental problems, but the volatile nature of this element was thought to cause insurmountable problems to formulating effective legislation. It was believed that by regulating the use of phosphate from manure nitrogen application could also be restricted.

In November 1984 the Interim Act was enacted. This law aimed to prevent further expansion of the numbers of cows, chickens and pigs. At the beginning of 1987, the Manure Act was issued. This Act is a legal framework enabling the government to take additional measures to abate the environmental effects of manure use. In accordance with the Manure Act the government, in May 1987, proclaimed phosphate standards. Until the end of 1990 the application of manure was to be limited to amounts equivalent to 250 kilogram phosphate per hectare for grassland, 350 kilogram per hectare for green maize, and 125 kilogram per hectare for all other arable crops. The amount of manure that, according to these standards, may not be used on farmland is called the *manure excess*. The manure excess can be calculated at various levels: farm level, regional level, and national level. The calculated excess levels depend on the amount of manure trade actually taking place or presumed to be (theoretically) possible. This has made public debates on the subject extremely complicated.

The manure levels were calculated in such a way that no manure excess would arise at the aggregated level of the whole country before the end of 1990. Meanwhile, regional excesses could be reduced by transporting the manure to regions with a relative shortage. The farmers, their organizations and the government hoped that at the end of 1990 new techniques would be available to reduce nutrient leakages into the environment, such as the industrial processing of manure and a substantial reduction of the nutrient content of animal feed. Anticipating these new techniques, the level of the manure standards were announced as decreasing in four successive steps (as shown in *Table 2*) until, by the year 2000, the final standards would be reached. The exact level of the final standards has still not been determined, but it should be equivalent to the amount of phosphate taken up by the various crops.

Table 2:   Legal standards for using manure in kilogram phosphate per
            hectare per year

Period	Grassland	Green maize	Arable land
1987-1990	250	350	125
1991-1994	200	250-150	125
1995-2000	175	125	125
2000-...	amount of phosphate taken up by the crops		

Source: Ministerie van Landbouw, Natuurbehoud en Visserij, 1989 and 1990b

The stages in the decrease of manure standards were also thought to comply with the policy objective for 1995, to reduce both the phosphate and nitrogen emissions into the North Sea by 50 percent on a 1985 baseline, which was agreed at the third conference of the North Sea countries in 1990 (van der Gaag, *et al.*, 1991, pp. 266-7).

Regarding the choice of policy instruments, current Dutch manure policy is dominated by direct regulation. The list of prohibitions and prescriptions is long, and only the most important measures are mentioned here. Apart from the phosphate standards already mentioned, farmers are not allowed to dump manure on their grassland between October 1 and December 1, and on sandy soils between October 1 and November 1. These restrictions have been progressively extended from 1991 to 1995 with as objective, a prohibition for grassland and for arable land on sandy soils and in valleys from September 1 to February 1. This implies that no manure dumping is allowed outside the growing season. Furthermore, farmers are initially obliged to plough the manure into their land within 48 hours of application in order to prevent the volatilization of ammonia. Since January 1, 1992, manure has had to be ploughed into arable land immediately and has to be injected into instead of spread on grassland. Also, the manure production on each farm is not allowed to be greater than that of 1986. New farmers or expanding farmers have to comply with even stricter standards: their total manure production is not allowed to exceed 125 kilogram phosphate per hectare. Moreover, all farmers are obliged to build accommodation for storing manure beyond the growing season. In addition, farmers have to keep an accounting system for their manure. Finally, special restrictions hold concerning farming practices in drinking water catchment areas. All these regulations are explicitly meant to reduce the nutrient leakages into the environment.

In contrast to these extensive regulations, economic instruments or financial incentives so far were hardly used. Where charges are imposed, they are intended to finance research and modifications at farm level. For this purpose the government created the "Manure Fund"; the *manure excess levy* brings in most of the respective money. A manure excess at farm level is taxed with a (relatively small) charge.[3] The object of the Manure Fund is to supply financial support for research and technological developments that might help to alleviate the manure problem. All efforts are concentrated along three lines:

1. development of manure processing plants;
2. transportation of excess manure to areas of shortage;
3. reduction of the phosphate (and nitrogen) content in animal feed.

Most of the money and attention has been given to the development of manure processing plants. It is hoped that these factories will turn the watery manure into a dry granular fertilizer that can compete with ordinary chemical fertilizers. In that way, manure would become another product that could be exported, which would both reduce the national manure excess and add to the balance of payments. Large-scale manure processing is the most ambitious element of the Dutch manure policy. After a period of research and demonstration projects it is intended to establish a network of manure processing plants, having a capacity of 6 million tons by the end of 1994.

The second line of approach is manure redistribution. To this end the "National Manure Bank" has been established. The primary function of the manure bank is to act as an intermediary, routing manure from farms with an excess to farms that wish to use the manure as fertilizer. The success of this redistribution strategy depends to a large extent on the quality of the manure offered. The less the amount of weed seeds, the more accu-

---

3 The first 125 kilogram phosphate per hectare each year is free of charges, the next 75 kilogram per hectare is subject to a levy of Fl 0.25 per kilogram, and any quantities above 200 kilogram per hectare are charged at a rate of Fl 0.50 per kilogram.

rately the nutrient content can be measured, and the higher the concentration of dry matter, the better is the quality of the manure. A high concentration of dry matter in particular is encouraged by a "quality premium system," because the water in the slurry only increases the transportation costs. In addition, the manure bank subsidizes manure transportation over long distances in order to alleviate the problems in excess regions.

The third line of approach is the reduction of the nutrient content in animal feed. To this end research is stimulated (by means of subsidies). The greatest potential for nutrient reductions seems to be the pig and poultry sector. Changes in the composition of concentrated feedstuff have already had modest success (Hartog, 1989). In order to stimulate the use of animal feed relatively poor in nutrients, the government in 1990 started the "Minerals Supply Registration System," a demonstration project to measure the effects which less nutrients in concentrated feedstuff have on the manure production of pigs and poultry.

Failures of the manure policy

Despite the development of a whole body of regulations, the Dutch manure policy is extremely ineffective as a method of abating nutrient leakages. To begin with, only the use of phosphate from manure is covered under the regulations, while the application of phosphate from chemical fertilizers is completely unrestricted. Moreover, the standards used for the maximum application of phosphate per hectare are, on the whole, far too high to be consistent with the capacity of nature to process nutrients sustainably. Most peculiar, however, is the exclusion of various categories of animals in the manure regulations. Until 1992 the regulations were only confined to cattle, pigs, and poultry. As could be expected, more and more farmers bypassed such regulations on manure by changing over to ducks, geese and, especially, sheep. Since January 1992 these categories (and fur-producing animals) have been included, but there are still categories that are free from regulation, such as horses and roes. A rise of the number of roes is now expected.

The idea of abating nitrogen leakages via a phosphate policy must be characterized as being either naive or wishful thinking. There is no connection between the two nutrients which would warrant such a policy, either in agricultural practice or in their impacts on the environment.[4] Meanwhile the Dutch government has admitted that a nitrogen policy is needed, and a process has been initiated to draw up legislation for nitrogen application in agriculture. However, at the moment of writing (summer 1992) it is still unclear which regulation will be chosen and when it will be implemented. For the time being, the use of nitrogen from both manure and chemical fertilizers is unrestricted.

Gaps in the existing legislation, as mentioned above, could quite easily be filled. Basically, what is needed is the introduction of environmental standards for the maximum application of nutrients, covering *all* nutrient losses from agriculture. It is, however, much more difficult to design an efficient policy once these standards have been set. The crux of the manure policy currently in effect is a set of "command and control" instruments, including various prohibitions and prescriptions at farm level which have been mentioned previously. This command and control approach, to my mind, considerably limits the options within farming practice, especially the option of how to reduce the nutrient losses.

The effects of nutrient losses vary greatly depending on specific local circumstances, which limit either the environmental effectiveness or the economic efficiency of generally prescribed abatement action. A set of uniform prohibitions and prescriptions which adequately prevent the washing-out of nutrients from one type of soil (e.g., clay) may prove inadequate on another type of soil (e.g., sand). If the set of prohibitions and prescriptions is made so restrictive that washing-out is prevented on all types of soil, the set will appear to be economically inefficient, because less restrictive measures will suffice at locations with lower levels of washing-out. At these locations the washing-out of nutrients can be prevented at a lower cost than that involved in the implemented set of prohibitions and prescriptions.

To prevent such inefficiencies in the abatement of nutrient losses, specific local conditions (such as the type of soil, level of groundwater, type of crop, amount of rainfall) should be taken into account. Consequently, a tailor-made set of measures is needed for each type of location which must be fitted to the specific circumstances of nutrient leaching. The accumulation of detailed and specific measures will, however, result in a very

---

4 This partly explains why the Netherlands in 1995 will not be able to comply with the aim to reduce the nitrogen emissions into the North Sea by 50 percent on a 1985 baseline, agreed upon at the third conference of the North Sea countries in 1990 (van der Gaag, *et al.*, 1991, pp. 266-7).

complicated system of regulation, as is already the case in the Netherlands. Apart from the tremendous costs that are incurred in gathering information about local circumstances as well as those incurred in maintaining all prohibitions and prescriptions, the command and control structure will also have paralyzing effects on farming practice, causing resistance from individual farmers and their organizations.[5]

Apart from the high costs of gathering information and maintaining the regulations (i.e., agency costs) as well as the paralyzing effects of the complicated command and control system used, there is no real incentive to decrease nutrient losses below the actual level of the standards imposed. As mentioned before, the present standards for applying maximum levels of phosphate do not correspond with a sustainable use of nutrients. Of course, the government intends to decrease the existing manuring and fertilizing levels step by step, until "end-state standards" are ultimately reached. But it is not yet clear what these "end-state standards" will look like, whether they will be sustainable and when they will have to be met. In the meantime, farmers who comply with the prevailing phosphate standards (which are far too high from an environmental point of view) have no incentive for decreasing their nutrient losses any further in the direction of sustainable levels.

To summarize, the Dutch manure policy is environmentally ineffective because standards for nitrogen use are lacking, while the current phosphate standards considerably exceed the carrying capacity of nature. Moreover, the unilateral choice of command and control instruments for abating nutrient leaching economically is an inefficient approach. In order to improve effectiveness and efficiency, environmental economists urge the use of economic instruments in environmental policy.

---

5 For example, Dutch arable farmers object fiercely to the prohibition on extending their intensive livestock if this results in a manure production larger than 125 kilogram phosphate per hectare. Arable farmers face declining prices of the main arable crops due to overproduction in the European Community and due to the international pressure in the GATT negotiations to decrease European price supports. Some of them would like to start or to switch to intensive livestock production, but they meet with the extension prohibition. They consider this prohibition unfair because intensive livestock farmers on the vulnerable sandy soils in the South and East of the country are temporarily allowed to produce more phosphate than 125 kilogram per hectare. In short, arable farmers feel themselves seriously restricted in their choices for production.

Pleas for economic instruments

Arguments in favor of the use of economic instruments in environmental policy originate from welfare economics. If applied to the case of nutrients leaching from agriculture, nutrient losses would be seen as an *externality problem*. Farmers using excessive amounts of nutrients do not take into account the increasing production costs of other producers and the decreasing utility levels of consumers due to the environmental degeneration caused by nutrient emissions. As Pigou (1920, p. 192) has already recommended, the activity causing the negative externality should be taxed at such a level that net social benefits will be maximized. However, optimization meets with fundamental problems, since it appears to be impossible to calculate *ex ante* the tax level which equals the marginal social costs and the marginal social benefits of decreasing the nutrient losses. Especially the estimation of the (marginal) benefits meets with problems due to the dynamics of nutrient leaching. So long as the marginal benefits of decreasing nutrient losses for current and future generations cannot be estimated, "optimality is not a policy option" (Hanley, 1990, p. 136).

This conclusion does, of course, not imply that economic instruments are useless for controlling nutrient losses. But it must be recognized that controlling nutrient losses by price manipulation alone cannot protect the environment adequately from high nutrient loads. Therefore, using economic instruments would, in practice, need to be accompanied by some form of regulatory control, especially over maximum nutrient losses. As Baumol and Oates (1971; 1988, pp. 159-76) demonstrated, a set of economic instruments can, in theory, achieve policy targets, such as emission levels, at lower total costs than uniform regulation. Economic instruments permit flexibility in the amount of pollution reduction achieved by each source, allowing polluters with low abatement costs per emitted unit to reduce emissions to a greater degree than polluters with high abatement costs per emitted unit.

In recent years several categories of economic instruments have been proposed for decreasing nutrient losses from agriculture. For example, Huppes and de Haas (1987) and Huppes, *et al.* (1992) developed a deposit-refund system for phosphorus and nitrogen: a deposit is imposed on the imports and newly produced goods containing phosphorus and/or nitrogen; the deposit is refunded if products containing phosphorus and nitrogen are exported or processed in such a way that the nutrients do not disturb ecosystems. Another category is advocated by Sandiford (1984) and Nentjes (1988) who, independently, proposed establishing a limited amount of tradeable permits (quotas) for the spreading of manure. They expect that quotas for manure spreading will achieve the desired maximum nutrient load per hectare at a lower cost than regulations based on standards. However, a levy on the use of nutrients seems most popular among agricultural economists and environmentalists, judging by the attention given to the input levy in the literature. The potential of an input levy will be examined in section 5.1. Objections to the input levy were among the motives for developing a specific emission levy, the nutrient surplus, which will be discussed in section 5.2.

Potential of an input levy

Levies on the input of chemical fertilizers have frequently been studied (cf. England, 1986; Dubgaard, 1987; Hanley, 1990; von Meyer, undated). Most of the studies only deal with nitrogen use, but could easily be extended to the application of phosphate and, if desired, to potassium. As far as I know, the price manipulation of concentrated feedstuff containing high levels of nutrients has not been considered. There is, however, no reason for excluding this category of nutrient inputs. Apparently, studies of this kind are exclusively inspired by the problem of excessive nutrient use on arable land and grassland.

The basic idea of nutrient price manipulation is to penalize the use of nutrients by a considerable increase in their prices relative to that of the output.[6] This is likely to have two effects: firstly, a reduction in the optimum rate of nutrients for each individual product, and secondly, a substitution effect at farm level away from products demanding high levels of nutrients (England, 1986, p. 14).

Although improvements in economic efficiency are anticipated in the literature, an input levy on nutrients as an instrument to abate nutrient leaching has some major disadvantages. A uniform levy on nutrients in fertilizers and concentrated feedstuffs does not differentiate between nutrients being utilized in farming products and nutrients being lost into the environment. Such a side-effect is only acceptable if the loss of nutrients varies proportionally with the degree of intensification. But as de Wit

---

6 The price rise has to be substantial because of the low elasticities of nutrient demands (Hanley, 1990, p. 138).

(1988) points out, this proportionality hardly exists in practice, which implies that a farmer who farms intensively but uses nutrients efficiently is penalized more than a farmer who farms extensively and uses nutrients less efficiently. Moreover, Dubgaard (1987) mentions a similar unintended and undesired effect of a levy on nitrogen fertilizer, namely that the least polluting crops (winter wheat and oilseed rape) are penalized more heavily than crops from which leaching is substantially greater (such as peas and spring cereals). This implies that marginal damage costs are not equal across arable activities. The same holds for the intensive livestock sector. A uniform levy on concentrated feedstuffs does not impose a higher penalty on farmers located on the vulnerable sandy soils than on farmers located on the less vulnerable clay soils. Therefore, a differentiation of the level of the levy is required in order to avoid these undesired effects.

Levy differentiation in this case would probably take the form of the allocation of levy-free quotas up to the appropriate level of nutrient use per hectare. However, this option meets with at least two problems. Firstly, the arrangement tempts farmers to trade nutrient quotas, probably resulting in excessive concentrations of nutrient applications in the areas with intensive forms of agriculture (Commission of the European Communities, 1989, p. 120); as a result, pollution rights will be concentrated in the most affected areas. Secondly, if such concentrations of pollution rights are considered to be undesirable, a prohibition on the trading of nutrient quotas would present a huge administrative task for the regulating agency, including the monitoring of the actual nutrient use per hectare.

The last objection to be dealt with here is the absence of any incentive to avoid nutrient leaching once the nutrients are bought. In intensive farming a levy on nutrients in purchased animal feed would considerably increase the nutrient efficiency in fattening pigs and chickens. Consequently, manure will contain less nutrients than previously. But farmers have no direct incentive to deal carefully with the remaining nutrients in manure. The prevention of nutrient leaching by, for example, careful storing of manure beyond the growing season means high additional costs for the farmer. On the other hand, farmers will probably receive a better price for nutrients from manure due to the price rise in fertilizers. However, arable farmers will not be willing to pay the same price for nutrients from manure as for nutrients from fertilizers because crops take up less nutrients from manure than from fertilizers (cf. Commission of the

European Communities, 1989, p. 37). Also, arable farmers may be reluctant to buy manure as long as the nutrient content cannot be guaranteed, and manure contains heavy metals and seeds from weeds.

To summarize, a uniform input levy on nutrients has substantial allocative disadvantages, while a differentiation in the levy rate invokes substantial agency costs. The most serious objection is, however, that the polluting activities themselves are not taxed, which causes incentive distortions.

Potential of an emission levy

To reduce the occurrence of incentive distortions as much as possible, a levy should be imposed on the emissions causing the environmental deterioration. To determine the proper basis for such a levy, the character of the nutrient problem must be kept in mind. A part of the nutrients used in concentrated feedstuffs and in fertilizers will be taken up in the agricultural products (like crops, milk, eggs, and meat). The remaining part of the nutrients used is redundant, because they are not essential to production.

These idle nutrients potentially jeopardize environmental quality. If farmers were aware of the dissipation of nutrients on their farm, they would look for methods of decreasing nutrient losses and thus saving money on nutrient inputs. Information about nutrient streams at farm level can be provided by systematic measurement of the input and output of nutrients. The introduction of such a *nutrient accountancy* would serve the interests of both individual farmers (savings on costs) and society (decrease in nutrient losses, i.e., environmental costs).

However, not all nutrient losses can be prevented. For example, crops only take up part of the nitrogen present in fertilizers or manure. This take-up varies across crops and seasonally. Whether the remaining nitrogen damages the environment depends on specific local circumstances, such as type of soil, rainfall, level of groundwater, denitrification, winter coverage, deposition of nitrogen compounds originating from other sources, etc. Thus, not all nitrogen losses lower environmental quality, but the capacity of nature to process nitrogen emissions varies across locations. It is common practice to consider nature's nitrogen processing capacity free to use for farmers.[7]

In contrast to nitrogen emissions, phosphate emissions from agriculture can be completely prevented. In general, soil has some phosphate combining capacity which acts as a buffer. As soon as this buffering capacity is used up, any additional phosphate emissions will completely wash out. However, as long as the phosphate buffer is not used up, it is technically feasible to attune the application of phosphates to the needs of the crops. By using nutrient accountancy, environmental deterioration due to phosphate emissions from agriculture can quite easily be prevented.

Nutrient accountancy would help farmers to track down nutrient dissipation. From society's viewpoint, nutrient accountancy offers an opportunity to establish a link between environmental deterioration and the nutrient losses of individual farmers, which is a prerequisite of an effective policy to abate nutrient leaching. However, a complicating factor is that in most cases individual losses of nutrients as determined by nutrient accountancy are not equivalent to nutrient emissions. Whether and to what extent nutrient losses affect the environment depends on local physical circumstances. To determine the emission level, we need to measure actual nutrient leaching on each lot. The amount of nutrients actually lost from the farm (that is, applied but not taken up by the crops) minus the amount of nutrients nature can sustainably process at the location concerned is called the *nutrient surplus*.

Although technically feasible, measurement of the nutrient surplus on each lot would appear to be a costly method. Besides, facilities for taking and analyzing all the soil samples needed are lacking as yet. Thus, for the time being, the nutrient surplus has to be partly calculated on the basis of average circumstances for and impacts of nutrient leaching. These average circumstances and impacts can be translated into a set of fertilizing and manuring standards, termed *sustainable standards* (to distinguish them from the standards used for farmers' information which are based on maximum output levels without any environmental considerations). Sus-

---

7 Apparently, the use of nature's nitrogen processing capacity is part and parcel of the bundle of usufruct rights of arable land. Basically, this right seems relatively scarce, implying a willingness to pay for it. For this reason we would expect that the price of land with a large nitrogen processing capacity (such as clay) is higher than that of land with a small nitrogen processing capacity (such as sand), other circumstances being equal. Empirical research on this hypothesis at least requires the existence of some sort of an abatement policy which makes farmers (as potential buyers or tenants of land) clear that nature's nitrogen processing capacity is limited.

tainable standards specify the maximum amount of nutrients that can be applied per hectare per year without causing damage to the environment, taking into account the type of crops grown and the type of soil present.

Table 3: *Sustainable standards for the use of phosphate and nitrogen*

	Grassland	Arable land*	Green maize*
Phosphate (kg P_2O_5/ha)	110	70	75
Nitrogen (kg N/ha)			
- clay soil	350	235	235
- sandy soil	330	130	130

* Including mandatory soil coverage by crops during the winter season.

Source: Dietz and Hoogervorst, 1991, p. 323

Dietz and Hoogervorst developed such sustainable standards (see *Table 3*). These standards are derived from the maximum losses of nutrients to soil, water and air that are acceptable from an environmental point of view. These maximum nutrient levels encompass all manures and fertilizers. The sustainable standards for application of phosphate are equivalent to the phosphate uptake by agricultural crops on different types of soil. The sustainable standards for the application of nitrogen are based on acceptable emissions of ammonia as well as on the European target guide level for nitrate in drinking water (see Dietz and Hoogervorst, 1991, pp. 323-4, for further details). A farm has a nutrient surplus if the *calculated* amount of nutrients used on the land is larger than the maximum nutrient load per hectare that may be applied according to the sustainable standards of *Table 3*.

It is almost impossible to compare the environmental standards in *Table 3* with the final standards the government is aiming for, owing to two reasons. First, the government has not (yet) developed final standards for the use of nitrogen. Second, the government remains rather vague about the precise level of the phosphate standards that will ultimately have to be attained by the year 2000.

The standards in *Table 3* are the goals of what could be called a "sustainable nutrient policy." The remaining issue is how to achieve these goals in the most efficient way. A bald announcement that the environmental standards will be in force as from a certain date in the future and that they will certainly be enforced if not complied with will certainly not work. Regarding the high level of nutrient leakages, farmers must be stimulated to modify their farming practices to an ecologically sustainable level long before the sustainable standards have to be attained. In this context, the Dutch government mainly applies command and control instruments for achieving the much weaker phosphate goals of the manure policy. The inefficiencies generated by this approach (see section 4) can be reduced by the use of the appropriate economic instruments.

Dietz and Hoogervorst (1991) propose using the nutrient surplus as a basis for a regulatory emission levy. This emission levy is called the *surplus levy* to distinguish it from the excess levy of the current manure policy. The latter only applies to the phosphate content of the manure from most but not all categories of animals, while the former includes both phosphate and nitrogen from *all* manures and chemical fertilizers. Moreover, the latter (the excess levy) has no regulatory target and is only meant as a means of financing abatement initiatives, such as the development of manure processing plants, while the former (the surplus levy) is meant to adjust the behavior of farmers.

Imposing a levy on the surpluses of phosphate and nitrogen acts as an incentive to farmers to prevent nutrient losses. This surplus levy confronts farmers with an additional trade-off: on the one hand, money can be saved by reducing the nutrient use, which decreases the leaching out of nutrients and, subsequently, avoids the costs of the surplus levy. On the other hand, farmers may fear a considerable reduction of output from a substantial reduction in the nutrients used, which would jeopardize income generation and outweigh the avoided costs of the surplus levy. However, several studies (Meyer and Lalkens, 1988; Tinker, 1988; Neeteson, 1989) suggest that considerable reductions in nitrogen application can be achieved with little or no reductions in crop yields.

Dietz and Hoogervorst (1991) calculated that a levy of 1.25 guilders per kilogram phosphate surplus and 1.25 guilders per kilogram nitrogen surplus is needed to give the surplus levy an allocative function. Unfortunately, it is almost impossible to compare the level of the proposed surplus levy and the level of the existing (ear-marked) excess levy on manure production, because the bases of the levies differ. However, as a rough indication it can be assumed that the level of the surplus levy is approximately ten times higher than that of the excess levy. The surplus levy will also increase the price of chemical fertilizers leaching into the environment. Nitrogen or phosphate emissions from fertilizers will cost a farmer

1.25 guilders per kilogram, which will increase the price of leached fertilizers by approximately 200 percent.

The introduction of the surplus levy would substantially reduce the costs of information for and maintaining of the current manure policy. On the whole, the individual farmer has much more knowledge about the specific physical conditions of his land than governmental agencies have. For decades this knowledge has been used for producing as much as possible (cereals, milk, meat), ignoring the loss of nutrient inputs in the hunt for higher production levels. The introduction of nutrient accountancy will make farmers aware of the (considerable) losses of nutrients. This knowledge alone will stimulate them to reduce nutrient losses, simply because it saves money on nutrient inputs.

There are numerous ways to decrease the nutrient surplus: reduction in the use of chemical fertilizers, substitution of manure by fertilizers, use of soil coverage during the winter season, reduction of the nutrient contents of concentrated feedstuff, transportation of manure to farmers who need nutrients, delivery of surplus manure to an industrial manure processing plant, etc. The choice of one or more methods of nutrient surplus reduction depends on the local physical circumstances, with which the farmer is most familiar (or which the surplus levy will stimulate him to explore).

The reaction of farmers to the introduction of this surplus levy is expected to vary with the amount of manure they produce. Farmers who produce little or no manure on their own farm will be discouraged from buying manure from other farmers. Farmers who produce substantial amounts of manure will be encouraged by the surplus levy to reduce their use of chemical fertilizers. Reducing the use of fertilizers means a reduction in production costs for animal feed (roughage) and possibly a (slight) reduction in the yield per hectare.

It is likely that the implementation of the sustainable standards in *Table 3* will generate considerable costs for the executing agency. To start with, an exact delineation of the clay and sandy soils is required. Furthermore, many farms are located on mixed soil types, which implies that using standards developed for pure clay or pure sand will either harm the environment or mean an unfair increase in production costs for the farmer. Finally, farmers may claim that specific local circumstances (low rainfall, low groundwater level, low deposition) and special measures taken on the farm (winter coverage, manure injection) have made the *actual* nutrient surplus much lower than the *calculated* nutrient surplus. If all these basically reasonable claims must be checked, agency costs most certainly will rise. Also, the character of the policy would change and could come to resemble the current situation: farmers feeling dependent on regulations they see as unfair and limiting their choice of farming practice. If this were to be the case, abatement policy would suffer severely from the noncompliance of farmers.

In my view, however, the information costs for the executing agency can be decreased considerably, while at the same time the compliance of farmers can be improved, *if* the burden of proof is put with the individual farmer! Then a farmer who claims a lower nutrient surplus than is calculated has to demonstrate this, for instance, on the basis of an analysis of soil samples by an independent laboratory. Of course, shifting the burden of proof will also shift the costs of proof to the farmer. However, as these costs need not be excessive (or could be reduced)[8], it may be expected that this institutional arrangement really will motivate farmers to comply with a system of nutrient accountancy, because most decisions concerning farming practice are left to the farmer.

At first sight, a levy based on nutrient accountancy of individual farmers seems extremely susceptible for fraud. Farmers are continuously tempted to "reduce" their nutrient surplus by registrating less fertilizer use and less manure spreading than actually is the case, and by recording a lower nutrient content of manure than is factual. However, the parties involved with nutrient transactions have incompatible interests. Arable farmers, (intensive) livestock farmers, dairy farmers, producers of fertilizers and concentrated feedstuff, manure banks, manure processing plants, they all have to register the inputs and outputs of nutrients. The interest of, for example, an intensive livestock farmer supplying manure to an arable farmer is to register the nutrient content of the manure delivered as high as possible, while the interest of the arable farmer is the registration of the nutrient content as low as possible. If none of the farmers has power over the other, the manure transaction will only take place if they both agree on the nutrient content, which will be very close to if not exactly the same as the actual nutrient content.

In general, it is essential for imposing a levy on the nutrient surplus that the (nutrient) gain of the one contracting party is the (nutrient) loss

---

8 In the Netherlands the costs of taking and analyzing soil samples currently varies between Fl 80 and Fl 100 per hectare. Rationalization of the procedures and economies of scale will likely reduce these costs.

of the other party. This is not to say that malversations can be excluded.[9]
But the incompatible interests of the contracting parties implicitly introduce mutual checks into the system, reducing the agency costs considerably.

To summarize, an effective nutrient policy requires a set of sustainable
application standards for nutrients from both manure and chemical fertilizers. The transition of current practices of manure dumping and overfer-
tilization into a sustainable use of nutrients seems most efficiently effected
by imposing a levy on the nutrient surplus of individual farms, supplying
industries and processing companies. In the literature a levy on the input
of nutrients has often been advocated. However, an input levy will generate certain incentive distortions. These distortions could substantially be
reduced by introducing the surplus levy. The ensuing agency costs can be
kept low if the burden of proof is laid with the nutrient holder.

The European context of the Dutch manure policy

So far the EC context of the Dutch abatement policy on nutrient leaching
has hardly been mentioned. Especially in the light of the current political
priority, the completion of the "Internal Market," the European Commission will critically evaluate existing regulations as well as additional measures or alternative instruments, such as economic instruments. The possibly complicated legal aspects will not be dealt with in this section. Here,
our modest intention is to shed some light on the EC pitfalls for both the
strategy of direct regulation (which the Dutch government has opted for
so far) and the alternative strategy of employing considerably more economic instruments, such as an input levy on nutrients or a levy on a nutrient
surplus.

According to the "principle of subsidiarity" of Article 130R of the EC
Treaty, environmental policy has to be formulated and carried out at the
lowest possible administrative level. Thus, without international environmental spillovers, national authorities have to deal with the problems of
nutrient leaching. The subsidiarity principle implies that a stricter abatement policy is permitted than in other EC member states, because the

---

9 For this reason nutrient accounts need independent inspection as is the case for
financial accounts.

nutrient leaching problem in the Netherlands is much more severe than in other EC countries.

However, this degree of freedom is restricted by Article 100A of the Treaty, which prohibits the national environmental authority from imposing arbitrary or hidden trade barriers. The issue here is to what extent environmental policy generates market segmentation arising from border controls and from market entry barriers (Siebert, 1991). On this basis, the European Commission raised doubts as to whether the Dutch government subsidizing up to 35 percent of the development and construction costs of manure processing plants is compatible with the Treaty of Rome (Official Journal of the European Community, September 1990). Finally, the Commission announced in December 1990 that this subsidy was permissible. The fact that about half of this subsidy is financed by the farmers themselves (by means of the revenue raised from the excess levy) was instrumental in the decision. The Commission nevertheless emphasized that there could be no question of subsidizing the operation of the manure processing plants, a subsidy which the farmers had tacitly hoped and also lobbied for.

The case of the Dutch subsidy for manure processing illustrates the growing concern in Europe about the adverse effects of (national) environmental regulations on fair competition. Generally speaking, the core of most regulatory approaches in EC member states is a licensing procedure, creating market entry obstacles which protect the existing firms against the competition of newcomers, as long as licences are not transferable (which is normal practice). To avoid segmentation of the European market, national licensing procedures must be harmonized. However, harmonization requires a European-wide definition of emission standards—either uniform or differentiated for specific regions—which are expected to be met by the application of the currently known abatement technologies. Instead of the European authorities defining the (continuously changing) currently known abatement technologies, it is clearly much more efficient to encourage individual firms to search for new technological solutions which meet environmental standards. As Siebert (1991) demonstrates, economic instruments reduce the role of regulatory procedures and thus make market entry easier. From the Internal Market perspective, economic instruments therefore have the appeal of reducing market barriers and segmentation.

Unfortunately, some economic instruments can also generate market segmentation in Europe. In this respect, proposals for an *input levy on nutrients* may meet with far more objections than the emission levy on nutrients, such as the levy on a nutrient surplus. In particular, the requirement that different environmental conditions have to be taken into account by a differentiation of the level of the input levy or a differentiation of the levy-free quotas means additional controls at the borders between member states. This could be interpreted as conflicting with Article 100A. If not, it is in any case incompatible with the aim to decrease tariff and nontariff barriers in the light of the completion of the Internal Market. Moreover, the introduction of a differentiated input levy on nutrients could also hamper the fiscal harmonization in the European Community, because such a levy is seen as an indirect tax.

A *levy on the emission of nutrients* into the environment does not have these disadvantages. The basis of the levy, the nutrient surplus, is the same for all member states. If trading in nutrients (e.g., manure from surplus regions to shortage regions) were to develop, border controls would not be required as is the case with the input levy. As far as I know, the European fiscal harmonization program does not apply to emission levies. But even if it did, a uniform levy would suffice, because the different environmental conditions do not need to be expressed in tariff differentiation.

So far, nutrient leaching has been discussed as a purely national problem which needs to be abated at the national level in line with the subsidiarity principle. Indeed, part of the nutrient problem concerns purely national, or often only regionally felt environmental effects, such as nitrate pollution of groundwater, eutrophication of streams and lakes, and acidification due to ammonia emissions. However, a substantial amount of the leached nutrients has impacts which are internationally felt, such as the pollution of groundwater in border areas and the eutrophication of rivers and marine waters, like the North Sea, the Baltic Sea, and the Mediterranean Sea. These international spillovers demand an international approach. The North Sea conference of 1990 was a step in that direction. However, noteworthy results did not accrue because national policies are as yet still dominated by the fear of the national agricultural sector losing international competitiveness if a strict national abatement policy were implemented.

The brief discussion above warrants the conclusion that the introduction of a regulatory levy on the nutrient surplus of Dutch farms, as advocated in the previous section, would not contravene existing European regulations concerning fair competition nor interfere with the aim of the Internal Market.

Concluding remarks

In Dutch agriculture excessive nutrient use is normal practice. The resulting nutrient emissions cause serious environmental problems, especially in areas where intensive livestock farms are concentrated. The existing abatement policy of the Dutch government falls short in both environmental effectiveness and economic efficiency.

The effectiveness is poor because the use of nutrients is only partly covered (especially the excessive application of nitrogen is not covered) and because much higher nutrient application levels are allowed than nature can carry sustainably. To improve the effectiveness of Dutch abatement policy, sustainable standards need to be introduced, indicating the maximum application of nutrients per hectare, covering all nutrients leaching from agriculture.

The efficiency of existing abatement policy is poor because regulating authorities have unilaterally chosen for "command and control" instruments. If the regulating authorities would like to take into account the specific local conditions of nutrient leaching, tremendous costs had to be made for collecting information and for maintaining all prohibitions and prescriptions. Such a tight command and control approach also would have paralyzing effects on the agricultural sector.

The efficiency of controlling nutrient leaching could, instead, considerably be improved by introducing economic instruments. In the literature an input levy on nutrients has frequently been proposed. A uniform input levy on nutrients, however, has certain allocative disadvantages—such as that least-polluting crops are penalized more heavily than crops from which leaching is considerably greater—while a differentiation of the rate of the levy invokes substantial agency costs. The most serious objection is, however, that the polluting activities themselves are not taxed, implying incentive distortions.

A levy on nutrient emissions could considerably reduce the chance for incentive distortions. However, to determine the amount of nutrient emissions of a farm nutrient accountancy is needed, which will generate costs for the individual farmer as well as for the regulating authority. The level and the distribution of these costs over the parties involved depend on which institutional arrangement is chosen. The proposal to shift the burden of proof to the farmers (implying a certain shift in property rights from farmers to society) will reduce the agency costs but will increase the production costs of farmers.

So far, there is no EC policy to abate nutrient emissions. According to the subsidiarity principle, regulation on the national (or even regional) level is preferred. However, the instruments used are not allowed to impose arbitrary or hidden trade barriers. As far as we can see the surplus levy, being the variant of a levy on nutrient emissions advocated here, does not generate such barriers, thus fitting in very well in the existing European regulations concerning fair competition as well as with the aim of a single European market.

Despite the highly celebrated subsidiarity principle, the European Community has to take policy initiatives in cases where nutrient emissions generate international spillovers. Regarding the increasing eutrophication problems in international waters, such an initiative is urgent. In addition, a European nutrient policy could probably prevent a dramatic shift of intensive livestock farms toward EC member states employing lower environmental quality standards.

References

Anderson, G. D. and R. C. Bishop (1986). "The Valuation Problem." In D. W. Bromley (ed.), *Natural Resource Economics. Policy Problems and Contemporary Analysis.* Boston, pp. 89-137.

Baumol, W. J. and W. E. Oates (1971). "The Use of Standards and Prices for Protection of the Environment." *Swedish Journal of Economics*, Vol. 73, pp. 42-54.

—— and W. E. Oates (1988). *The Theory of Environmental Policy.* Cambridge, MA.

Centraal Bureau voor de Statistiek (1989). *CBS '90. Negentig jaren statistiek in tijdreeksen.* The Hague.

—— (1991). *Maandstatistiek voor de landbouw.* Vol. 39 (January). The Hague.

Commission of the European Communities (1989). *Intensive Farming and the Impact on the Environment and the Rural Economy of Restrictions on the Use of Chemical and Animal Fertilizers.* Brussels.

Dietz, F. J. and N. J. P. Hoogervorst (1991). "Towards a Sustainable and Efficient Use of Manure in Agriculture: The Dutch Case." *Environmental and Resource Economics*, Vol. 1, No. 3, pp. 313-32.

Dubgaard, A. (1987). "Reconciliation of Agricultural Policy and Environmental Interests in Denmark: Regarding Controls on Nitrogen Fertilizer." In M. Merlo, *et al.* (eds.), *Multipurpose Agriculture and Forestry.* Kiel.

England, R. A. (1986). "Reducing the Nitrogen Input on Arable Farms." *Journal of Agricultural Economics*, Vol. 37, No. 1, pp. 13-24.

Erisman, J. W. and G. J. Heij (1991). "Concentration and Deposition of Acidifying Compounds." In G. J. Heij and T. Schneider (eds.), *Final Report Second Phase Dutch Priority Programme on Acidification.* Report No. 200-09. Bilthoven, pp. 51-96.

Gaag, M. A. van der *et al.* (1991). "Fluviale milieuproblemen." In RIVM, *Nationale Milieuverkenning 2: 1990-2010.* Alphen aan den Rijn, pp. 235-86.

Hanley, N. (1990). "The Economics of Nitrate Pollution." *European Review of Agricultural Economics,* Vol. 17, No. 2, pp. 129-51.

Hartog, J. den (1989). "Mest- en ammoniakproblematiek. Een bijdrage aan de oplossing door de veevoedersector." In Nederlands Studiecentrum, *Tweede jaarcongres mestoverschot en ammoniakbestrijding.* Wageningen.

Hoogervorst, N. J. P. (1990). "International Influences on Agricultural Pollution in the Netherlands." *Netherlands Journal of Environmental Sciences,* Vol. 5, No. 6, pp. 217-24.

—— (1991). "Nutrientenbeheer en voedselproduktie." In RIVM, *Nationale Milieuverkenning 2: 1990-2010.* Alphen aan den Rijn, pp. 103-17.

Huppes, G. and H. U. de Haas (1987). "Stofstatiegeld." *Economisch Statistische Berichten,* Vol. 72, No. 3615, pp. 684-86.

—— *et al.* (1992). *New Market-Oriented Instruments for European Environmental Policies.* London.

Langeweg, F. (ed.) (1988). *Zorgen voor Morgen (Concern for Tomorrow).* Alphen aan den Rijn.

Mansholt, S. (1990). "Nederlandse boeren in een Europees milieu. Naar een duurzame landbouw." In N. J. M. Nelissen (ed.), *Het milieu: denkbeelden voor de 21ste eeuw.* Zeist, pp. 339-57.

Meyer, B. J. M. and P. F. Lalkens (1988). "Economische analyse van de bedrijfssystemen op het proefbedrijf 'OBS'." In PAGV, *Themadag Gentegreerde Bedrijfssystemen.* Lelystad.

Meyer, H. von (undated). *The Common Agricultural Policy and the Environment.* WWF International Discussion Papers, No. 1. Gland.

Ministerie van Landbouw, Natuurbeheer en Visserij (1989). *Structuurnota Landbouw.* The Hague.

—— (1990a). *Feiten en cijfers.* The Hague.

—— (1990b). *Notitie Mestbeleid Tweede Fase.* Handelingen Tweede Kamer 1989-1990, 21502, Nr. 3. The Hague.

Ministerie van Verkeer en Waterstaat (1989). *Derde Nota Waterhuishouding.* Handelingen Tweede Kamer 1988-1989, 21250, Nrs. 1-2. The Hague.

Nentjes, A. (1988). "De economie van het mestoverschot." *Netherlands Journal of Environmental Sciences,* Vol. 3, No. 5, pp. 159-63.

Neeteson, J. J. (1989). "Evaluation of the Performance of Three Advisory Methods for Nitrogen Fertilization of Sugar Beet and Potatoes." *Netherlands Journal of Agricultural Science,* Vol. 37, No. 2, pp. 143-55.

Olsthoorn, C. S. M. (1989). "Stikstof in de landbouw, waarheen?" *Landbouwkundig Tijdschrift*, Vol. 101, No. 12, pp. 22-6.

Pigou, A. C. (1920). *The Economics of Welfare*. London.

Sandiford, F. (1984). "Controlling Water Pollution from Animal Wastes: A Reconsideration of Economic and Legislative Approaches." *Agriculture, Ecosystems and Environment*, Vol. 11, No. 1, pp. 15-27.

Siebert, H. (1991). "Europe '92. Decentralizing Environmental Policy in the Single Market." *Environmental and Resource Economics*, Vol. 1, No. 3, pp. 271-87.

Stee, A. P. J. M. M. van der (chairman) (1989). *Om schone zakelijkheid*. Perspectieven voor de agrarischer sector in Nederland. The Hague.

Tinker, P. B. (1988). "Efficiency of Agricultural Industry in Relation to the Environment." In J. R. Park (ed.), *Environmental Management in Agriculture - European Perspectives*. London, pp. 7-20.

Wijnands, J., H. Luesink, and M. van der Veen (1988). "Impacts of the Manure Laws in the Netherlands." *TSL*, Vol. 3, No. 3, pp. 242-62.

Willems, W. J. and N. J. P. Hoogervorst (1991). "Vermesting van bodem en grondwater." In RIVM, *Nationale Milieuverkenning 2: 1990-2010*. Alphen aan den Rijn, pp. 285-314.

Wit, C. T. de (1988). "Environmental Impact of the Common Agricultural Policy." In F. J. Dietz and W. J. M. Heijman (eds.), *Environmental Policy in a Market Economy*. Wageningen, pp. 190-204.

Part III.

**Restraints and Advances
in Technology**

Innovative Technologies for a Sustainable Development

Gerhard Angerer

Introduction

Sustainability characterizes a new kind of economic system in which preservation of raw materials and environmental resources are of high importance. The contribution of technologies for sustainable development is discussed controversially in the public. Whereas one group feels that environmental technologies hinder or postpone necessary behavior change of individuals, the other claims that only with innovative technologies the existing environmental problems can come under control. It is an open question where the truth between these extreme positions may lie.

In the following, an answer shall be given taking Germany as a case study. The German Federal Ministry for Research and Technology spends about 200 million DM in support of research and development (R&D) on environmental technologies. The Ministry wanted that those fields should be identified where sponsoring of R&D is most effective. Thus, the Institute for Systems and Innovation Research of the Fraunhofer Association was asked to identify the technology gaps in the emission control technologies (Angerer, Böhm, *et al.*, 1990).

Air pollution control in Germany

German air pollution control policy has focused in the last two and a half decades on the so-called bulk agents. These are dust, sulfur dioxide, and nitrogen oxides. These agents are characterized by a comparatively small toxic potential but are emitted in large quantities. *Figure 1* shows the emissions since 1966.

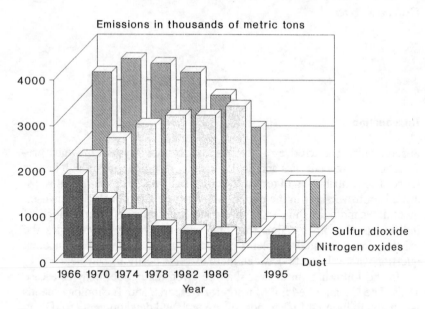

Figure 1:   Emissions of bulk pollutants

The emissions of dust in the Federal Republic of Germany (West Germany) dropped in the twenty years between 1966 and 1986 by 70 percent, from 1.8 to 0.5 million metric tons. For sulfur dioxide the reduction was 35 percent, from 3.4 to 2.2 million tons. Since all West German power plants meanwhile are equipped with desulfurization devices, emissions will further decrease by 1995 to approximately 1 million tons, which would then correspond to a reduction since 1966 of over 70 percent.

A special problem, at least in the past, was with nitrogen oxides. As the FRG and the European Community failed for many years to enforce an electronically controlled three-way catalytic converter in cars, the traffic sector became the major emitter of this pollutant. Therefore, the emissions of nitrogen oxides increased after 1966 by 60 percent, from 1.9 to 3 million tons. Fortunately, the policy was changed. With the help of financial incentives, meanwhile over 98 percent of all *new* gasoline powered cars are equipped with catalytic converters. Owners of *old* cars got a grant in case they added a device to their car; this offer, however, was only marginally accepted. In 1992, therefore, more than 50 percent of the stock of running cars still were polluting cars. However, by 1995 the emissions of nitrogen oxides may drop to 50 percent of the 1986 level.

Generally speaking one can say that for the bulk pollutants effective techniques have been developed in the past to reduce emissions. Among these are scrubbers for desulfurization, fibrous filters for dust extraction, and selective catalytic denitrification. With these techniques some 90 percent and more of the pollutant content can be separated from flue gases. By consistent utilization of the available techniques it would be possible to reduce emissions of sulfur dioxide further to 0.3 million tons, or 9 percent of the 1966 emissions, dust to 0.1 million tons, or 6 percent of the 1966 emissions, and nitrogen oxides to 1 million tons. Half of this amount comes from diesel engines for which effective reduction techniques are not yet available.

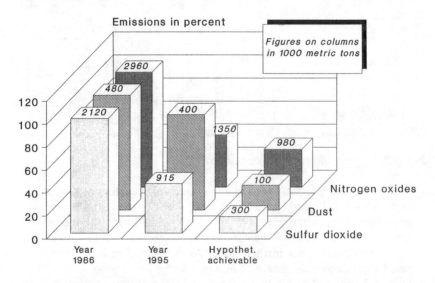

Figure 2:   Hypothetically achievable emissions of bulk pollutants

Figure 2 confirms that the development of emission control technologies has been quite successful in the past. Therefore R&D to generate new environmental technologies can now concentrate on other agents. The question is on which. A method is needed to help answer this question.

Method to identify R&D demand

To assess the effectiveness of the available environmental technologies for each of the selected pollutants three emission levels were used: first, the actual emissions in 1986, the last statistically available data at the beginning of our assessment; second, the expected emissions for the year 1995; and third, the hypothetical emission level, the level achievable if in all cases the best available technologies for emission control were used. By so doing, three different emission patterns emerge which indicate the effectiveness of available technologies or, conversely, the demand for further R&D to close the existing technological gaps.

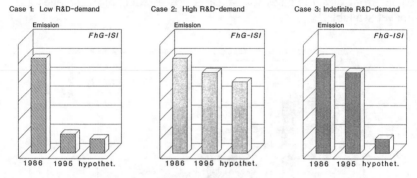

Figure 3:   Three different emission patterns

- In *case 1* existing technologies allow a powerful reduction of the emissions. This is indicated by the low emission level hypothetically achievable. Moreover, as the emission level for 1995 indicates, the technologies will be widely used in the coming years. *Case 1* pollutants therefore have a low demand for further R&D. As mentioned earlier, this is the case for sulfur dioxide, dust, and nitrogen oxides.
- In *case 2* powerful technologies for emission control are obviously not available. The emissions do not change very much till 1995, and the hypothetically achievable level is not very much below that. For *case 2* pollutants a high demand for further R&D is indicated.
- In *case 3* the R&D demand is indefinite. The situation is characterized by a considerable hypothetical potential to reduce emissions by technical means, but only a small actual reduction up to 1995. Two different

causes explain this situation. First, it may be that the available technologies are not adequately used. In this case, there is no demand for further R&D but a demand for policy to enforce application of available technologies. A second reason for poor technology use may be that the financial expenditures involved are too high. In this case, there is a certain R&D demand to lower the application costs.

Research results

What are the major R&D fields indicated by this method? *Table 1* shows the pollutants (and the respective emission levels) included in the survey. We were not successful in quantifying the emissions of dioxines and furanes, and in estimating the hypothetically achievable emission level for nonhalogenated solvents.

Table 1: *Pollutants and emission levels in metric tons*

Pollutant	1986	1995	At present hypothetically achievable
Sulfur dioxide	2,120,000	915,000	300,000
Nitrogen oxides	2,960,000	1,350,000	980,000
Dust	480,000	400,000	100,000
Cadmium	35	25	9
Mercury	38	35	25
Arsenic	185	150	80
Lead[1]	890	665	160
Gasoline[1]	100,000	60,000	13,000
Benzene[1]	6,610	5,400	2,250
Chlorofluorocarbons	90,000	40,000	30,000
Chlorinated solvents	245,000	160,000	95,000
Non-chlorinated solvents	510,000	250,000	?
Polychlorinated biphenyls	575	275	275
Benzpyrene	32	25	13
PCDD and PCDF	some 0.1	?	?

1 traffic not included

Source: FhG-ISI Karlsruhe

As can be seen, the emissions vary considerably; from nearly 3 million tons for nitrogen oxides to some 32 tons for benzpyrene. It would be very desirable to make these emissions comparable by using a "weighting factor" which characterizing the different toxic effects of the pollutants, such as health effects, phytotoxic effects, effects on the stratospheric ozone layer. At present, no such weighting factor is available, and it is questionable if it ever can be found.

Having this assessment problem in mind, we do not try to make the emissions of different pollutants comparable but looked simply at the relative emissions for each pollutant, based on the emission level in 1986. By so doing we got the figures shown in *Table 2*.

Table 2:   Relative emission levels and R&D demand

Pollutant	1986	1995	At present hypothetically achievable	Case	R&D demand
Sulfur dioxide	100	43.2	14.2	1	low
Nitrogen oxides	100	45.6	33.1	1-2	medium
Dust	100	83.3	20.8	3	low
Cadmium	100	71.4	25.7	3	low
Mercury	100	92.1	65.8	2	high
Arsenic	100	81.1	43.2	2	high
Lead[1]	100	74.7	18.0	3	low
Gasoline[1]	100	60.0	13.0	1	low
Benzene[1]	100	81.7	34.0	3	medium
Chlorofluorocarbons	100	44.4	33.3	2	high
Chlorinated solvents	100	65.3	38.8	2	high
Polychlorinated biphenyls	100	47.8	47.8	1-2	medium
Benzpyrene	100	78.1	40.6	3	medium

1 traffic not included

Source: FhG-ISI Karlsruhe

With the graphical visualization of these results, in *Figure 4* for anorganic pollutants and in *Figure 5* for organic pollutants one can easily identify the fields where the R&D priorities should be.

A high R&D demand is obvious for chlorofluorocarbons (CFC), chlorinated solvents, mercury, and arsenic.

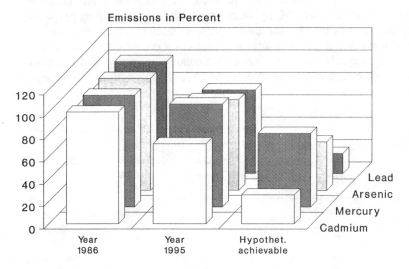

Figure 4:   *Hypothetically achievable emissions for anorganic pollutants*

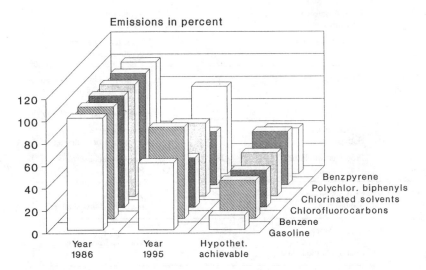

Figure 5:   *Hypothetically achievable emissions for organic pollutants*

Some of the priority R&D fields are listed in *Tables 3* and *4*. Among these are the substitution of CFC by water-based solvents for cleaning purposes; the recovery of CFC blowing gas for polyurethantial-foam production; the substitution of halogenated solvents by water-based cleaning systems or by other organic solvents, like benzine or alcohols; the recovery of these solvents from outgoing air; the trapping and recovery of mercury and arsenic from flue gases.

Table 3:   R&D fields with high priority

Pollutant	Application	Share of hypothetical emission level in %		R&D
CFC	PUR-hard foams	26		Substitution of blowing gas
	PUR-soft foams	9	1. 2.	Substitution of blowing gas Recovery of blowing gas
	Solvents for cleaning purposes	51		Substitution by water-based solvent systems or non-halogenated agents like alcohols, acetone, benzine
	Fire-extinguisher substances	5		Substitution by water or CO_2
	Refrigerating agents	5		Substitution by nonhalo-genated agents
Chlorinated solvents	Cleaning purposes	70	1. 2.	Substitution by water-based solvent systems or nonhalo-genated agents Recovery from outgoing air
	Dry-cleaning of clothes	10	1. 2.	Substitution by benzine Recovery from outgoing air
	Processing of plastics	18	1. 2.	Substitution of solvents Recovery
Mercury	Coal combustion plants	77		Trapping from flue gas (e.g., with charcoal filters)
Arsenic	Glass industry Metallurgical industry Coal combustion plants	30 37 26		Trapping from flue gas

Source: FhG-ISI Karlsruhe

A somewhat lower priority emerges for polychlorinated biphenyls (PCB), benzpyrene (B(a)P), benzene (CH_6) and nitrogen oxides. As the PCB containing hydraulic oils were substituted in the German coal mining industry, all emissions originate from old loadings, like waste disposal sites or older electrical transformers. Therefore, the elimination of these sources by decontamination is necessary to reduce PCB emissions. Also, the development of low-emission stoves and boilers for the abatement of benzpyrene emissions; the improvement of burners and furnaces to reduce benzene emissions; the sealing of coke ovens combined with trapping and recovery of benzene from flue gases; and the reduction of nitrogen oxides emissions from diesel engines are tasks for further R&D activities.

Table 4: **R&D fields with medium priority**

Pollutant	Application	Share of hypothetical emission level in %	R&D
Polychlorinated biphenyls	Old loadings	100	Exploration of sources and decontamination
Benzpyrene	Domestic boilers and stoves	46	Low-emission combustion
Benzene	Small sized furnaces	38	Improvement of burners
	Coke ovens	20	Improvement of sealing, trapping, and recovery
	Solvent	22	Substitution
	Distribution of gasoline	11	Improvement of sealing and recovery
Nitrogen oxides	Diesel engines	37	Catalytic reduction to nitrogen

Source: FhG-ISI Karlsruhe

Conclusion

To estimate actual and hypothetical emissions is not an easy task, particularly not for pollutants poorly documented, which is the case for all agents not belonging to the group of bulk pollutants. Nevertheless, there is no other option to put R&D activities on a rational basis. We hope that our method will be adopted for other environmental compartments too, and the method be developed from its present crude status to a higher level of sophistication.

Environmental technologies will play an important role in the transition process to a sustainable economy. They offer a chance to get environmental loadings under control, without essential losses in the living standard achieved. However, one should keep in mind that technology use must be accompanied by behavior change on all levels of decision-making, and it should not be forgotten that improved technology will tie up considerable financial resources.

Reference

Angerer, G., E. Böhm, *et al.* (1990). *Möglichkeiten und Ausmaß der Minderung luftgängiger Emissionen durch neue Umweltschutztechnologien.* Research report of the Fraunhofer-Institut für Systemtechnik und Innovationsforschung. Karlsruhe.

Sustainable Development—Will the Technology Option Work?

Udo E. Simonis

> "... a fundamental problem with economics is the inflated view that economists have of the very real but limited success of their discipline."
>
> *Paul R. Ehrlich*

Introduction

The topic of this workshop[1] reminds me of an American economist and a German philosopher. The American economist (E. G. Dolan) once said:

> Two thirds of the job of the economists in conserving the environment would already be done if they succeeded in establishing reliable accounting systems at the national and the business level that include the environmental costs of production and consumption.

The German philosopher (A. Schopenhauer) once gave a definition of happiness:

> To be happy and to remain happy you have two options: Either decrease your expectations or increase your efforts!

Regarding our topic, there is probably a third option, i. e., a combination of the two:

> Let us decrease our expectations *and* increase our efforts!

Why to ask for such a modest approach? There are several reasons, all of which have to do with the *real* world which is so much different from our *ideal* world.

In a background paper to our workshop Robert Repetto and John Pezzey say: "Sustainable development requires improvement of policy failures no less than of market failures." I cannot but fully agree to that judgment. But we have to add one additional failure, with which I would

---

1 Intervention at the Workshop on "The Economics of Sustainable Development," Washington, D.C., January 23-25, 1990.

like to start my contribution, and that is the failure of the economists to treat ideal for real worlds!

Ideally, pollution could be prevented and emission-free technology and products be promoted, by emission charges or resource taxes or transferable emission permits or different tariff systems, etc., etc.

In the real world, however, those various theoretical concepts have been traded against each other by the politicians and the business people. None of these concepts actually was bought by them implemented in practice in full scale.

Ideally, it is possible to construct improved information systems that facilitate sustainable development by incorporating the environmental dimension into the relevant accounting systems. However, I know of only two empirical studies on a Net National Welfare (NNW) indicator (by American and Japanese colleagues); and I know of only two countries in which systematic analyses of the defensive (or compensatory) expenditures in the GNP have been undertaken (Japan and Germany). But I know of a dozen sophisticated social indicator systems that were developed to complement the traditional national accounts, all of which sooner or later were abolished and never implemented.

For these, and probably for some other reasons, one might declare the economics profession as one that is, in actual fact, not very much interested in the implementation of its own proposals. If we really were, the state of the world could not be as it is!

And it is exactly for these reasons that when talking about "sustainable development" my plea is for more modest expectations and for some more serious efforts.

Being asked for operational dimensions of sustainable development in general, and technological improvements in particular, I would like to make that plea somewhat more specific by focusing on three levels, on which a real break-through is possible if our expectations are not too high and our efforts high enough: (1) information base, (2) environmental principles, (3) economic instruments. Put differently, one could say that the task is to correct certain information failures, market failures and policy failures.

Information base

The Brundtland Commission has stated that it is theoretically possible to achieve increased output with decreased energy and materials consumption. The evidence of this *decoupling* of GNP growth from the growth of environmentally harmful effects is, however, not well established and not widely spread.

Several approaches are possible, one or two of them should be implemented worldwide and on a continuous basis. My personal priorities are the following:

Model 1: Decoupling
In a study undertaken in Berlin on 32 countries from East and West, we have focused on four input factors (or industries) whose negative environmental impacts are self-evident: energy, steel, cement, and transport.

We asked whether there was a (relative) decoupling of these factors from the GNP or even a (absolute) decrease of production and pollution in these industries since the early 1970s. The result of the research was that there are cases of rapid decoupling (Sweden), slow decoupling (FRG, Japan), and no decoupling (CSSR, GDR).

I would like to see similar studies commissioned on other environmentally important input factors (industries) and the results published on a regular basis. In particular, the agricultural sector should be included, and also chemical industry.

Model 2: Environmental productivity
Environmental productivity can be measured by levels of output per unit of natural resource input and/or per unit of waste discharged. Such productivity indicators should be compiled and continuously monitored.

Repetto and Pezzey observe that traditional productivity studies ignored an important dimension, namely the efficiency—better: the inefficiency—with which materials and services generated by nature are being used. Particularly, energy efficiency should be measured and published for all countries on a yearly basis.

All of us know, or would expect, that the ranking of the countries of the world would be very much different if energy productivity became a major indicator of economic success instead of the GNP indicator. Repetto and Pezzey rightly demand that governments and economists should at least devote the same attention to measuring and analyzing these aspects of productivity as to conventional indicators of economic efficiency.

Model 3: Net national welfare-indicator
I am still very much in favour of the NNW-approach and of related approaches of an improved measurement of welfare. And I am grateful that some Japanese colleagues have continued work on that welfare indicator although they got nearly no support for their efforts from the international academic community. To be sure: without an alternative understanding and measuring of welfare we will neither reach ecological sustainability nor pollution-free technology.

For some reasons of methodology but mainly because of shortage of resources, in my institute we somewhat modified the NNW-approach and studied thoroughly the growth of the "defensive (or compensatory) expenditures" in the GNP. The share of such expenditures in the Federal Republic of Germany rose from 5 percent in 1975 to some 12 percent in 1988! I would like to see more studies of this type in all the OECD countries.

Economists are not technicians. But with these kinds of qualified information they could provide helpful guidelines for the technicians on the question in which direction technical innovations should be pursued.

For instance, the NNW is focusing on the services (!) from private consumer goods and government infrastructure, and is declaring environmental protection expenditures as defensive, and environmental damages and costs of urbanization as losses, not benefits of industrial development.

Several new accounting systems were developed, but only a few of them were empirically tested. A common effort seems needed to establish what the priorities of further research on that topic should be. Most certainly, an international project on improved environmental information systems is required and should be funded by one of the international institutions.

There is a special East-West aspect involved here, not yet mentioned. Recently we often hear, "the East should learn from the West." However, there might also be something to be learned from the East. For instance, there is a long tradition in the East in using materials balances which in some way are needed to link economic and environmental accounting.

Environmental principles

In the background paper mentioned Repetto and Pezzey say:

> Decisions made by enterprises (and households) in response to perceived economic advantage largely determine the direction of technological change; market incentives dominate the search for and diffusion of new technologies.

I think, no one will oppose to this hypothesis. Unfortunately, however, there are only few or no market incentives to seek and adopt low-emission technologies. On the contrary, there are still considerable incentives to save priced inputs at the expense of greater environmental damages that are not paid by the polluter but by nature or the public at large (the tax payer). In the paper it is said: "perverse incentives" that lead to resource-intensive production technology.

> The good news is that many emerging technologies offer exciting opportunities. The bad news is that no "hidden hand" is operating to guide technology ... The needed transformation is technological, but the drive for it will come from another realm ..., particularly from the people's insistence that some things that seem to be wrong are just that! (Gus Speth)

Environmental policy of some kind has been established in more than 120 countries in the world, and that makes quite a difference to 1972, when only 17 were counted. But there is strong evidence that this environmental policy predominantly is a react-and-cure policy. Despite all the talking and writing on the "polluter-pays principle," in the real world it is mostly the taxpayer (and future generations) that bear the costs, and not the polluter himself. "Preventive environmental policy" is up to now not much more than a metaphor.

This state of environmental policy means that the larger part of environmental technology still is of an add-on-type, or "end-of-pipe technology," and not integrated, "low-emission technology." As to Germany, we have some evidence that approximately 70 percent of what can be classified as environmental technology is add-on-technology. (A study on the USA, a few years ago, showed a similar percentage.)

So, the transformation of technology, the "greening of technology" (Gus Speth) has at best just begun. There are promising solutions, no doubt. But guiding and speeding the application of solution-oriented technology will require strong institutional innovation.

Gus Speth recently promoted the idea of having an EPA that is not organized according to the environmental media (air, water, soil), but according to the main polluting activities—transportation, manufacturing, agriculture, energy, housing, the sectors of the economy that are technology-based and technology-driven.

Regarding the future of environmental policy, I think that contrary to what most economists believe there will be only limited trade-offs between environmental regulations on the one hand and economic instruments on the other. Technology-forcing regulations and economic incentives must both be harnessed. And this is so for various reasons.

First, countries with an established administrative culture (like Western Europe) and high enforcement potential (like Japan) will never give up regulation, though they might be willing to employ some additional economic instruments. Secondly, with an increasing environmental awareness and pressure from below, governments in the future will be forced to phase out certain products and technologies. Where the exhaustion of resources and the extinction of species is at stake, quantitative restrictions, not taxation and pricing are needed. Thirdly, preventive planning and action will be promoted by actively introducing liability rules and by shifting the burden of proof, a field mainly hold by law-making and law-interpreting people who are very much inclined toward regulation.

Still, there are many tasks for economists. I would particularly like them to establish more and better evidence on the "greening of technology." I would like to see more work on promoting and disseminating low-emission technology, because I still have trust in the "power of information" and also in the educational role of the "good example." Modern information and communication technology could be used to spread the idea and the economics of "clean technology" to all the technology-based and technology-driven sectors of the economy. Such need for dissemination of knowledge, of course, has an international dimension. Day by day, too many of the "old mistakes" are being repeated throughout the world.

To some extent, however, this state of affairs is a consequence of the fact that there is no clear-cut definition and no consensus on what "clean technology" really is. This is particularly due to one inherent problem: There is clean technology leading to dirty products, and there are clean products relying on dirty production technology.

Economic instruments

Robert U. Ayres recently wrote the following:

> The current resource-intensive and energy-intensive technology of the industrial world has been shaped by decades of cheap energy (and resources) ... This history determines its present appetite for energy and mineral resources ... But this is exactly the same technology that would be exported to the developing countries if they only could afford it.

Ayres concluded:

> ... although there is no necessary link between GNP and energy/materials consumption, there is certainly an actual one.

No doubt, we need a tighter economic linkage between energy and resource use and the damages attributable to that use—regardless of where the resources are obtained and how and where they are used. It is particularly the intensive international trade of material resources that makes resource taxation an international task.

Theoretically, I am quite in sympathy with "grand designs" for a global resource tax, or a system of "green taxes." But, coming back to my initial warning, we better should lower our expectations because the efforts needed for such designs are rather high. However, we have to "put the prices right" in order to encourage and promote low-emission technology and products. Prices must reflect the true costs to society, the environment, and future generations.

As Johannes B. Opschoor and colleagues have shown, so far there are only a few countries that effectively use resource taxes and emission charges on a larger base and to a greater degree. There is even one case (Japan) where an emission charge was abolished after a few years in use.

In Germany, in a strict sense, there is only one emission charge in effect, namely in the water sector (*Abwasserabgabe*). Through strict regulation it was possible to decrease the sulphur dioxide (SO_2) emissions. But the great problems are with the increasing nitrogen oxide (NO_x) emissions, the still high carbon dioxide (CO_2) emissions, and particularly the increasing toxicity (not the volume) of waste.

In view of climate change, the German environment minister is actively favouring a CO_2 emission charge; but so far he has no sufficient support, neither in the cabinet nor in his own party, nor in the European Community and the OECD. In contrast, two opposition parties (the Social Democrats and the Greens) are favoring a resource tax (energy tax) and four to six emission charges. So, if the current government stays in power, in Germany we at best will get a CO_2-emission charge, depending on whether the other European countries will join respective agreements. If, instead, the opposition parties gain power, we have two major proposals at the moment:

- SPD: special tax on gasoline, providing approximately 10 percent of the federal budget (30 billion DM) and four to six emission charges (8 billion DM). These funds shall enter the general government budget without specified spending prescriptions. Parallel to this, the wage tax shall be reduced accordingly.

- Greens: tax on primary energy (including coal and nuclear energy) in the range of approximately 27 percent (80 billion DM) of the federal budget. These funds shall be allocated for the promotion and application of low-waste technology, particularly public transport and renewable energy.

The message of these proposals is clear: Make energy and extractive resources more expensive and human labor cheaper! The substitution of cheap energy for expensive labor and capital must be reversed (see Ayres).

When taking past experience, present public debate and future needs into consideration, a medium-rage approach of using economic instruments for inducing technology change seems most likeable: Not comprehensive, perfect, ideal models will be implemented but pragmatic, well-defined models might get a chance. However, quite some coordination effort is needed to get such a medium-range approach going, particularly if we not only think of the OECD countries alone, but of the world as a whole.

Conclusion

I would like to end by quoting a Norwegian peace researcher who once said:

> A policy proposal that cannot be understood by somebody with ten years of education within ten minutes, is not a democratic proposal but an academic or political power instrument. (Johan Galtung)

To paraphrase this quotation with regards to the topic of our workshop: The message of "sustainable development" will not reach its addressees, the people in general, and the technicians and the politicians in particular,

Part II.
Restraints and Advances in Policy

Part IV.

Restraints and Advances in International Relations

Global Institutions for Sustainable Development[1]

Jonathan M. Harris

Dimensions of the global ecological crisis

The rapidly escalating environmental problems of the late twentieth century have a common characteristic: their increasingly global nature. Attention has recently been directed to problems affecting the atmosphere: the CO_2 build-up and resulting climatic change, and the depletion of the ozone layer. But other environmental problems which have in the past been more often analyzed as specific or local issues are also taking on global scope. Erosion and the degradation of soil productivity is a worldwide problem, most intense in parts of the developing countries. Groundwater pollution and overdraft is increasing in all parts of the world. Deforestation and desertification, toxic agricultural run-off, acid precipitation, and the exponentially rising generation of toxic wastes by industrial processes are all global phenomena. Most of these ecological threats are driven by inexorable world population growth. Since 1950 world population has more than doubled, from 2.5 billion to 5.4 billion; by 2050 it is projected to double again, to more than 10 billion. Whereas the ecological impacts of human economic activity have in the past generally been limited, specific, and local, it is becoming increasingly evident that the scale of world agricultural and industrial production is now such that the entire global ecology is affected, sometimes in ways which are unpredictable and possibly irreversible.

Despite growing public and professional awareness of this reality, there has until recently been an almost complete absence of global institutions designed to respond to ecological issues. Existing organizations, such as the United Nations Environmental Program (UNEP), are limited in scope and lack any enforcement powers. International organizations which do have some financial power, notably the IMF and the World Bank, have until recently promoted projects and policies which have hastened environmental degradation. Public protest and pressure from environmental

1 An earlier version of this article appeared in *World Development*, Vol. 19, No. 1. Reprinted with the permission from Pergamon Press Ltd., Oxford, UK.

groups have recently compelled the World Bank to modify or withdraw some of its support from environmentally disastrous mega-projects (the Polonoroeste road-building project in Brazil, the Singrauli energy complex in India, transmigration projects in Indonesia, cattle-ranching and mechanized agriculture projects in Botswana and the Sudan, etc.) The IMF has yet to acknowledge a significant role for environmental issues.

In the campaign to modify World Bank and IMF policies, the main achievements to date have been in limiting destructive policies. By contrast, the effort to reorient the lending policies of the banks toward ecologically sound development has encountered heavy institutional resistance. The strong bias of the banks is still toward large-scale centralized projects using technology which is often environmentally destructive ("hard" rather than "soft" technology, to use the terminology popularized by Amory Lovins). While adding some environmentally-oriented staff members may modify some bank policies, it does not alter the basic thrust and underlying economic analysis governing bank lending.

In the wake of the 1992 U.N. Conference on Environment and Development, this institutional picture has changed only slightly, despite lofty rhetoric. The newly created Global Environmental Fund (GEF), formally coordinated by UNEP, UNDP, and World Bank, is dominated financially and in policy direction by the World Bank. It is thus unlikely to represent a shift in basic funding priorities or strategic goals away from the Bank's traditional emphasis on increasing economic output. Rather, it will provide a "green" veneer to development strategies whose essential emphasis is still on large-scale energy projects, "modernized" agriculture, timbering operations, and the like.

This experience in the limits of institutional reform is not surprising, given the origins and constitutional purpose of the IMF and the World Bank. Their purpose is to promote economic development and the stable expansion of world output. But this objective, originally formulated in the immediate post-World War II period, is derived from an economic analysis which essentially ignores ecological realities.

Since awareness of environmental issues first took hold in the early 1970s, economists have devoted some attention to the internalization of "external" costs (environmental damage) through pollution taxes and similar market modifications. This approach to environmental problems, however, fails to capture the global effects of economic expansion, concentrating instead on specific, measurable impacts which can be factored into cost-benefit analysis.

If we consider some of the ecological issues mentioned above, we can see how standard economic analysis misses the essence of the problem.

Virtually all industrial processes and transportation depend on energy inputs which are overwhelmingly drawn from *fossil fuel* sources (coal, oil, and gas). While various pollutants such as sulfur dioxide and nitrogen oxides can be reduced by fuel selection and technological modifications (scrubbers, fluidized bed combustion), the emission of carbon dioxide (CO_2) is inherent in fossil fuel combustion. The increase in CO_2 emissions and atmospheric concentrations has been exponential since the beginning of the industrial revolution. Evidence is mounting that the resulting global warming effect may have already begun. Regardless of scientific differences in evaluation of this evidence, the danger of irreversibly altering the composition of the atmosphere, with unknown but potentially catastrophic effects on weather and planetary ecosystems, is obvious. Thus an effective response to the CO_2 build-up must involve a fundamental change in the nature of industry and transportation. Greatly improved energy efficiency and renewable energy technologies are feasible possibilities, other than a cessation or reversal of economic growth. The massive project of capital replacement that would be required for such technological change is not now motivated by any market price signals—nor will it be until the exhaustion of fossil fuel sources approaches. The limiting environmental constraint, however, is not the supply of fossil fuels but rather the ability of the ecosphere to absorb their waste products. Without government or institutional intervention on a massive scale worldwide, the global warming process will continue unabated. Here the 1992 Rio conference offered only statements of good intention, with no binding timetable or institutional mechanism for CO_2 reduction.

The destruction of the stratospheric ozone layer by *chlorofluorocarbons* (CFCs) is now well documented. These long-lived catalytic gases continue to destroy ozone for decades, and are still making their way to the stratosphere so that even if all CFC production ceased immediately, the ozone depletion would continue to an unknown degree. Destruction of the ozone layer threatens all life on earth. Market signals are relatively ineffectual in dealing with this threat; the only effective policy is complete prohibition. The Montreal Protocol of 1987, initiated by UNEP, mandated a 50-percent reduction in CFC production in industrial nations by 1999. While this was hailed as a victory for international environmental cooperation, scientific evidence of more rapid damage soon required a shift to a complete phase-out by 1999, or earlier. Even the limited Montreal agreement required long and difficult negotiation and substantial compromise of goals. Compliance by developing countries is in doubt; the United States in particular has been extremely reluctant to provide even minimal compensation which developing countries have demanded as the price of for swearing CFCs. This record, to my mind, is not conducive to optimism in assessing our capacity to respond to the continued threat from CFCs and related ozone-depleting chemicals, let alone the multifaceted environmental threats of the coming decades.

In the area of global agricultural expansion, a complex of problems threatens the future viability of much *agricultural production*. Erosion and soil degradation is a worldwide phenomenon which has reached critical proportions in many areas of the developing world (World Resources Institute, 1992; Worldwatch Institute, 1990). Water pollution from agricultural run-off affects all high-fertilizer application farming areas; this non-point pollution has increasingly been identified as a leading problem in industrial countries, one which is not susceptible to the standard remedy of point-source emission controls. Due to the strong correlation between fertilizer use and yield, run-off pollution will intensify throughout the developing world as output must rise to match population-driven demand (Harris, 1990). Water overdraft has reached dramatic proportions in irrigated agriculture areas of the United States and the former Soviet Union; depletion of the Ogallala aquifer and the Aral Sea water system threaten the future of agriculture in those areas. Water shortages present an absolute barrier to agricultural development in much of Asia, and present overuse of existing supplies has led to extremely severe water pollution and soil salinization in China and other Asian nations (Worldwatch Institute, 1990; Harris, 1990). Pollution and ecological damage from pesticide use are widespread, especially in the developing world, with the emergence of resistant pest species a rapidly growing problem (Pimentel, 1980).

Many of the problems which now plague global agriculture are a direct result of yield-increasing, "Green Revolution" technology of intensive cultivation. Yet continuing population momentum and limited arable land means that yields must continue to rise for the next half-century. Research, development and promulgation of low-input, sustainable agriculture techniques is urgent, yet market incentives generally point in the opposite direction, toward rapid adoption of present high-yield systems. Some U.N. agencies (UNEP and the International Fund for Agricultural Development) are promoting sustainable techniques, but their very limited budgets mean that they have only a minor impact on world production patterns.

The rapidly growing problem of *toxic waste disposal* presents another environmental issue which is essentially out of control worldwide. Most industrial production has toxic by-products, and the growth in output of toxic synthetic compounds has been on the rise since World War II. Attention has been focused on major toxic chemical accidents (at Seveso, Italy; Bhopal, India; and Basel, Switzerland), but the long-term accumulation and inadequate disposal of wastes is of much larger scope. In the United States, some funding (so-called Super Fund) has been devoted to attempts to clean up existing toxic waste sites holding wastes from past production, with mixed results. But the question of how to handle ever-increasing toxic wastes, or whether their production can be reduced, has barely been addressed. Recently there have been several examples of industrialized countries attempting to "bribe" developing nations to act as major toxic waste disposal sites; as development proceeds these countries will become significant toxic waste producers themselves. Long-term solutions to this problem can only lie in extensive alteration of production techniques and development of recycling processes. Massive research and development and new capital expenditures are needed. The systematic promotion of what has been referred to as "industrial ecology" (Duchin, 1992) and "industrial metabolism" (Ayres and Simonis, 1992) will require deliberate government planning, taxes on virgin materials and other modifications of market incentives, as well as extensive technology transfer to the developing world.

An emerging awareness of environmental issues on the national level during the 1970s led to the creation of national agencies and ministries for environmental management. Most nations now have some institutional mechanisms for formulating and carrying out environmental policy. But these agencies are primarily designed to respond to specific, local, or national issues. Their mandate also defines environmental issues relatively narrowly. Typically, they have the power to promulgate regulations, standards, and penalties related to specific environmental problems. But their purview does *not* include the relation of environmental protection to economic growth, technical progress, income distribution, or industrial organization. This has often led to conflicts between government agencies concerned with the environment and those concerned with budgetary and economic issues. In some developing countries and formerly communist states, this division has often led to almost complete subordination of environmental goals. Also, there is significant disparity and conflict between different countries, regions, or jurisdictions when environmental problems transcend boundaries.

In the decade of the 1990s, it has become apparent that the existing patchwork of environmental agencies is inadequate to deal with the globalization of environmental problems. The national agencies operate within national boundaries, and under the assumption that environmental protection is a separate concern from broader issues of economic development. At the global level, the powers of UNEP and other existing international agencies dealing with environmental issues are extremely limited. A strengthening of the powers of existing agencies, while helpful in some areas, will not resolve the basic problem—and might well exacerbate conflicts with national and international institutions whose mission is the promotion of economic development. What is clearly needed, therefore, is a rethinking and restructuring of global institutions in light of the emerging reality: a world in which ecological sustainability will be the dominant factor in future economic development.

This necessity becomes apparent at a time when the present structure of international institutions is showing its age. In the area of economic development, even setting aside environmental concerns, there are very significant strains on the global economic system associated with trade policies, international debt, North-South relations, and regional economic balance. To these must be added both the opportunities and the problems resulting from the integration of formerly communist states into the world economic system. To approach a solution to the global environmental crisis, we must consider the mandates, limitations, and shortcomings of the existing global institutional system.

The obsolescence of present international institutions

Most of the global institutions presently in existence date from the period immediately following the Second World War—the International Monetary Fund, the World Bank, the General Agreement on Tariffs and Trade, the United Nations and its various agencies. These institutions are by now so much a familiar part of the landscape of international relations that we tend to assume their permanence. Their origins and constitutional mandates, however, were a product of specific political and economic forces, and embody a particular vision of world political structure and economic development. Since the 1940s, the international order based on these institutions has been through a period of dramatic success in the 1950s and 1960s, marked by rapid world economic growth and trade expansion, then a period of increasing strains during the 1970s and 1980s. The role of the IMF, the World Bank, and GATT has altered from one of guiding and shaping world economic development to one of struggling to manage problems and keep up with often destabilizing events.

Thus GATT, after remarkable achievements in lowering tariffs worldwide, has been grappling with a worldwide trend to nontariff barriers and neomercantilist policies, with at best limited success. The IMF and the World Bank have been drawn into crisis management of the Third World debt problem, while the Bank has come under fire for the ecologically devastating effects of many of the major projects it has financed. The United Nations has only a marginal effect on international relations, though some of its specialized agencies perform important, though limited functions. The deterioration in the ability of present international organizations to shape events is clear. What is not so clear is the future of global institutions. Will we "muddle through" with the present structures, create new ones, or simply allow them to decline further, leaving significant policy-making to national governments? To understand the present situation it is necessary to examine the origins of existing institutions.

The creation of the IMF and World Bank at Bretton Woods in 1944 has been aptly characterized by Frances Stewart as "an attempt to institutionalize at an international level the revolution in economic ideas brought about by John Maynard Keynes" (Stewart, 1987). The same strong Keynesian influence was present in the formation of GATT. Economic growth, in the Keynesian vision, required government guidance; to avoid a recurrence of the protectionism and worldwide deflation of the 1930s, both activist national macroeconomic policies and international coordination were needed. The international economic agencies, in their original form, were assigned a clear Keynesian mission: to promote world economic expansion. Their spectacular success in the earlier postwar period, characterized by the economic dominance of the United States, the reconstruction of Europe and Japan, and exponential growth in world trade, seemed to fulfill the Keynesian vision and amply justify their existence.

During the later period of growing strains, however, theorists and policy-makers have moved away from the Keynesian perspective. The dominant trends in recent economic theory minimize the role and effectiveness of government policy. In practical terms, the main policy prescription of the IMF in responding to the international debt problem has been deflationary and contractionary rather than expansionary. Thus the legacy of Keynes has been turned upside-down: the use of contractionary policies in an economic situation of faltering growth and high debt is, of course, precisely what Keynes warned against in *The Economic Consequences of the Peace* and the *General Theory*.

Many economists today would doubtlessly view this abandonment of the Keynesian perspective as being a step in the right direction. Excessive reliance on Keynesian prescriptions has been repeatedly indicted as responsible for worldwide inflationary conditions in the 1970s. In this view, the harsh monetarist policies which led to the recession of the early 1980s (and the emergence of the international debt problem) are seen as a needed corrective. But this perspective depends for its credibility on a resumption of vigorous growth after the recessionary shake-out. Was there such a resumption?

One could argue that it occurred in the economically advanced nations, but definitely not in the developing world. The expansion of the world economy in the later 1980s was strongly dependent on the continuing U.S. trade deficit. Europe, Japan, and the export-oriented newly industrialized countries have all benefitted from the U.S. role as an international consumer with a trillion-dollar credit line. The continued, but lopsided, expansion of the world economy was thus a function of a kind of global Keynesian demand creation—but on an unplanned basis leading to major structural trade imbalances and stagnation or decline for many nations. The recessionary conditions now again affecting the United States, Europe and Japan will prove less tractable on account of the 1980s legacy of debt and unbalanced overexpansion in construction and other industrial sectors.

The uneven character of the world economic expansion of the 1980s, and the stubborn nature of the subsequent slowdown, has left the international economic agencies in a position of trying to alleviate the symptoms of economic distress with inadequate policy tools. The IMF decries structural trade imbalances and urges budget-balancing on the United States and expansionary policies on Japan and Germany, but lacks any real authority to make international macroeconomic policy. At the same time, it imposes austerity on debtor nations, helping to make the 1980s a "lost decade for development" in Latin America and Africa, and increasing the U.S. trade deficit. The World Bank's long-term development goals have been undercut by the overwhelming debt burden, so that the Bank too is drawn into short-term policy-making in response to the debt emergency (and sometimes into policy conflict with the IMF). The GATT negotiations at the Uruguay Round have focused on attempts to limit trade-restricting and neomercantilist policies even as such policies proliferate, given impetus by the desires of nations to manage their trade to gain market share, or to pay off debt. Is it time to return to a more overtly Keynesian approach to global macroeconomic policy management—and to strengthen existing institutions or create new ones with greater power?

A number of economists, less enamored of laissez-faire and monetary stringency than the majority of the profession and the policy-makers at the IMF, have made specific proposals along these lines. Jeffrey Sachs has proposed an "International Debt Facility" to resolve the seemingly intractable debt crisis by purchasing or guaranteeing the debt in return for significant write-offs by the banks, reducing the outstanding debt to its secondary market value plus a small premium (Sachs, 1989). Frances Stewart has suggested a restructuring of the IMF and World Bank, giving the IMF more power to channel trade surpluses into long-term capital outflows to the developing world and issue more "Special Drawing Rights" (Stewart, 1987). This would be accompanied by a shift in IMF and World Bank policies toward a more expansionary approach, and a broadening of "conditionality" to include indicators of social and economic progress, investment, and sectoral productivity rather than a narrow monetary focus. Paul Streeten has proposed more sweeping institutional innovations including an International Central Bank, international income or consumption tax, and an international investment agency for coordination of long-term investment plans and recycling of surpluses (Streeten, 1989). Stewart and Streeten also proposed international institutions for-commodity price stabilization. Robert Kuttner has argued that the problems of GATT cannot be resolved without a specific orientation toward managed trade, planned reduction of excess capacity, and negotiated quota systems—a quite different approach from the Ricardian free-trade logic which has hitherto provided GATT's theoretical basis and shaped its trade policy agreements (Kuttner, 1991).

These policy proposals have so far met a cold reception from governments and international institutions. So long as it seems possible to muddle through with the existing system (and so long as the most devastating costs are borne by the politically weaker developing nations), there is a strong political bias toward the status quo. But the question must be asked: do our present international structures provide a stable basis for sound world development into the twenty-first century? It is difficult to conceive of any other than a negative answer.

This becomes even clearer when we add the global ecological crisis to the problems of international economic coordination. Either issue taken separately provides a strong case for restructured international organization. Taken together, the case becomes overwhelming. The unwillingness of the world's present political leadership to accept this conclusion in no way lessens its trenchancy; continued procrastination and denial by national governments merely increases the likelihood of economic and ecological crisis.

A revitalized Keynesian vision

The story of the success and decline of the international Keynesian institutions founded in the post-World War II period makes it clear that we stand at the end of an era. Numerous analysts have described the characteristics of the present period: the decline of United States as hegemonic power, the rise of neomercantilist states, the persistence of structural economic imbalances and international debt, the growing disproportionality of military and economic power among the United States and its allies, as well as the shifting East-West balance with the crumbling of communist systems and Cold War shibboleths (Calleo, 1987; Gilpin, 1987; Mead, 1987; Garten, *et al.*, 1992). Some have also tackled the challenging question of shaping the next era of world history. Calleo, Gilpin, and Kuttner discuss policies for a "soft landing" and smooth transition from a U.S.-dominated to a more pluralistic world order. Plans for military burden-sharing, a shift to commercial rather than military-dominated industrial policy in the United States, and a greater role for Japan in international institutions, are essential elements of this transition. The policies of macroeconomic coordination among major powers and the internal economic reforms needed in the United States are discussed by Bergsten (1988) and Friedman (1988). All of these analysts, however, are principally concerned with responding to a deteriorating international situation. If new global institutions are to have at least the staying power of those conceived forty-five years ago, they must be based on a more sweeping and positive vision of the future.

It seems to me that the failure of present world economic institutions is not a failure of the Keynesian vision which inspired them. Rather, these institutions succeeded brilliantly in performing the tasks for which they were intended. But now the balance of economic and political forces, and the essential problems, have altered. In 1944 the urgent issues were the rebuilding of war-devastated nations and the maintenance of political and economic stability to provide a climate for world economic expansion. The problems of the present period arise partly from the very success of that economic expansion, partly from the imperfect inclusion of the less developed nations in world economic development, and increasingly from environmental issues unforeseen by the architects of the postwar world.

What is needed, therefore, is a renewed global Keynesianism which will focus on the unsolved problems of the less developed nations and which must be integrated with an analysis of the ecological basis of economic activity. If we can sketch the outlines of this Keynesian/ecological perspective, the shape of new world institutions and policies for the twenty-first century will follow.

The essential insight of Keynes was that market capitalist systems are prone to instability, imbalance and disequilibrium, requiring government intervention and guidance to maintain stability and growth. In this Keynes stands in the Malthusian tradition in economics, in opposition to the Ricardian view of a self-equilibrating economic system. Malthus, of course, also emphasized problems of disproportionality between economic and ecological systems in his famous theory of population. As Robert Dorfman points out (1989), the Ricardo/Malthus dispute was essentially a conflict between the pure theorist (Ricardo) and the practical economist (Malthus). This division persists to the present day, with an increasing tendency recently for the Ricardian/equilibrium approach to dominate. This is consistent with the monetarist/laissez-faire policy approach which, as we have noted, governs present international policy-making, in particular at the IMF. Historically, however, the disequilibrium/interventionist approach has made major gains at times of economic crisis with the clearest example being, of course, the Keynesian revolution. We have presented a case that such a crisis situation exists again today, with its most urgent dimension being the ecological threat. If we reject the course of muddling through with laissez-faire, then we need to examine the possibilities for revitalized Keynesian policies adapted to the present situation.

As some post-Keynesian theorists have stressed (Eichner, 1979), the policy implications of the Keynesian perspective go well beyond the areas

of fiscal and monetary policy. The limited neoclassical version of Keynesianism derived from Hicks and systematized by Samuelson and others
focuses on these two policy areas almost exclusively. But other important
forms of government intervention or guidance are suggested by a
thoroughgoing Keynesian analysis. These include policies for income distribution, greater social management of investment, specific market stabilization policies, and managed trade policies. Some of these were proposed or implied by Keynes (e.g., in Chapters 23 and 24 of the *General
Theory*), and others have been developed by writers in the post-Keynesian
tradition (Eichner, 1979; Minsky, 1986; Kuttner, 1991). Resource management and environmental protection policies are also strongly consistent
with the Keynesian tradition (Davidson in Eichner, 1979), and of course
were a prominent part of new government programs serving the dual functions of employment creation and environmental protection.

The present global crisis demands the full range of Keynesian policy
tools, but with a special emphasis on environmental policies. Here a different theoretical grounding is needed. Environmental analysis is underdeveloped in economic theory (see Dietz and van der Straaten, in this volume), usually consisting primarily of setting monetary values on environmental damage to analyze costs and benefits. The scope of global ecological issues suggests that this perspective, while useful in some specific policy analysis, is inadequate to conceptualize ecosphere disruptions which
threaten the very basis of life on earth. However, work has been done
toward the development of a consistent theory which places the economic
system within the context of the earth's biological and geophysical systems,
notably by Nicholas Georgescu-Roegen (1974) and Herman Daly (1991).
Their work analyzes economic activity as subject to the fundamental
physical laws of entropy (the Second Law of Thermodynamics). It is this
approach which holds the key to understanding the dynamics of environmental problems of global scope. Therefore, it is necessary to delve into
this body of theory—still unfamiliar to most economists—to see how it
may be synthesized with Keynesian analysis and policy tools. Its special
applicability to the current global ecological crisis provides the catalyst
necessary to initiate a second Keynesian revolution in national and international economic policy.

Ecology, entropy, and economic theory

The "circular flow" is a fundamental concept in economic theory. Labor flows into the production of goods; the goods thus produced are consumed by the population who then supply more labor for further production. Some of the goods produced are capital goods; these too enter the next cycle of production as inputs. Natural resources also enter the circular flow; but the processes by which natural resources are reproduced is less clear. Metal ores, for example, may be produced through mining, but at the same time the stocks of ore in the ground are depleted. So long as ore is abundant, its use is limited only by the costs of extraction. Over time, technological progress may lower these costs, so that resource availability increases. At the same time, however, the rate of depletion accelerates. What results is not a circular flow but a race between technological progress and resource exhaustion. Economists tend to assume that technology will win this race in the future as it has in the past, assuring a continual supply of resources for economic use. Ecological and physical principles, however, suggest a somewhat different analysis.

The circular flow of the labor and capital in the economy takes place in the midst of, and subject to, the flows of natural resources, energy, and biological systems. Some of these flows are circular, such as the water cycle and the nitrogen, carbon, and oxygen cycles. Others, in particular the flow of energy as governed by the workings of the law of entropy, are unidirectional. In most standard formulations, economic theory takes little account of the equilibrium processes of these natural systems. Yet, with the development of industrial production, the interrelationship of the economic system with these other systems, and its dependence on them, becomes ever more complex.

We can conceive of the economic, biological, and geophysical systems as being linked in a kind of triple circular flow (*Figure 1*). Each of these systems, of course, has its own internal laws of development. But one central principle regulates the whole complex of geophysical, biological, and economic processes: the principle of entropy, the "Second Law of Thermodynamics." This law states that the available energy in any system tends to decrease over time. Entropy is a measure of unavailable energy; thus useful resources (for example, a deposit of coal) have a low entropy; waste products (ashes and waste heat after the coal is burned) have a high entropy. All life processes require a stream of low entropy, and raise the entropy of their environment by emitting higher-entropy waste products.

Low entropy can be obtained from two sources: a stock of planetary resources and a flow of sunlight.

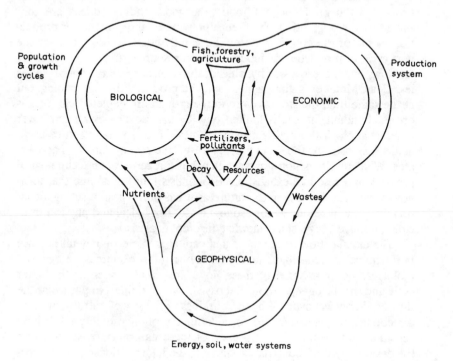

Figure 1:   The circular flow in economics and ecology

Existing ecological systems are precisely organized for the efficient capture of low entropy. Millenia of evolution have developed complex and interdependent life systems which draw low entropy from the environment, using the solar flux. The fundamental process in ecosystems is photosynthesis, by which green plants use the sun's energy to produce the organic compounds essential for life. All animal life is completely dependent on plant photosynthesis, since animals lack the ability to utilize the solar flux directly.

Viewed from the perspective of the entropy law, the economic process is essentially an extension of the biological process of capturing low entropy to support life activity, while at the same time increasing overall entropy. This fundamental point is developed in detail in Georgescu-Roegen's *The Entropy Law and the Economic Process* (1974) and in Herman Daly's *Steady-State Economics* (1991).

Industrial systems greatly increase the use rate of low entropy. Low-entropy mineral deposits and stored low entropy in the form of fossil fuels are mined to support the industrial process. Intensive agriculture also "mines" the stored resources of the soil. At the same time, the industrial system greatly increases the emission of high-entropy waste products into the environment.

There are thus two conditions for the operation and growth of an economic system: an ample supply of low entropy and an environment capable of absorbing high-entropy wastes. But as industrial processes expand, the planetary stock of low entropy is gradually depleted, and progressively replaced by high entropy in the form of pollution and waste products. Ultimately, the only sustainable world economic system is a steady-state economy, using the low entropy available from the solar flux.

Clearly this perspective differs fundamentally from the traditional economic view of production as a process of increasing wealth by transforming resources into capital and consumption goods. According to the *entropy theory*, much of modern economic production irreversibly decreases our wealth in terms of available resources. We may sustain economic growth for a certain period by absorbing low entropy from the biological and geophysical systems and returning to them our high-entropy wastes. But at some point this process will cause unacceptable stress to these systems, destroying their ecological stability. It may be possible temporarily to subsidize one system with low entropy from another (for example, by using fossil fuels to fix nitrogen in fertilizer to restore depleted soil) but in doing so we deplete low-entropy resources in the second system, and increase the high-entropy waste stream.

The entropy theory thus creates a presumption that there are limits to growth. Economic systems must operate within the constraints of:

- limited stocks of low-entropy resources, in particular high-grade ores and easily-available fossil fuels;
- limited capacity of soils and biological systems to produce food and other biological resources;
- limited capacity of the ecosystem to absorb high-entropy waste products.

As the global ecosystem approaches these interrelated limits to growth, signs of stress have become evident. Prices and incentives within the economic system, however, are not sufficiently sensitive to ecological degradation, and the ability of asset and futures markets to reflect impending resource exhaustion or environmental collapse is questionable, especially if common property resources and/or fairly long time periods are involved. This leads to the likelihood of an overshoot/collapse syndrome (Meadows and Randers, 1992) with irreversible damage to ecosystems and squandering of essential resources.

To avoid this catastrophic conclusion to economic development, the entropy theory clearly implies that new and efficient institutions for the management of economic development are required. As Daly proposes in *Steady-State Economics* (1991), the functions of such institutions would include:

1. resource management—minimizing resource depletion and promoting recycling;
2. controlling population growth;
3. maintaining ecosystem equilibrium; and
4. redistributing income for social equity, emphasizing needs overwants.

Rather than having the status of subsidiary agencies dealing with "externalities," which is essentially the role of the present national environmental agencies, the functions of these ecologically-oriented institutions would be fundamental to the shaping of long-term economic development.

As their common roots in the Malthusian tradition might imply, the Keynesian and the ecological perspective are compatible. Both are concerned with the stability of macroeconomic circular flows: of labor and goods in the Keynesian analysis, and of natural resources in the entropy analysis. Both stress the need for guidance and management of economic systems to avoid instability, imbalance, and potential collapse. In the Great Depression of the 1920s/1930s, the problems of cyclical instability and mass unemployment compelled the adoption of Keynesian policy-making institutions which in turn shaped the world after World War II. Fifty years later, it is the problems of population, development, and environment which dominate the global picture. Can a new set of institutions based on a synthesis of Keynesian and ecological perspectives provide an alternative to a grim future of growing global inequality, economic conflict, and further environmental degradation?

New institutions for global development

The case for a global system of Keynesian institutions has been made by Paul Streeten (1989). He calls for an international central bank, an international income tax/redistributive institution, investment planning and financing organizations, and commodity price stabilization plans. To this must be added institutions to address the interrelationship of the economic, biological, and geophysical systems. If we are to take seriously the message of the entropy analysis, the focus of economic policy must shift from promoting economic growth to managing growth and maintaining sustainable forms of economic activity. This means major technological transformation in the industrially advanced countries—specifically away from dependence on fossil fuels, synthetic chemicals, and high-input, chemical-dependent agriculture. In the developing countries, it means a shift away from reliance on overall GNP growth and trickle-down development toward the basic needs approach (advocated by Streeten and Stewart), combined with a systematic effort to develop production systems in agriculture and industry which are ecologically balanced, rather than imitating the ecologically disastrous high-input, high-waste-generating systems characteristic of the industrialized nations.

Global institutions for the twenty-first century must thus fulfill two sets of functions: the traditional Keynesian functions of employment creation, income redistribution, and economic stabilization; and the new functions of resource conservation, waste management, environmental protection, and planning for ecological stability. Fortunately, the two functions are complementary in many respects. Most ecologically sound agricultural practices, for example, are labor intensive and well suited for generation of stable employment. Ecologically-oriented public works also provide significant opportunities for employment and training.

The global scope of the problems indicates that transnational public institutions are essential. Dorfman (1991) suggests a case-by-case approach to international environmental agreements based on the model of the Montreal Protocol on protecting the ozone layer. While this pragmatic policy may reflect the present international political realities, the analysis presented above, in particularly the entropy perspective, suggests that it is inadequate to provide long-term economic and ecological stability. In the following, I will sketch the outlines of world institutions to accomplish these dual functions; presumably these would be complemented by similar national institutions.

1. An *International Financial Institution* based on the present IMF but with greater powers of liquidity creation. The mandate of this "world central bank" would be to provide ample liquidity in particular for developing countries and for the integration of the formerly communist states into the world financial system. Debt management and debt reduction would also be a function of this institution: conditionality programs would be oriented much more to elimination of corruption and environmental abuse, and improvement in social equity and basic needs indicators, rather than requiring contractionary policies.

2. An *International Development Institution* along the lines of the World Bank but with a greatly expanded capacity, to focus on projects for ecologically sustainable development and reclamation of environmentally damaged areas. Such projects could include efficient irrigation and sustainable water supply management (rather than expansion of irrigated area and large dam construction), agroforestry and forest management (rather than forest clearance), crop diversification and organic, labor-intensive agriculture (rather than increased chemical dependence), "soft" or intermediate level technology for industry and agriculture, and population management projects centered on education and employment creation for women.

3. A *Global Public Works Institution* which would directly fund and operate public health, education and literacy, waste management and recycling, population control, and environmental protection and restoration projects in developing countries. The programs would employ skilled personnel from developed countries (teachers, medical personnel, engineers, etc.) as well as providing extensive training for local people. This could be linked to national service programs in developed countries and might function as an alternative to military service.

4. A *Global Environmental Protection Agency* with a mandate to conduct environmental monitoring, set standards for emissions, create regulations and incentive systems such as charges and transferable emission permits, and penalize violators in economic activities affecting the global environment, particularly the atmosphere, the oceans, and the soils.

5. A *Global Resource Management Agency* charged with the creation and management of "World Parks" through negotiation with national governments, the management of common property resources (oceans, fisheries, seabed, Antarctic) with the power to impose depletion taxes

and quotas, and possibly also the power to impose depletion taxes on environmentally sensitive, internationally traded commodities.

6. An *International Research and Technology Transfer Institution* to promote and disseminate ecologically sound technology for industry, agriculture, and transport. This would include a strong focus on tropical agriculture, regional crop diversification, integrated pest management, and efficient irrigation; also on solar and other alternative energy systems and on environmentally benign synthetic materials.

7. An *International Trade Organization* dealing with questions of managed trade, including development of labor-intensive industries in developing nations, export of capital goods from developed to developing and communist nations, balanced agricultural trade avoiding overproduction and providing incentives for land conservation, commodity price stabilization and conservation of strategic commodities.

8. An *International Peacekeeping Institution* with more extensive powers than present U.N. forces, which would also provide a forum for agreements on the control of nuclear proliferation, chemical and biological weapons, and reduction of nuclear and conventional arsenals. Some of the present military spending and military personnel of individual nations would be redirected into the international forces.

This world institutional structure is as sweeping and may be as "unthinkable" in today's international politics as U.S. national institutions for social security, unemployment compensation, protection of unionization rights, active fiscal policy with massive federal spending, and expansionary monetary policy would have been in the 1920s; or a U.S. national income tax, antitrust laws, and a Federal Reserve system in the 1890s. Once again we are at a stage in history where economic development has outrun the institutions which manage it. But this time the issues are of global rather than national scope, and can only be resolved at a global level. The best precedent is the creation of the present set of international institutions in the 1940s, with its strong Keynesian inspiration. That process, laying the foundations for the postwar world, was facilitated by the clearly hegemonic role of the United States. Can a more powerful set of institutions come into being in a more pluralistic—and conflict-ridden— world? Measured against the urgency of the problem, especially the ecological crisis, the political and economic barriers may be less insuperable than a conventional perspective would lead us to expect.

Political and economic feasibility

Creation of such a strong set of international institutions first of all requires agreement among the major market capitalist powers: the United States, Japan, and the European Community. If agreement could be reached, this trilateral force could act as a new global "hegemon." There would be powerful inducements for the former Soviet Union, Eastern European nations, and China to participate (whatever the future forms of their governments) in that enormous economic development benefits would accrue to them. Clearly, environmental issues are of primary importance in the vast undertaking of rebuilding the former Soviet and East European countries. Similarly, the developing countries would have a strong incentive to endorse the new institutional structure since it would promise an end to a crushing debt burden and major continuing financial, trade, and technological benefits. These political benefits would have to be weighed against the obstacles—disputes over political control and funding responsibilities, unwillingness to yield some national control on environmental and resource issues, unwillingness to accept international jurisdiction or contribute to an international military force, etc. But if such a sweeping proposal, with clear economic and environmental benefits, could be powerfully advocated, it would alter the nature of world political discussion and could generate its own momentum. A parallel is the growth and integration of the European Community since its original proposal by Jean Monnet after World War II. At each stage significant obstacles, opposition, and conflict have been overcome by the strength and economic benefits of integration (although the embattled Maastricht treaty probably represents the high-water mark of this process). I think the historical moment is right for initiation of a similar thrust toward more integrated global institutions.

If narrow, short-term interests were to prevail, the United States, Japan, and Europe would be against a bold global initiative. These powers would presumably have to provide most of the funding for the new institutions. The United States in particular would have to yield some strategic dominance in favor of a more pluralistic structure. Japan would have to break out of its insularity in world affairs, and Europe to overcome its internal preoccupations to achieve a stronger world role. Unfortunately, these narrow concerns have up till now prevented a serious advocacy of a new world institutional structure. But as we have noted, further delay has a very high economic and environmental price. Growing awareness of this may change the political climate sufficiently to generate a breakthrough— a political leadership in the economically advanced nations willing to take the necessary efforts to confront ecological crisis and provide a strong basis for the world economy of the twenty-first century.

Once the barriers of status-quo politics are broken, the issues of funding the new institutions and integrating their economic and environmental functions would not be of overwhelming difficulty. In part, funding for their operations could come from reduced military budgets. Investment capital for the development finance institutions would be available from the surplus nations including some newly industrialized countries. Other sources of financing could come from global resource depletion taxes (energy tax and CO_2 charge), auction of quota rights, and possibly taxes on some multinational corporations. A significant pool of human resources could be made available at relatively low cost either through national service programs or through volunteer programs for young people who would willingly participate for low compensation in work to guarantee the global future.

Of course, this would require the replacement of the 1980s "yuppie" ethic with a revitalized "Peace Corps" ethic—but such a shift in political mood is not unprecedented (and may already have begun). Economists tend to underrate the importance of idealism in the course of history, assuming that all individual calculations are made on the basis of self-interest. But a radically reforming political movement, offering individuals a framework to contribute to the solution of the problems which threaten the planetary future, would have enormous worldwide appeal.

As Joan Robinson has pointed out (in Eichner, 1979), it is the question of the link between present and future which is at the heart of the Keynesian perspective. It is here that the Walrasian vision of a self-regulating multimarket equilibrium most clearly breaks down due to the relatively short-term time horizon of unregulated market economies. Keynes spoke of the need for conscious public policy "to defeat the dark forces of time and ignorance which envelop our future." An ecologically-oriented perspective places even greater emphasis on the issue of long-term sustainability, and points up the inadequacy of a laissez-faire system to provide this. The convergence of the two perspectives defines the need for global public policy-making, without which economic drift and environmental degradation will continue. The outlines of the new institutions are discernible, the possibilities are great, the economics are sound. But the global institutions for sustainable development still await the constellation of political forces which can bring them into being.

References

Ayres, Robert U. and Udo E. Simonis (eds.) (1992). *Industrial Metabolism: Restructuring for Sustainable Development*. Tokyo.

Bergsten, C. Fred (1988). *America in the World Economy: A Strategy for the 1990s*. Washington, D.C.

Calleo, David P. (1987). *Beyond American Hegemony: The Future of the Western Alliance*. New York.

Daly, Herman E. (1991). *Steady-State Economics*. 2nd edition. San Francisco.

Dorfman, Robert (1989). "Thomas Robert Malthus and David Ricardo." *Journal of Economic Perspectives*, Vol. 3, No. 3, pp. 153-64.

—— (1991). "Protecting the Global Environment: A Modest Proposal." *World Development*, Vol. 19, No. 1, pp. 103-10.

Duchin, Faye (1992). "Industrial Input-Output Analysis." In U.S. National Academy of Sciences (ed.), *Proceedings*, Vol. 89, pp. 851-5.

Eichner, Alfred S. (ed.) (1979). *A Guide To Post-Keynesian Economics*. White Plains, NY.

Friedman, Benjamin M. (1988). *Day of Reckoning: The Consequences of American Economic Policy Under Reagan and After*. New York.

Garten, Jeffrey E. (1992). *A Cold Peace: America, Japan, Germany, and the Struggle for Supremacy*. New York.

Georgescu-Roegen, Nicholas (1974). *The Entropy Law and the Economic Process*. Cambridge, MA.

Gilpin, Robert (1987). *The Political Economy of International Relations*. Princeton, NJ.

Harris, Jonathan M. (1990). *Environmental Limits to Growth in World Agriculture*. New York.

Kuttner, Robert (1991). *Beyond Laissez-Faire*. New York.

Mead, Walter Russell (1987). *Mortal Splendour: The American Empire in Transition*. Boston.

Meadows, Donella, Dennis Meadows, and Jorgen Randers (1992). *Beyond the Limits*. Post Mills.

Minsky, Hyman P. (1986). *Stabilizing an Unstable Economy*. New Haven.

Pimentel, David *et al.* (1980). "Environmental and Social Costs of Pesticides." *OIKOS*, No. 34, pp. 126-40.

Sachs, Jeffrey (1989). "Testimony to the Subcommittee on Foreign Operations, Export Financing, and Related Programs of the House Appropriations Committee." Washington, D.C., February 28, 1989.

Stewart, Frances (1987). "Back to Keynesianism." *World Policy Journal*, Vol. IV, No. 3, pp. 465-83.

Streeten, Paul (1989). "International Cooperation." In H. Chenery and T. N. Srinivasan (eds.), *Handbook of Development Economics* (Chapter 2). Amsterdam.

World Bank (1984). *World Development Report*. New York.

World Resources Institute (1992). *World Resources 1992-93*. New York.

Worldwatch Institute (1990): *State of the World 1990*. New York.

Savage Capitalism: International Market Alliances to Conserve Neotropical Forests

Peter H. May

> There is a fear that . . . increasing the economic productivity of forest-based societies . . . is a vain dream, a Faustian pact with the devil; that the commercialization of forest products will undermine and destroy the very societies it is intended to save . . .
>
> *Colchester, 1989*

Introduction

Forest peoples and progressive international entrepreneurs willing to invest venture capital in new markets for tropical forest products recently emerged as partners in the struggle to preserve indigenous cultures and biodiversity in the Amazon region. Such alliances seek to harness forces driving modern capitalism—profits, growth, and income enhancement—while simultaneously respecting the value of indigenous knowledge, irreplaceable gene pools, and pristine ecosystems. This paper traces trends and anticipated consequences of this improbable alliance with regard to both tropical resource conservation and the participation of previously marginalized social groups in sustainable economic development.

Their organizational capacity and degree of control over the natural resource base determine the relative benefits forest peoples may derive from a market-oriented strategy. The trade-off between capitalist objectives and distributive objectives of forest peoples movements illustrate possible contradictions in sustainable development. Nevertheless, these international alliances represent a new and perhaps replicable model of global cooperation to manage threatened common pool resources.

The context of trade partnerships

Accelerating pressures for tropical deforestation and recent burning in the Brazilian Amazon have alarmed observers in developed nations already reeling from confirmation of a long-threatened global warming. Tropical forest burning contributes only marginally to climate change, but it is becoming increasingly apparent that population growth, frontier occupation, and permanent forestland conversion in Brazil and other tropical nations can only add fuel to a burgeoning tragedy of the global commons. The brutal slaying of labor leader-environmentalist Chico Mendes—who represented forest peoples in their struggle to halt deforestation—only added to concern that, in the Amazon, matters were out of control.

Although international environmental groups worked vigorously to block expansion of public infrastructure to serve isolated forest regions, this tactic only aroused animosity in government circles, and appeared to justify arguments that environmentalists are the handmaidens of foreign interests opposed to competition from Brazil. Pressure for policy shifts that might have protected the Amazon against encroachment by colonists and cattle ranchers (Repetto and Gillis, 1988) has been seen as too little, too late; by the mid-1980s, the process of regional occupation and devastation had taken on a dynamic of its own, driven along by land speculation, gold fever, and the drug trade (Hecht and Cockburn, 1989).

To counter the unfettered forces that threaten the last strongholds of biological diversity on the planet, conservationists have begun to suggest that a market-oriented approach may be more effective than policy adjustments in harnessing the very forces of modern capitalism that have kindled deforestation. Ethnobotanists have long proclaimed the importance to subsistence of tropical tree products for forest-dwelling peoples (Balick, 1985; Posey, 1983) while recent studies show that the value of products extracted from the Amazon jungle exceed what could be gained if the land were converted to pasture or crops (Peters, Gentry, and Mendelsohn, 1989; Hecht and Schwartzman, 1988; Rose, 1988). Such products are derived from harvesting fruits, nuts, latexes or fibers of tropical trees without requiring that the trees themselves be cut. Yet, very few such products derived from tropical forests reach the Northern consumer. Already preoccupied with the possible relationship between Amazonian burning and his air conditioning bill, this consumer could be attracted by commodities marketed in an effort to conserve rainforests and benefit forest-dwelling peoples.

Besides furnishing excellent propaganda for entrepreneurs willing to explore the potential of these new markets, forest peoples could benefit both from the growing popularity of their products in more lucrative non-traditional markets, and from the promise held out by some of the investors to plow-back a share of their profits into "sustainable development" projects (The Economist, 1989). Expanding markets for these products would protect resources of global concern while at the same time generate profits for both forest peoples and Northern capitalists: in effect, a positive sum result from the internalization of market failures heretofore contributing to forest devastation.

Product pitfalls

The question arises whether turning capitalism loose in the jungle is either sustainable or politically tenable for forest peoples. In theory, "sustainable" processes of development ought to simultaneously meet biogeophysical conservation criteria and socioeconomic needs and can be maintained indefinitely, so that future generations as well as immediate resource users may benefit and species may survive (Barbier, 1987; WCED, 1987). There are several reasons to fear that growth in forest product marketing may not be sustainable.

The history of forest product extraction in the Amazon suggests that such products are subject to the vagaries of narrow, fickle markets. If output in these highly inelastic markets expands, prices may plummet, thus negating a broadening in social benefits from market development. Consumers of these products are quite finical; quality control to assure purity of content, extended shelf life, and assurances that products are in fact derived from "sustainable" sources may be beyond the immediate capabilities of forest peoples. Furthermore, changing tastes and altered preoccupations of Northern consumers that shift in line with global priorities may make it no longer "chic" to serve rainforest products over cocktails, especially if there are doubts regarding the integrity of indigenous leaders or their Northern counterparts.[1]

---

1 Here we refer to such revelations as the scurry over movie rights to Chico Mendes' life among rubber tapper leaders, and the sordid rape accusations against Kayapó chief Paiakán that stunned participants in the Global Forum at UNCED in Rio de Janeiro in June 1992. No less harmful to credibility are squabbles among Northern

Even if market demand expands fortuitously for extractive tropical forest products, it is possible that this expansion could spur biotechnological innovation to develop fast growing clonal varieties of these species as tree crops.[2] These could then be produced on areas cleared of native vegetation, and eventually drive extractive producers out of the market by undercutting costs, and through improved product uniformity and quality control.[3] A further source of product displacement arises when synthetic substitutes are discovered.

The threat of such innovations is particularly acute when forest peoples have become overly specialized in their market portfolio. Some authors suggest that such displacement would not in the long run be harmful to diversified forest economies (Nations, 1992). However, it takes time and imagination to develop new products, find market channels, and test new production systems. It thus may be necessary to adopt a strategy of simultaneous multiple product development combined with constant market research and development to stay out in front of the plant breeders and pharmaceutical laboratories.

The hazards to sustainability of competition with planted varieties are associated with who's doing the planting. Market stimuli and improved stock for production of tree crops in agroforestry systems could fortify smallholders, who might then be convinced to protect forestlands from further degradation by adopting more sedentary perennial cropping patterns. Such a strategy could conceivably be achieved without seriously undermining forest product extractivism in the medium term. These outcomes would be reversed if large-scale commercial plantations were to dominate the scene. Massive plantation operations not only threaten traditional extraction but smallholder agriculture as well, thrust onto infertile lands and into the forest when influential agrobusiness firms are offered preferential access to land resources and credit (May, 1990).

---

environmentalists and would-be forest product vendors for market share, and accusations from their indigenous clients that the money raised in their names has not arrived at its purported destination.

2 Such processes have already occurred or been initiated in the case of *Hevea brasiliensis* (rubber), *Bertholletia excelsa* (Brazil nut), and *Paullinia cupana* (guaraná) (see Homma, 1989).

3 Unpredictable quality characteristics and foreign matter content make it particularly difficult to secure overseas markets which insist on product uniformity and purity. Brazil nuts, for instance, have a tendency to attract fungi that cause salmonella, making it necessary to assure complete vacuum storage after shelling.

Moreover, it is not only a question of who's doing the planting, but also who controls the market channels and processing industries. Extractive products in the Amazon have historically wended their way through complex marketing chains whose intermediaries reap the lion's share of the profits. If the benefits of market opening are captured principally by large landowners or merchants who already dominate commercial and processing channels, this could cut into the benefits of new markets to forest peoples. Such merchants may be able to capture the bulk of the price differential created by innovative marketing tactics, thereby undermining cooperative marketing efforts. In summary, nontimber forest product development requires identification of alternative marketing channels, low-cost processing systems and means to segment markets so as to reward sustainable sources and counteract decades of exploitation.

Finally, even if all these hurdles are bypassed, forest peoples currently face the prospect that trade liberalization policies may sweep away any of the advantages they had hope of earning through market development. To comply with the demands of the international financial system as a condition to obtain trade credit, tariff barriers are evaporating in the developing countries. Although these policies make imported goods more accessible to the populace at large, they threaten to undermine sustainable forest production systems unable to compete with plantation produced substitutes obtainable in the international market. To ensure their continuing economic viability, such products may require region-specific subsidies or direct transfers to producers.

Risks and opportunities

Research into the impacts of commercialization of forest products by Amazon peoples suggest that market integration can indeed be a two-edged sword. For example, even where Indians have achieved secure control over demarcated reserves, they run the risk of fatal disruption of their traditional cultures if they become too dependent on commodities only obtainable through trade or if they have only one or two commodities of their own to trade (Colchester, 1989). Comparative case studies of Amazonian indigenous peoples that have brushed with capitalist markets show mixed responses, but suggest that the most successful were those groups that took their time, had control over their resource base and were able to make informed decisions to ensure that market integration took place on their own terms.

Market pressures have been particularly responsible for degradation of forest resources where local communities have not maintained common property institutions that dictate the rate and intensity of extraction (Repetto and Holmes, 1983). The disintegration of common property resource management can also occur as a result of pressures arising from privatization, leading to intensification of harvest in areas remaining under common property regimes, and a "tragedy of the non-commons" (May, 1992). In Eastern Guatemala, for example, market penetration in extractive economies has increased the rate of harvesting of native palm leaves used in a multimillion dollar floral industry. There, the absence of land rights or local organization of palm harvesters demonstrate that unmanaged common pool resources can be subjected rapidly to over-exploitation when markets expand (Nations, 1992).

A case can be made, however, for utilization of less fragile secondary forests as a basis for product marketing. Some particularly aggressive species that form dense, easily managed stands and generate useful products, such as babassu palms (*Orbignya phalerata*), could be used to recuperate degraded areas through reforestation (Anderson, May, and Balick, 1991). Arguments for use of secondary successional vegetation as a focus of rural development include the fact that much land converted to pasture has already returned to second growth, and that such areas are already occupied or near to settlement areas. Development in such areas would thus reduce pressures on untouched forest, but would also require that land and tree tenure be defined, and that marketing structures be organized so as to benefit extractivists (Hecht, Anderson, and May, 1988).

In summary, besides access to better prices in foreign specialty markets, local organization and land rights thus appear to represent crucial variables for ensuring that forest peoples do in fact benefit from expanded markets for tropical tree products. The structure of marketing channels through which such products make their way to the consumer, and the extent to which producers possess secure usufruct rights over trees or land may strongly affect the sustainability of their production systems.

Markets and objectives of Amazon social movements

Stewardship by forest communities has become increasingly viable as a bargaining chip in indigenous struggles to guarantee secure resource control, by quelling global fears over climate change. Alliances between human rights activists, environmentalists, and forest peoples have been effective in this sense, in focusing pressure to demarcate so-called "extractive reserves" in the Western Amazon of Brazil and to constitutionally guarantee Indian land rights.

Extractive reserves, a proposal of the rubber tappers' movement, consist of public lands granted in long-term collective usufruct to extractivist households, respecting historical forms of land occupation while advancing objectives for social and economic improvement. This proposal altered the common perception of forest dwellers as marginal and itinerant social groups who had occupied rubber trails as squatters. The rubber tappers' movement changed this perception, first through nonviolent sit-ins to protect threatened forests, and later through negotiations toward definition of a new form of property in federal land reform regulations. The extractive reserve concept recognizes rubber tappers' temporal property rights to sustainable resource products, while retaining permanent public control and responsibility for conserving the native forest (Schwartzman, 1989).

The movement sparked the imagination of environmentalists yearning for panda-like folk who could occupy and protect tropical forests, but few of the donations generated help the forest residents. Furthermore, land rights and political organization, while important first steps toward development, are not enough. Forest residents need to make a living; they need good prices for their products. Thus it was the more people-oriented human rights and development organizations such as *Cultural Survival*—not the larger environmental groups—that were able to catch the eye of progressive entrepreneurs concerned with global environmental problems, but unsure how to help aside from the donations they had made to environmentalists.

Entrepreneurs readily acknowledge that they are incompetent to help overcome the underlying market structure or land rights and, hoping to avoid accusations of meddling in sensitive regions, channel their support for "sustainable" local projects through organizations historically more closely engaged with indigenous rights or environmental issues. Entrepreneurs who have begun to engage themselves in these new markets have thus sought out representatives of indianist organizations to serve as intermediaries. The latter, on the other hand, have little experience with marketing, and stand to benefit from the business acumen of entrepreneurial sponsors.

A new marketing chain, founded on the premises outlined above, was forged through the intermediation of *Cultural Survival*, which brought samples of more than 300 forest products to testing labs of scores of businesses, including Community Products, Ben and Jerry's Homemade (ice cream), Loblaws, Ralston Purina, and the Body Shop. Pilot enterprises and cooperatives were then supported, with processing facilities placed under the direct control of rubber tappers and indigenous peoples. Trade was initiated with Brazil nuts—a product widely available and only obtained from natural forest stands—thus guaranteeing that beneficiaries of trade would be forest peoples, whether organized or not. Profits from the nut trade were used to help bring new products into the market place.

Political contradictions and prospects for development

There is now a growing recognition by rubber tappers and Indians that they might autonomously alter production and marketing patterns, and in so doing improve their welfare while at the same time preserve cultural values and the environment. Yet, such a recognition could represent a denial of the collectivist values that have inspired forest peoples' movements, and undermine their identification with socialist political currents at home.

The rubber tappers' movement has among its origins the Amazon penetration of the labor-oriented Partido dos Trabalhadores (PT) and the union federation Central Unica dos Trabalhadores (CUT) that organized rural workers' unions in the states of Acre, Amazonas, Pará, and Amapá. The rhetoric of the movement has always been shared with political objectives of the PT, and union representation by the CUT, on the surface at least antithetical to interests of foreign capital. Reconciliation of socialist goals with the concept of international market alliances is one of the challenges facing the forest peoples' movement (Almeida, 1989).

Today, progress in developing new markets for tropical forest products is still in an incipient stage, in which the relationships among protagonists in trade partnerships are undergoing definition. Altruism is all very well, but the returns on these investments must eventually be perceived as financially positive, even if the yield is greatest from propaganda campaigns and "green marketing." On the other hand, for centuries forest products have been traded under considerably more exploitative market structures, and such conditions are still the principal route through which forest goods reach consumers. Only time will tell if modern trade alliances can improve conditions of forest peoples, by adding value while helping to conserve the resource base upon which we all depend for our survival.

In conclusion, it must be recognized that the naive optimism which spurred this quest to inject economic vitality toward remote marginalized social groups has by now been tempered by a strong dose of realism. The lessons learned by incipient forest product cooperatives in the Amazon serve as important models for groups elsewhere in the humid tropics, who may also seek to sustain their resource base in part through a market orientation.

Such models can hope to be replicable in restricted cases, where a combination of economic, cultural, and biological factors enable resources to be extracted at a sustainable pace, and where product markets are amenable and not likely to encounter high volume substitutes in the near future. Such markets are rare, making product diversification desirable from the outset. Bringing processing closer to the producer and under community control also holds promise, although the commitment of resources and managerial talent to this task may overwhelm even the most capable leaders.

In the end, effective lobbying to secure better relative product prices, subsidies or credit may be a more powerful strategy than devising innovative market channels.

Nevertheless, the involvement of progressive entrepreneurs in expanding awareness of the options and barriers to sustainable forest management has had an important role in ensuring attention to the conditions and needs of forest peoples throughout the tropics.

References

Almeida, A. W. (1989). "Universalização e Localismo: Movimentos Sociais e Crise dos Patrões Tradicionais de Relação Política na Amazônia." *Reforma Agrária*, Vol. 19, No. 1, pp. 4-16.

Anderson, A. B., P. H. May, and M. J. Balick (1991). *The Subsidy from Nature: Palm Forests, Peasantry and Development on an Amazonian Frontier*. New York.

Balick, M. J. (1985). "Useful Plants of Amazonia: A Resource of Global Importance." In G. T. Prance and T. E. Lovejoy (eds.), *Key Environments: Amazonia*. Oxford, pp. 339-68.

Barbier, E. (1987). "The Concept of Sustainable Economic Development." *Environmental Conservation*, Vol. 14, No. 2, pp. 101-10.

Colchester, M. (1989). "Indian Development in Amazonia: Risks and Strategies." *The Ecologist*, Vol. 19, No. 6, p. 249.

The Economist (1989). "The Month Amazonia Burns." London, September 9, pp. 15-6.

Hecht, S. and A. Cockburn (1989). *The Fate of the Forest*. London.

———, A. B. Anderson, and P. H. May (1988). "The Subsidy from Nature: Shifting Cultivation, Successional Palm Forests and Rural Development." *Human Organization*, Vol. 47, No. 1, pp. 25-35.

Homma, A. (1989). "A Extração de Recursos Naturais Renováveis: O Caso do Extrativismo Vegetal na Amazônia." Doctoral thesis. Agricultural Economics Department. Federal University of Viçosa, Brazil.

May, P. (1990). *Palmeiras em Chamas: Transformação Agrária e Justiça Social na Zona do Babaçu*. São Luís, Brazil.

——— (1992). "Common Property Resources in the Neotropics: Theory, Management Progress and an Action Agenda." In K. Redford and C. Padoch (eds.), *Conservation of Neotropical Forests: Working from Traditional Resource Use*. New York, pp. 359-78.

Nations, J. (1992). "Xateros, Chicleros, and Pimenteros: Harvesting Renewable Tropical Forest Resources in the Guatemalan Petén." In K. Redford and C. Padoch (eds.), *Conservation of Neotropical Forests: Working from Traditional Resource Use*. New York, pp. 208-219.

Peters, C., A. Gentry, and R. Mendelsohn (1989). "Valuation of a Tropical Forest in Peruvian Amazonia." *Nature*, Vol. 339, pp. 655-6.

Posey, D. A. (1983). "Indigenous Ecological Knowledge and Development of the Amazon." In E. Moran (ed.), *The Dilemma of Amazon Development*. Boulder, pp. 225-57.

Repetto, R. and M. Gillis (1988). *Public Policies and the Misuse of Forest Resources*. Cambridge, MA.

Repetto, R. and T. Holmes (1983). "The Role of Population in Resource Depletion in Developing Countries." *Population and Development Review*, Vol. 9, pp. 609-32.

Rose, D. (1988). *Economic Assessment of Biodiversity and Tropical Forests*. Washington, D.C.

Schwartzman, S. (1989). "Extractive Reserves: The Rubber Tappers' Strategy for Sustainable Use of the Amazon Rainforest." In J. Browder (ed.), *Strategies for Management of Fragile Lands in Latin America*. Boulder, pp. 223-45.

World Commission on Environment and Development (WCED) (1987). *Our Common Future*. Oxford.

Poverty and Sustainable Development

Deonanan Oodit and Udo E. Simonis

> "We must begin to think of poverty in terms of income poverty, asset poverty, and public service poverty."
> *Bertrand M. Gross*

Introduction

Generally, the relationship between poverty, environment, and development is perceived as a "vicious circle." Poverty leads people to overutilize and overburden their natural environment on which, in the end, all development depends. In reality, however, there are certain structures behind the aggregates of this relationship. And structures should be studied when searching for solutions to escape vicious circles. In this chapter, therefore, both poverty and environmental problems are structurally defined in order to detect options for development that may simultaneously contribute to alleviate poverty and to prevent further environmental deterioration. Both national and international options are considered.

Sustainable development—task of the future

Sustainable development is a concept that so far has eluded a simple and precise definition. The concept arose as a reaction to certain negative experiences, both in the developed and the developing countries. In an ecological sense, sustainable development calls for development patterns that maintain the natural capital stock and overall ecological integrity. Strictly speaking this would imply that development be based only on renewable resources, used at a rate at which they regenerate, and leading to emissions and wastes that can be decomposed and digested by nature.

A more pragmatic view places the emphasis on development first and on ecological integrity to the extent that it is important for sustained development.

In this view, key ingredients for sustainable development are seen to be (a) eradication of poverty so as to prevent further resource degradation, which calls for changes in the sociopolitical structures; (b) clean or cleaner technologies to mitigate environmental pollution, which would call for R&D investment and technology transfer, and for environmental impact assessment of all new projects; (c) slowing-down of population growth, so as to relieve the pressure of population on natural resources; (d) internalization of environmental costs, so as to reduce discharge of harmful emissions and disposal of hazardous wastes, implying a change in lifestyles that are both resource-destroying and environmentally polluting.

Such principles and respective measures, it is believed, would mitigate the negative effects of current patterns of economic growth, prevent further degradation of the natural resource base, and at the same time contribute to the alleviation of poverty, and would give a decent but sustainable development perspective for all.[1] How valuable are such considerations *vis-à-vis* rural and urban poverty in the developing countries?

Environmental degradation and the rural poor

Extent and causes of land degradation

In the rural areas of the developing countries, poverty defined as severe deprivation of basic needs, and most importantly by inadequacy of nutrition, is first of all, linked to landlessness. According to recent estimates, 73 percent of all rural households in the developing countries are either landless or near-landless. Assuming an average household size of five to six people that translates to an estimated 935 million rural people who have too little land to meet the minimum subsistence requirements of food and fuel. (This estimate excludes China which could add 200 million absolute poor.) To this must be added another 1,000 million people who are living on the borderline of absolute poverty. Land scarcity on account of popula-

---

1 The 1992 Report of the Committee for Development Planning (CDP), that includes a chapter on poverty, environment and development, will be available by the end of 1992 as a United Nations publication.

tion pressure and skewed distribution of land are the prime causes of landlessness.

A second characteristic of the rural poor is that the majority of them have become increasingly clustered on low-potential land. Pushed into marginal areas, the poor have no chance but to overexploit resources available to them in order to survive. Survival thus takes precedence over concern for the future viability of land. Some 60 percent of the developing countries' poorest people live in highly vulnerable areas—arid and semi-arid lands, steep slopes and poorly serviced urban lands. The "retreat" of the poor to fragile lands with low agricultural potential is the result of a combination of several factors: industrialization and urban sprawl, privatization and commercialization of previously common land, modernization of agriculture with reduced labor inputs, population pressure in previously sparsely populated areas, and inappropriate macroeconomic policies which have distorted relative prices against labor-intensive technologies and products.

Desertification

Land degradation is reflected in a decline of land productivity due to depletion of the vegetable cover, exposure of the soil to wind and water erosion, reduction of the soil's organic and nutrient content, and deterioration of the soil structure and its capacity to retain water. This process is referred to as desertification. It may be the result of natural phenomena, most importantly, frequent and prolonged droughts. In recent times, however, desertification has been aggravated by the action of man. Large-scale deforestation, slash and burn agriculture, overgrazing and overcultivation of marginal lands are among the main causes.

By the early 1980s, some 1,987 million hectares of productive dryland had been desertified. Of this, 1,536 million hectares were to be found in the developing countries. At the regional level, Africa is the most affected, accounting for 37 percent of the area desertified worldwide, followed by Asia, accounting for 29 percent (World Resources Institute, 1988, p. 291).

What should be of great concern is that the rate of desertification continues to accelerate in parts of the Sahelo-Sudanian Africa, the Near-East, Iran, Pakistan, and North East India. The semi-arid area of North East Brazil and parts of Argentina are subject to similar conditions. Morocco, Tunisia and Lybia are losing some 100,000 hectares of rangeland and cropland each year through desertification. Worldwide it is estimated that desertification is claiming 6 million hectares of land each year.

Desertification is likely to be exacerbated if the process proceeds unchecked[2], particularly if cleared land is put to unsustainable use. Deforested land is subject to soil erosion which is slowly undermining about one-third of the world's cropland. According to FAO, soil erosion could reduce agricultural production in Africa by one-fourth by the year 2000.

Deforestation

Deforestation affects agriculture in many ways. It alters the local hydrological cycles by increasing run-off and affecting rainfall inland. The former effect is starkly evident in the Indian subcontinent where deforestation of the Himalayan watersheds has raised rainfall run-off, causing increasingly severe flooding. The area that is subject to annual flooding in India has more than tripled since 1980, from some 19 million hectares to 59 million hectares.

Another effect of deforestation is increasing scarcity of energy supply for the poor. Fuelwood and charcoal supply over 75 percent of the total energy use in several developing countries, such as Bangladesh and Ethiopia, and even oil producing Nigeria. In Central America it supplies over 50 percent of total household energy consumption, and exceeds 72 percent in the rural areas. In terms of people involved, over 2,000 million use wood for domestic heating and cooking. Projections for the year 2000 suggest that without remedial action, 2,400 million people will be unable to obtain their basic energy requirements.

While there may be room for increasing efficiency of use, the problem is obviously daunting. Sources of cheap fuel for the poor, such as dung and biomass, are not in plentiful supply either, and their use may have the effect of depriving agricultural land of vital nutrients. Other alternative sources, such as solar and wind energy, are still too expensive and will not

---

2 According to the 1990 FAO resources assessment interim report, the annual rate of deforestation in 87 developing countries including all the medium and large countries in the period 1981-90 was 16.9 million hectares—8.3 million hectares in Latin America, 5 million hectares in Africa and 3.6 million hectares in Asia. A comparison of these assessments with those of an FAO/UNEP assessment done in 1980 shows a dramatic acceleration of deforestation in the 76 countries common to both assessments in the period 1981-90 over the period 1976-80, when the annual rate of deforestation was estimated at 11.3 million hectares.

come within the reach of the rural poor if vigorous initiatives are not taken, both nationally and internationally, to improve and disseminate them.

The causes of deforestation are many and vary from region to region, with the expansion of agricultural production being the most important single factor, followed by ranching and infrastructural investments (mainly in tropical America), colonization programs (mostly in tropical Asia), and overexploitation for fuelwood (particularly in the dry zones of Africa).

The absolute number of people living in tropical forest areas has been on the rise. Estimates put the current number at 200 million. A high proportion of these people are recent poor immigrants who have been forced into forest areas due to increasing land scarcity in the existing agricultural areas. Tropical forest areas thus have become »safety valves" for countries facing a rising tide of landlessness because of population pressure on high potential land, for instance in Indonesia; limited urban absorption of people displaced by agricultural modernization, for instance in Brazil; or grossly inequitable distribution of existing agricultural land, for instance in Central America. Nearly 75 percent of the annual deforestation of tropical forests is attributed to slash and burn agriculture.

In the face of population growth, massive poverty and landlessness in many developing countries, it is not easy to imagine how deforestation can be stopped and reversed. The problem has, however, received great international attention in recent years, mainly in connection with the loss of biodiversity and reductions of the size of carbon sinks. This attention could be channelled towards new solutions of international support, like compensation schemes, for instance.

Waterlogging and salinization

Land degradation is occurring not only in areas of low agricultural potential but also in irrigated fertile areas and rain-fed areas. Efforts at raising agricultural yield through large irrigation schemes without adequate provision for drainage have resulted in widespread waterlogging and salinization, which again have reduced productive lands to virtual deserts in many countries.

Estimates indicate that some 267 million hectares of land have been salinized to various degrees in the developing world—20 million in South East Asia, 40 million in South Asia, 43 million in West Asia, 40 million in North and Central Asia, 71 million in Latin America and 53 million in Africa. According to a recent case study by the World Bank, waterlogging and salinity have reduced yields of major crops by 30 percent in the 15 million hectares of irrigated croplands in Pakistan, and 3.5 million hectares in Egypt. FAO estimates that because of salinity and poor drainage as much as 45 million hectares of irrigated land in developing countries need immediate reclamation or will have to be removed from agriculture.

Salinity problems are to be found not only in irrigated areas but also in rain-fed areas. Again according to FAO, without conservation measures some 544 million hectares of rain-fed cropland in developing countries which are affected by soil erosion and soil fertility problems would cease to be viable for production in the medium term.

Part of the 250 million of the poorest people who still live in agricultural lands of high potential are located in rain-fed areas, and thus could be the prime victims of land degradation in those areas.

Water scarcity

Water scarcity is increasing rapidly in most of the developing countries (Oodit and Simonis, 1992). Regionally, Asia and Africa are facing the greatest problems. In Asia, water supply per capita is less than half the global average. In Africa, the situation is mainly one of underdevelopment of water resources, and uneven distribution. In South America, water resources are abundant in relation to requirements, but wide disparities exist from place to place.

Over the years, the limits set to freshwater availability by nature have been exacerbated by man. Expansion of irrigation and industrial use of water have led to increased water withdrawal. On account of leaks in the distribution systems, a high proportion of water is lost.

Irrigation is heavily contributing to water scarcity. More groundwater has been withdrawn from aquifers than is recharged naturally. Excessive pumping of groundwater has possibly disastrous long-term consequences for agriculture in the arid and semi-arid areas of the developing world.

Altogether more than 50 developing countries are thought to face severe water scarcity by the year 2025, 19 are already in that situation. In most of these countries, industrial and household demand for water strongly compete with the agricultural sector for the limited water supply, making food self-sufficiency a goal increasingly difficult to attain.

Concern about water relates not only to its quantity but even more so to its quality. Problems of water pollution must be seen both in the context of rural and of urban health problems.

Environmental degradation and rural health

The rural poor suffer from ill-health mainly on account of undernutrition and/or malnutrition. Their health is further affected by various forms of pollution and agricultural hazards, most importantly by water pollution, in-door air pollution and direct exposure to pesticides and herbicides.

High proportions of the rural poor depend for drinking water on water bodies that are heavily polluted. Storm water run-offs carry herbicides, pesticides and chemical fertilizers as well as human and animal wastes into the water bodies. Rivers flowing through urban areas to rural areas are contaminated with industrial pollutants and sewage directly discharged into the rivers. Diseases caused by microbial pollution of water and related to inadequate sanitation are widespread.

According to WHO, up to 2,000 million people are at risk from diarrheal diseases, 800 million from diseases affecting skin and eyes, 500 to 600 million from bilharzia, over 100 million from Guinea-worm, 50 million from sleeping sickness, 900 million from Filaria, 2,100 million from Malaria, 85 to 90 million from river blindness, most of them in the rural areas of the developing countries.

In spite of some progress made during the International Drinking Water and Sanitation Decade in the 1980s, large numbers of the rural as well as the urban poor are still without safe drinking water and adequate sanitation facilities. In Africa, for instance, safe drinking water is inadequate for about 50 percent of the rural population, or about 240 million people. In view of the fact that the poor are generally the last to benefit from services provided by government, high proportions of the rural dwellers still without safe drinking water and adequate sanitation facilities would be the poorest people.

While air pollution is a major problem in urban areas, the rural poor also suffer from it because they rely heavily on biomass fuels. Instead of turning biomass into gas, the fuels are usually burnt in primitive cook stoves. The combination of inefficient stoves, absence of chimneys and poor ventilation leads to in-door air pollution which has severe effects on health, particularly on women, infants and children. Data on exposure is still limited. According to WHO, however, an estimated 700 million women are affected by in-door air pollution arising from biomass fuels. This constitutes the largest single health problem for women in the world.

The problem of direct poisoning of agricultural workers by pesticides is serious in many developing countries. Many individual cases have been documented but overall quantitative assessment is meager.

Sustainable rural development

Slowing down population growth

In the face of persistent degradation and depletion of natural resources in the developing countries, no strategy is likely to succeed unless the day to day pressure of poverty that forces the poor to overuse the resource base is removed (World Commission on Environment and Development, 1987, pp. 95-117). To achieve poverty alleviation without adverse impacts on the environment, any effective rural development strategy therefore to be supplemented by policies to slow-down population growth.

In the 1980s, the population of the developing countries grew by 770 million, and according to the United Nations medium variant projections will increase by an additional 900 million in the 1990s, and by over 3 billion between 1990 and 2025. This implies a further increase of pressure on the natural resource base, especially in the rural areas, where today some 63 percent of the population reside.

The impact of population growth on the environment will be severe in the rural areas, but urban problems will also be aggravated. As will be discussed later on, the developing countries are in a process of rapid urbanization. By the year 2025 the scale of urbanization in the developing countries is expected to increase by more than 60 percent from the current 1.5 billion people.

The dominating policy stance of most of the developing countries on population growth is shown in a recent survey by the United Nations: more than 74 developing countries (or more than 50 percent of the countries surveyed) consider their rate of fertility to be too high. Out of the total of 131 developing countries, 10 have policies in place to raise fertility, 12 intervene to maintain the rate, 64 have policies to lower the rate, while 45 do not intervene.

In countries that have policies in place to lower the fertility rate, implementation is hampered by cultural, financial and administrative constraints. These constraints are the most severe in the poorest countries, obviously on account of the lack of resources to launch and staff the institutional arrangements required.

Slowing down population growth because of ecological reasons thus is not going to be easy, but efforts are needed so as to relieve the pressure on land and resources. Here, the promotion of rural infrastructure, industries and services would provide alternatives to eking out a living on marginal land. Rural off-farm employment focused on small towns and villages could have the benefits of urbanization most people are looking for, without putting undue additional stress on the large cities. Improvement of productivity and equity through land reform in economically viable units would have a direct effect on the alleviation of poverty. High potential land could be allocated to the landless and near-landless through reform of property rights. Why is all this not done, or not done in a sufficient manner?

To be sustainable, rural development must be based on land use planning and environmental impact assessment. The fragile land, where the bulk of the rural poor is concentrated, needs to be protected, and impact assessments are necessary to prevent individual projects having negative effects on the environment. It is a matter of some urgency that legislation and regulatory mechanisms in respect to land and natural resources be enacted and economic instruments employed to ensure sustainable development. There is also an evident need for establishing institutions to deal with land use issues and to define their responsibilities at the national and local levels.

Sustainable development of high potential land

Both to improve agricultural productivity and to take the pressure off from marginal land, greater attention needs to be paid to the high-potential land. Under optimal conditions these areas alone could produce enough food to meet the demand of the growing populations. High potential land can generally sustain intensive crop production, as long as exploitation does not exceed the regenerative capacity of the soil.

Substantial increase in production is still possible in such areas as the central plains of India, the fertile plains and the Savannah belt of Africa, and the high Savannah and Pacific lowland plains of Central and South America, through intensive cultivation. The ecological challenge in those areas is to implement land and water management that will ensure that increased agricultural productivity does not cause land degradation in the long term.

Some 250 million of the very poor people of the world live in areas of high potential land and could quickly benefit from increasing agricultural productivity. To do so it must be ensured that agricultural modernization does not result in the eviction of the poor from these areas, either through land consolidation, privatization of common land, or as a result of mechanization.

Sustainable development of low potential land

Low potential lands are generally dry lands, often subject to drought and desertification, mountain ecosystems and saline lands. Hundreds of million of poor people live on those lands, and much could be done in their favor through a change in the mode of farming.

Land degradation in those areas has occurred primarily because the poor have not been provided with the physical, social, and institutional infrastructure necessary to move beyond subsistence farming and herding, which deplete soil fertility. It is well known that the type of farming that is economically and ecologically sustainable on marginal land consists of intensive cultivation of nonfood crops: perennial bush and tree crops such as coffee, nuts, cocoa, rubber, fruits, vines, etc., and not field crops such as rice, beans, squash, maize, tubers, etc. Poor farmers should therefore be enabled to switch from subsistence field crop farming to sustainable commercial farming. This type of farming calls for better transportation, for marketing, and for stable property rights, and holds out the promise of raising the incomes of the poor *and* providing plant cover to the land, preventing further degradation.

Some amount of traditional food crops can still be grown on marginal lands through new techniques. For instance, the combination of rows of leguminous trees alternated with rows of annual crops provide organic nutrients that prolong productivity of acid, infertile soils found in much of the humid tropics. Examples of these modes of farming exist in many parts of the world, but only on a small scale. The main challenge thus is in multiplying the successful small scale initiatives.

A reorientation of the use of lowpotential land will also fit in with the objective of desertification control which is to promote the use of drylands in such a manner that it ensures a sustainable livelihood for those who depend on them. In the global convention on desertification, envisaged to be prepared for 1994, such goals and instruments will have to be fixed.

Rehabilitation of degraded land

In view of the constraints on increasing cropland in most developing countries, the prevention of further degradation needs to be supplemented by measures to rehabilitate the already degraded land, both in high-potential and low-potential areas. Although not much has been accomplished by way of rehabilitation so far, efforts are underway in a number of countries to restore the productivity of degraded land. A few examples might serve to illustrate of what is possible.

In China, rehabilitation of saline soil by natural and artificial drainage, land levelling, and adding clay to the soil has been tried with good results. Soil structure and fertility have been improved by harvesting flood water and cultivating green manure such as sweet clover and alfalfa. Terracing has made possible cropping with nominal erosion, while cash crops such as apple, and leguminous shrubs good for fodder have been planted to stabilize the remaining sloping land.

In Burkina Faso, land has been restored in the Yatenga Province by building stone bunds, digging deep planting holes to collect and concentrate run-off water, and placing manure or compost in each hole. The combination of contour stone bunding and deep planting have proved highly beneficial to farmers. Yields improved by 40 to 60 percent in the first season after the rehabilitation work was done. Even in dry years these techniques ensure moderate yields.

In Syria, a very successful example of rangeland restoration has been the revival of the ancient "Hema" system, a cooperative management, in which each cooperative has the sole grazing right to a demarcated area of rangeland, and each family member of a cooperative is granted a license to graze a certain number of sheep within that area. By reducing overgrazing, the system has enabled the revegetation of some 7 million hectares of rangeland.

These and numerous other examples indicate that conservation needs to involve local communities in the planning and maintenance of those projects designed to benefit local people. If the local communities see no short-term advantage, conservation projects are likely to be abandoned.

Reforestation and afforestation

Since most of the deforestation is occurring for purposes of agricultural production, any effective approach to arrest and reverse this process must try to increase agricultural productivity, as discussed above. Intensification of agricultural production in the high potential areas will make it unnecessary to clear more forests and will free marginal land from agriculture, which than can be reforested. Switching from field crops to tree and bush crops in the marginal areas would at the same time amount to reforestation and afforestation.

In many countries deforestation has been and still is encouraged through direct or indirect subsidies (Enquête-Commission, 1990), among them agricultural and pasture incentives, logging concessions and road construction. The identification and removal of such incentives is indispensable to prevent further deforestation.

Reforestation and afforestation are badly needed not only to stabilize global climate but, at the same time, to meet local energy demand. Estimates of the rates of reforestation needed are somewhat staggering, however. A World Bank estimate suggests that the rate of tree planting in Africa would have to increase 15 fold by the year 2000 if demand for fuelwood were to be met.

Reforestation is also necessary for the restoration of degraded watersheds so as to increase water supply for agriculture and other uses, and has the additional advantage of preventing floods by slowing down run-off. Such reforestation would not only generate environmentally positive effects but also economic benefits.

In view of the growing scarcity of wood resources, afforestation in the form of plantation forestry is a financially viable option. Such afforestation could instantly provide gainful employment to the poor and in the medium term would increase the supply of timber for the domestic and the export market as well as that of fuel wood. Plantation forestry has been established in several countries with good results, notably in Southern Brazil and Southern Chile on land degraded by past agricultural activities.

Whenever afforestation and reforestation are undertaken by the private sector on a commercial basis, it would seem to make the venture profitable; secure land tenure would help, through the creation of vested interests, to maintain the forest cover. In other cases, such as reforestation for watershed restoration and climate protection, hovever, the government may have to take the initiative, hopefully in the future with the help of an *International Forest Fund*.

Environmental stress and the urban poor

Extent and causes of the problem

In 1975, the rural poor of the world outnumbered the urban poor by about three to one; this relationship could be reversed by the year 2000. Why could this happen?

Urbanization is a most dramatic social and material transformation that is taking place in the developing countries since the mid-century (World Commission on Environment and Development, 1987, pp. 235-58). The urban population rose by 450 million between 1975 and 1985, and demographers expect that by the year 2010, some 52 percent of the population of developing countries will live in urban agglomerations, as compared to 37 percent in 1990. By the turn of the century, there might be as many as 37 cities in the developing countries with a population of over 5 million.

Urbanization initially was propelled by rural-urban migration. Although this is still important, migration in general has ceased to be the driving force behind urban growth. The urban poor are increasingly born in the urban areas, and urbanization has thus been accompanied by an increase in the number of the urban poor. Over 130 million of the developing countries' poorest poor now live in urban areas.

Manufacturing industries, services and commercial centers are located at the core of the big cities. Large numbers of the urban poor cluster in slums and squatter settlements around such centers or at the urban periphery, be it due to absolute shortage of land or to the high rents on serviced lands. These areas are prone to hazardous natural and man-made environmental conditions, such as flood plains, slopes, or land adjacent to industries using polluting technologies.

Most of the urban poor thus live and work in hazardous exposure situations, shunned by the more affluent. They have to contend with bad sanitation, contaminated water, floods, or chemical pollution. According to WHO, an estimated 600 million urban dwellers in the developing countries live in what is termed life and health threatening circumstances.

Water pollution, air pollution and hazardous wastes

In particular, the urban poor are affected by water pollution, inadequate sanitation facilities, insufficient collection and disposal of solid and toxic wastes, in-door and out-door air pollution. A WHO estimate for 1988 suggests that 170 million urban inhabitants lack access to safe and adequate water supply, and 330 million lack adequate sanitation. The urban poor depend on water from inland water bodies that are contaminated by human excreta, and industrial toxic wastes. Many urban agglomerations in the developing countries have even no sewerage systems at all.

Large numbers of the urban poor depend for subsistence on urban waste, i.e., gathering materials from dumps and the streets. In so doing, they are exposed to a variety of hazards—bacteria, diseases and, most importantly, toxic wastes from industries, hospitals, and utilities.

While by and large the quality of urban cooking fuels is better than that used in rural households, not everybody in the urban areas can afford clean fuels. Poor households still depend on traditional biomass fuels which they burn in unventilated shacks. In the large urban agglomerations increasing numbers of people (both poor and nonpoor) are being exposed to out-door air pollution caused by uncontrolled industrial and automotive emissions.

The problem of hazardous wastes in developing countries has been exacerbated by the import of inappropriate products and technologies from industrial countries. In many cases it is cheaper to relocate such industries to the developing countries than to meet the increasingly stringent environmental standards and regulations at home. Officially, "codes of conduct" on environmentally sound management have been signed, but in actual life such agreements on the national and international level all too often do not reach local decision-making.

Sustainable urban development

Ecological urban restructuring

Urbanization has put considerable stress on the natural environment and the health of the urban poor. To stop or reverse the process may well be impossible. What is needed, however, and what should be possible, is to find ways of providing cost-effective infrastructure and services, to prevent a further decline in the environmental conditions, and to contain existing environmental hazards. Given that international mass migration is impossible, these are the only ways to relieve the pressure on the environment, to ensure income growth, and to alleviate poverty.

The spatial concentration of production in urban areas can bring many cost advantages on account of "economies of scale." Urbanization in developing countries, however, has proceeded in a rapid and haphazard manner in the absence of appropriate institutional and legal structures, turning economies of scale into diseconomies of scale. What is needed, therefore, is a new paradigm for urban development (*urban ecology*), appropriate institutions and a legal framework conducive to environmentally sound city planning (Hahn and Simonis, 1991).

Assuming an effective city governance, highest priority should and could be given to the urban poor who are directly affected by the negative side effects of urban dynamics. The urban poor have benefitted little if at all from the industrial and commercial activities that degrade the environment, but bear the full consequences of their adverse effects. They are the primary victims of sewage discharged in water bodies, of polluted air, of dumped solid and toxic wastes.

Providing safe sanitation and drinking water

First and foremost, the urban poor need to be protected from the immediate threats to life posed by unhealthy sanitation facilities, water supplies and cooking facilities. A full-scale attack on urban problems using conventional capital-intensive technology would, however, require large increases in investments. For example, to meet the WHO targets for water and sanitation in Latin America by the year 2000, a threefold increase in the levels of annual investment (some $50 billion) would be needed. Moreover, conventional techniques require large amounts of freshwater, often as much as 40 percent of the average daily water consumption. At such costs the need of urban sanitation cannot be met. There exist, however, a wide range of alternative options that are much cheaper but equally efficient, and use locally manufactured hardware—plumbing, concrete caps, etc. Labor for such activities could be provided by the beneficiaries in the form of "sweat" equity.

Both the social and the technical factors of such basic sanitation facilities have been tested in Africa, Asia and Latin America. Much headway has been made in recent years in modifying conventional sewerage designs to reduce costs. Examples are the shallow sewerage system and the small bore sewerage system. The modified systems cost as little as a quarter of conventional sewerage. What is needed, is wider diffusion of these low-cost alternatives.

As far as safe drinking water supply is concerned, cities can encourage water conservation in water intensive industries as well as in the services and residential sectors, by ensuring that the water consumer pays a realistic price for water, and also by better maintenance of existing distribution systems to prevent leakage. A survey of 14 large Latin American cities found that unaccounted for water ranged from 39 to 67 percent. These measures alone could suffice to provide safe drinking water to most of the still unserved urban poor. For instance, in the city of Sao Paolo, a program to reduce water leakages in the distribution system succeeded in reducing the unaccounted for water from 35 percent in 1977 to 27 percent in 1986. The resulting water savings enabled the increase in the number of home connections without the need for additional water development by 46 percent.

Reducing air pollution

Solutions to in-door air pollution are more difficult to find, but several possibilities exist. For instance, charcoal or biomass when fermented to produce wood alcohol provide more energy per unit of fuel than raw biomass, and reduce air pollution at the same time. The impact of biomass fuels burned in-doors can also be reduced by improved cooking stove design that concentrates the heat. Another possibility is the use of solar stoves. Until now, however, such alternatives have largely failed to meet affordability criteria. While technologies to use energy more efficiently and to mitigate adverse health effects are available, their use requires financial resources that the poor often do not have. The ultimate solution thus lies in measures to quickly raise the income of the poor, or to drastically reduce the cost of such alternative techniques.

In order to mitigate the effects of out-door air pollution, in most developing countries there is urgent need for regulations on industrial and automotive emissions. New industrial plants and automobiles should be required to be fitted with state-of-the-art pollution control devices and allowed to operate only if they meet strict pollution standards. Leaded gasoline should be banned, price differentiation favoring cleaner gasoline could be introduced. Within city limits, better use of public transportation systems would reduce air pollution, cut transportation costs and save energy.

In many developing countries, the price of gasoline is already rather high. Still, a moderate gasoline tax would be useful for raising revenue which could be spent for financing public transport. In countries where gasoline is subsidized, such subsidies should be removed instantly. Vehicle tax and license fees need to be redesigned to discourage the ownership of energy-intensive and polluting vehicles. Compulsory inspection and regular maintenance of vehicles are still unknown in many countries, but could, if introduced, cut automotive pollution substantially.

Improving waste management

To effectively deal with the growing waste problems, emphasis needs to be placed on waste prevention, minimization and reuse—and preferably in that order. There is not only need for more stringent environmental laws, there is room also for economic instruments and, of course, many forms of local action.

Hazardous toxic materials may have to be banned outright. Solid waste minimization can be achieved through modification of industrial processes and through changes in the design and use of products. Already many options are available at the processing stage to reduce waste through raw material substitution. Additional recycling, such as the recirculation of cooling water through a closed loop, is also possible to a substantive amount. Durable packaging instead of single-use packaging can be made mandatory. Establishing strict quantitative and qualitative criteria for discharging industrial waste water into the sewer networks and enforcement of these criteria would drastically cut the cost of sewage treatment by municipal authorities.

One possible instrument to reduce waste is the application of user charges. To be effective in changing behavior, however, charges need to be sufficiently high. Various mechanisms such as "pay-per-bag," or "charge-per-can" have proved to be successful in reducing solid waste. The "deposit-refund system" for certain kinds of packaging is quite common in many countries. Concessional loan and tax incentives can encourage the application of waste minimization technologies, etc.

Generally, the environmental costs are not or not fully integrated in the price of a product. As a result, market signals do not provide sufficient incentives for waste minimization. Therefore, efforts need to be under-taken for the full internalization of environmental costs also in order to promote new technologies. Charges on the disposal and treatment of wastes can play a useful role in helping to recover the costs associated with waste management.

With regard to municipal sewage treatment plants that ensure the elimination of pathogens, technology is well developed. Cost-effectiveness and affordability, however, remain critical. An effective waste water tech-nology suited to the climatic conditions of many developing countries is the stabilization pond system. Unfortunately, this system requires large space which is not always available in high density urban areas.

Solid waste management which includes storage, collection, transport and disposal poses different problems. The collection techniques imported from industrial countries are often not appropriate. UNCHS (Habitat) therefore promotes the use of appropriate equipment in solid waste man-agement. In most developing countries, as much as 40 percent of the refuse can be reprocessed, the rest being primarily organic matter which may be composted and sold to the agricultural sector.

National environmental policy

Until recently, direct regulations were at the center of national environ-mental policy (Enyedi, *et al.*, 1987). Regulatory instruments aim at influ-encing the behavior of polluters by imposing norms or standards on prod-ucts, technologies and discharge of pollutants. Their use is likely to persist, particularly as regards hazardous and toxic substances. Increasingly, however, economic instruments are being introduced, though in most cases they are used only in conjunction with direct regulations. In theory, economic instruments offer the advantages of flexibility and efficiency in inducing polluters to internalize the costs of pollution and to develop cleaner technologies.

Several major economic instruments for environmental policy have been conceived, namely (a) charges, such as effluent charges, user charges, product charges, tax differentiation; (b) enforcement incentives, such as noncompliance fees and performance bonds; (c) subsidies; (d) deposit-refund systems. A variety of problems arise when trying to introduce such instruments. Economic efficiency can be achieved only if heavy polluters are charged more than low polluters, which calls for a scale of instruments, based on detailed monitoring. The administrative costs of enforcing such a system can be high, even in a developing country.

The discussion on economic instruments for environmental policy so far is based on rather few experiences in developed market economies. A general conclusion from that experience is that if inspite of the sophisticated institutions of these economies economic instruments play only a modest role, they cannot be expected to do better in the developing countries. For the time being, developing countries, most probably, will rely mainly on regulatory instruments to achieve environmental policy goals. Still, some preliminary answers can be given on the role of economic instruments regarding the relation between poverty, environment, and development:

1. The application of *charges,* particularly *user charges* seems not very viable in situations of extreme poverty. The poor contribute to certain types of pollution, but they are the ones who suffer most from it. The provision of safe drinking water and sanitation facilities to the poor at low cost would be a useful social function since such services give rise to positive externalities in terms of health and productivity. Charges on household water and for discharge of sewage into municipal facilities need not be based on the amount of use or discharge but could be based on the ability to pay (income).

2. Regarding solid-waste management, the *deposit-refund system,* as applied to bottles and other reusable containers, seems to be a viable mechanism. The deposit-refund system makes possible lower prices for energy and raw materials. The system is already in widespread use in developing countries. *Tax differentiation or command and control measures* could be used to extend the deposit-refund system by inducing

the production of reusable containers for as many products as feasible. Metallic waste reuse is not a big problem in most developing countries because it is already remunerative and provides an income to the poor. What is needed, however, is sanitary treatment, prior to collection, to prevent adverse health effects.

3. Elimination or reduction of *subsidies* for products brought directly into the environment, such as fertilizers and pesticides, particularly where they are being overused, would help in reducing their impact on water quality, soil, biodiversity, and on human health.

4. A major consideration as regards the application of *effluent charges* is the viability of industries. Even in developed market economies such charges are often kept low in order not to undermine the competitiveness of industries producing for the export market. The main emphasis in developing countries, as far as industrial pollution is concerned, would have to be placed on the use of *cleaner technologies*, particularly in new plants. While the provision of funds from the budget generally is not compatible with the "polluter-pays principle," subsidies would be justifiable in cases where environmental problems are severe and costly, as for instance, water pollution treatment, restoration of hazardous waste sites, and emissions from fossil fuels combustion.

5. *Product charges* can be effective in controlling pollution if environmentally sounder products are available at prices that will induce polluters to switch to these substitutes, i.e., when the cross price elasticity of demand is high.

Global environmental policy

Global warming

There are good reasons that global warming figures high on the international policy agenda, even so there are quite a few who still ask for more scientific evidence before action is to be taken. The evidence on the fact of global warming is authoritiative, and evidence on the regional and sectoral impacts of global warming is rapidly growing, due to unprecedented cooperative scientific efforts (IPCC, 1991). Still, there is a twofold dilemma: ecologically, global warming leads to irreversibilities; economically, delayed action will mean higher costs for future generations.

As is well known, global warming is due to the emission of several greenhouse gases, notably carbon dioxide (CO_2), chlorofluorocarbons (CFCs), methane (CH_4), and nitrous oxide (N_2O). The emission of CFCs leads to the destruction of the stratospheric ozone layer, what is potentially harmful to plants, animals, microorganisms, and to human health. Global warming with the resulting climate change will alter rainfall patterns and increase the incidence of droughts and floods. It will lead to a sea-level rise, affecting numerous small island countries but also large countries, like Bangladesh. While the consequences of global warming would be felt worldwide, the poor in the developing countries could suffer the most, as many of them live on fragile land and along the coasts.

Until now, global warming is largely caused by the industrial countries through the burning of fossil fuels and the extensive use of CFCs (Benedick, 1991). At the end of the 1980s, the industrial countries were responsible for some 75 percent of the CO_2 and more than 90 percent of the CFC emissions. Unless preventive action is taken, however, the contribution of the developing countries to global warming will increase rapidly. So far, the largest proportion of the CO_2 emissions in the developing countries results from deforestation and burning of biomass fuels; industrialization and motorization will take over in the future. Clearly, the industrial countries have the responsibility to lead the way, both in their national policies and through bilateral and multilateral assistance, in implementing the climate convention signed in Rio de Janeiro by altogether 155 countries. How this should best be done, by direct regulations or by using economic instruments, however, is an open question.

Forests as habitats of biological diversity and as carbon sinks

Concern about deforestation has centered on two main issues, namely, loss of biological diversity and reduction of the size of carbon sinks. The tropical rain forests contain a wealth of plant and animal species, including wild relatives of important varieties of crops. Benefits of preserving biodiversity are seen in its potential to respond to specific problems, such as new pests and plant diseases, and to the possible need to develop new plant varieties in the future (Enquête-Commission, 1990; Wilson and Peter, 1988).

The preservation of biodiversity has assumed increased importance also in the light of recent advances in biotechnology. Under strict safety precautions, biotechnology might help develop improved varieties of culti-vars and raise crop yields. A prerequisite for that is adequate support for all biological diversity—intra-specific and inter-specific—and the existence of efficient institutions for assessment and control.

Forests also contribute to the slowing-down of the rate of climate change by absorbing atmospheric carbon, i.e., by serving as global carbon sinks. Current international efforts at reforestation and afforestation center mostly on this role of forests. Economically viable approaches to afforestation need to be accompanied by increased efforts at decreasing and finally halting the process of deforestation so as to achieve a net gain in forest cover.

It must be borne in mind, however, that the major source of carbon dioxide remains the burning of fossil fuels. This means that unless the share of renewables in energy use is multiplied and that of fossil fuels drastically cut, even a rapid expansion of forests will not solve the problem of global warming. Natural gas, hydrogen, solar and wind energy are eminently clean sources of energy and therefore deserve greater attention, at the national but particularly also at the international level.

International mechanisms for preventing and slowing global warming

A number of mechanisms have been proposed to deal with global warm-ing, among them (a) a global carbon tax; (b) tradeable emission permits; and (c) international environmental offset programs (Lashof and Tirpak, 1990).

The chief objective of a carbon tax is to stabilize and decrease green-house gas emissions, according to the "polluter-pays principle." The tax is actually intended to alter the behavior of polluters by making fossil fuels more expensive, by inducing them to reduce energy demand, encourage energy conservation, enhance efficiency, and promote renewables. One version of the proposal advocates the levying of taxes at varying rates according to such criteria as current emissions, historic emissions, or pop-ulation size. A global carbon tax could be part of a "CO_2 protocol" to implement the climate convention signed in Rio de Janeiro, 1992.

To be effective in achieving a significant reduction in energy consump-tion and CO_2 emissions, the tax would have to be rather high, what obviously runs contrary to certain vested interests, not only in low-income countries. Moreover, a high tax rate could lead to shifts from fossil fuels to charcoal, firewood and biomass scavenging, with implications for further deforestation and deprivation of nutrients to the soil. It is here that international arrangements must come in to soften such distributional and substitutional problems.

Perhaps, a feasible use of the mechanism would be to impose a moderate but progressive carbon tax in the industrial countries (in Europe, for instance) in order to generate revenues which could be used for the transfer of environmentally sound technology to the developing countries on a preferential basis. The intent of the mechanism would be to place the greater financial burden on the wealthier nations which is where life style changes are most necessary if the threat of global warming is to be substantially reduced.

Another mechanism that has received much attention in the literature, but not so much in practice, is emissions trading. This calls for establishing markets for emission permits (quotas), to be issued (by an international agency) for transboundary pollutants based on current emissions, past emissions (for instance, 1980), levels of income or population size. Under this mechanism, the permission to release stipulated safe levels of pollutants, would be made available for a fee. Those who do not fully utilize their quotas could sell or lease the balance to third parties anywhere in the world at a price to be determined by the market (*market for emission permits*).

While practical experience with tradeable permits is limited, in principle the mechanism offers an efficient solution to reduce the levels of pollution. It runs, no doubt, against the vested interests of the heavy polluters, the industrial nations, the rich, who would have to pay for what they are doing to the global environment. Establishing markets against those (the rich) who so far benefitted most from growth and trade will, of course, be not an easy undertaking. Regarding those vested interests and the remaining uncertainties of setting targets, assessing emissions, etc., tradeable permits may not be introduced at the international level in the very near future. From the point of view of resource transfer from North to South, however, a market for emission trading would be a major breakthrough.

A mechanism that could be viable in the short run is an international environmental offset program, i.e., realization of the *compensation principle*. In such a case, an industrial country could invest in environmental protection in a developing country whose harmful technologies would tend to undermine established global emission-reduction targets. Recently, the modernization of two nickel smelting plants in the former Soviet Union near Murmansk were funded by the governments of Finland, Norway and Sweden. This is an interesting, though only regional case of concessional transfer of environmentally sound technology that benefits both the donor and the recipient—and the natural environment.

International mechanisms for protecting biodiversity and enlarging carbon sinks

As pointed out above, deforestation is partly due to absolute poverty. Since tropical forests save biodiversity and serve as CO_2 pollution sinks to the rest of the world, they could be taken to internationally exemplify the compensation principle. To the extent that tropical forests are important for the state of the global environment, *countries with* and *people in* tropical forests are providing free economic services to the rest of the world and should, therefore, be compensated by the international community for preserving these forests. The modalities of preservation of tropical forests, through appropriate regulations and policies, seem to be of secondary importance and can certainly be devised, once the *commitment to preservation* and the *willingness to pay for it* have been agreed upon internationally.

Other mechanisms, such as *debt-for-nature swaps* and *international environmental offset programs*, have been used, but are limited in number and extent. Debt-for-nature swaps initiated by NGOs in industrial countries have been successful on a small scale but are not viable on a large scale. One major problem is the unavailability of funds for swaps, but there are others. Countries that predominantly have public debt are reluctant to sell them on the secondary market at a discount for fear that this would undermine their credit rating with the international finance system. Moreover, the mechanism is often seen as a device to force developing countries to relinquish national sovereignty on natural resources to foreign NGOs.

International environmental offset programs so far also have been limited. One example was given above; another is the financing of afforestation in Latin America by the government of the Netherlands to offset current CO_2 emissions at home. To the extent that more industrial countries want to invest in reforestation and afforestation in the developing countries, this mechanism could become quite powerful. If, however, forestry measures in developing countries were financed only to offset the effects of *additional* polluting plants in the industrial countries (i.e., *future* emissions at home), this would be rightly perceived as fake.

International agreements on transboundary air pollution

Because of their transboundary impacts certain air pollutants can best (or only) be controlled through concerted international action. Some efforts have been made in this direction in the last fifteen years (Benedick, 1991).

The "Convention on Long-Range Transboundary Air Pollution" which has been signed by 31 of the 34 member states of the UN Economic Commission for Europe, was concluded in 1979, and was followed by four protocols. One protocol, signed in 1984, dealt with financial contributions to a European cooperative program, one, in 1985, established the targets for reducing SO_2 emissions by at least 30 percent (the so-called "*30-percent Club*"), one, in 1988, established the targets for NO_x emissions to 1987 levels by the end of 1994 at the latest, and another, signed in 1991, established targets for the emission of volatile organic compounds.

The "Vienna Convention for the Protection of the Ozone Layer" was concluded in 1985 and supplemented by the "Montreal Protocol," signed by 53 countries in 1987. This protocol at first required a 50 percent reduction of CFCs by the end of the century. In recognition of the special situation of the developing countries, the protocol concedes a grace period to delay their compliance for up to ten years (until 2010), and provides a fund for information and technology transfer. The Montreal Protocol was strengthened by the "Helsinki Agreement" and the "London Declaration" in 1989 and 1990, respectively, signed by 80 countries and aiming at banning all CFC production by the year 2000. Individual countries, like Germany and the Netherlands, meanwhile have announced to phase out CFC production totally by the year 1994.

International agreements on transboundary movements of hazardous wastes

The "Basle Convention on the Control of Transboundary Movements of Hazardous Wastes and their Disposal" was approved by 116 countries in 1989, but only 36 signed it at that time. Its effectiveness is marred by the fact that it does not strictly prohibit the transfer of hazardous wastes, but only specifies the conditions under which such transfers may be allowed.

In 1991, African countries adopted the "Bamako Convention on the Ban of the Import into Africa and the Control of Transboundary Movements of Hazardous Wastes within Africa." This convention imposes an outright ban on the import into Africa of all hazardous wastes. It also prohibits ships of nonsignatory countries from dumping hazardous wastes in the seas, internal waters or waterways of the signatory states and requires that all waste generation in Africa meets certain safety requirements.

Theoretically, at least, the poor (the poor countries) are thus prevented to fall victim to the toxic left-overs of the rich (the industrial) countries. In practice, however, "environmental dumping" is a reality, or must be expected to become reality in a quantity-oriented throughput economy (Kenneth Boulding).

International support measures for sustainable development in developing countries

Putting sustainable development on the agenda without increasing commitment to global environmental policy would certainly lead to serious political cleavages. However, there are no quick fixes to this endeavor. Feasible solutions are available or can be found, but the costs involved may be high and the returns somewhat uncertain. No doubt, achieving a socially necessary rate of economic growth and alleviation of poverty in the developing countries while at the same time maintaining the integrity of the environment will call for new thinking on international burden-sharing and for *additional* financial resources.

While parts of the additional financing will represent a cost to ensure sustainability by way of curing environmental degradation, parts of it will represent investments rather than costs. In many cases, such investments will simultaneously produce economic return and environmental relief. Also, the costs of timely (*preventive*) action will be less than the eventual costs of delayed (*adaptive*) action. In a broader sense, financing for environmental protection can be viewed as an investment in maintaining the productive capacity of the global ecological system.

Estimating the additional financial resources needed to cope with the environmental issues involved is beyond the scope of this paper. Some estimates are available, however, which at least give an order of magnitude of the financial requirements. Particularly, attempts were made in the preparatory meetings for the 1992 UNCED conference to provide comprehensive and consistent estimates of sectoral and overall financial needs.

As is well known, the net capital inflow requested for development of the poor countries, in terms of efforts by donors, has been set at 0.7 percent of the GNP of the industrial countries. This target, if met, would amount to approximately US$ 120 billion in 1990 prices, exchange rates and GNP levels. In terms of the needs of the developing countries to attain a socially necessary rate of economic growth of 5.5 percent, a WIDER study has estimated that an *additional* $ 40 billion over the actual flows of $ 55 billion would have been required in 1990, and would rise to $ 60 billion in the year 2000. To achieve both the goals of socially necessary rate of growth *and* environmental protection, *additional* flows over current levels would have to rise from $ 60 billion in 1990 to $ 140 billion in the year 2000. In other words, the cost of environmental protection would have been $ 20 billion in 1990, rising to $ 80 billion in the year 2000. An estimate of the Worldwatch Institute puts the financial needs of developing countries for environmental conservation at US$ 20 to 50 billion per year during the 1990s. The World Resources Institute has also arrived at about the same estimate. The secretariat of the UNCED conference in March 1992 came out with a figure on the necessary annual funds for environment *and* development in the South of US$ 600 billion and on the necessary transfers from *North to South* of 125 billion annually (Strong, 1992). This is more than twice the sum of current transfers (55 billion) but only US$ 5 billion avove the theoretical volume of the old but never reached 0.7 percent goal of development aid.

Estimates of financial requirements at the *sectoral* level have also been made, but shall not be presented here.

Current efforts at the bilateral and multilateral levels

Most multilateral agencies meanwhile have started to integrate environmental considerations into planning, budget allocation, implementation and assessment of their work. For instance, the World Bank now requires an environmental impact assessment for all their new projects. UNDP in one year increased its budget allocation for environmental protection activities by over 100 percent. Some 55 percent of IFAD's projects reflect concern about the environment.

In addition, several multilateral and bilateral programs have been established with an explicit environmental thrust. The largest is the *Global Environmental Facility* (GEF), established in 1990 as a pilot scheme of the World Bank, UNDP and UNEP, to provide grants and low interest loans to developing countries to help them carry out environmental programs. The UN conference in Rio de Janeiro gave a push to expand this program. Several sectoral efforts are also underway, for instance, the *Tropical Forestry Action Plan* (TFAP), the *Consultative Group on International Agricultural Research* (CGIAR), the *Metropolitan Improvement Programme* (MEIP), and the *Environment Programme for the Mediterranean* (EPM).

The TFAP, initiated in 1985 in collaboration with FAO, UNDP, World Bank and World Resources Institute to prepare national action plans for sustainable management of land and forests in 80 countries, has been criticized and is now under review. CGIAR's mandate is to carry out research on drought and stress-resistant crop varieties as well as on environmentally sound alternative farming. The MEIP, launched in 1990 with the assistance of UNDP, World Bank and the government of Japan, aims at arresting and reversing environmental stress in five major Asian cities—Beijing, Bombay, Colombo, Jakarta, and Manila. The EPM, a long-term technical assistance plan financed by the EC-Commission, European Investment Bank, UNDP, and World Bank, aims at improving environmental conditions in the Mediterranean Basin.

Thus, the trend at the bilateral and multilateral levels regarding environmental protection expenditure is positive. The present efforts, however, certainly do not constitute adequate responses, given the magnitude and urgency of the problems.

Potential sources of additional funding

In view of the substantial volume of *additional* funding required for sustainable development in the developing countries, it does not seem realistic to rely only on increases in voluntary contributions. Instead, or in conjunction, emphasis should be placed on additional long-term commitment. The potential for redeployment of funds within national budgets, through reduction in military spending (the *"peace dividend"*), elimination of subsidies for activities that are environmentally destructive and for changes in the outmoded taxation systems seems to be great. Also, a number of new, innovative approaches to funding environmental protection activities have been proposed. Examples are, notably, debt relief, charges, energy or carbon tax, tradeable emission permits (Chandler, 1990; Grubb, 1989; Sand, 1990).

Debt relief through debt-for-nature swaps has been tried on a small-scale basis. What is needed, however, is comprehensive debt relief for the poor countries. The World Resources Institute has proposed a "Multilateral Authority" which would purchase debt at a discount and then negotiate for phased forgiveness in return for the implementation of sustainable development programs.

Charges for the use of the global commons—like ocean fishing, use of the high seas by shipping, use of the atmosphere for air transport and other economic activities—could yield substantial financial resources. These charges could be levied and collected nationally or through an international taxing authority established under the United Nations (ITF - *International Taxation Fund*), and the revenues could be used for environmental protection measures, particularly to finance the transfer of clean technologies to developing countries.

An *energy tax* or a *carbon tax* have been proposed and meanwhile are widely debated, particularly in Europe. The primary objective of such taxes would be to alter the behavior of polluters by raising the cost of highly polluting products and technologies. Behavior modification, however, would require the tax rate to be rather high, which could make many current economic activities unprofitable. But it should not be forgotten that the willingness of implementing environmental taxation in many industrial countries does exist and has never been as high as it is at present.

Tradeable emission permits offer the potential of effectuating substantial transfer of resources from one country to another, from the North to the South. It implies establishing a market where no market exists so far. And it would be a market where the poor (countries) could gain, the rich (countries) would have to pay, and the environment (nature) would win.

References

Arrhenius, E. A. and T. W. Waltz (1990). *The Greenhouse Effect*. Implications for Economic Development. World Bank Discussion Paper 78. Washington, D.C.

Benedick, R. E. (1991). *Ozone Diplomacy*. New Directions in Safeguarding the Planet. Cambridge, MA.

Chandler, W. U. (ed.) (1990). *Carbon Emission Control Strategies*. Case Studies in International Cooperation. Washington, D.C.

Enquête-Commission (1990). "Preventive Measures to Protect the Earth's Atmosphere" of the 11th German Bundestag: *Protecting the Tropical Forests. A High-Priority International Task*. Bonn.

Enyedi, G. et al. (1987). *Environmental Policies in East and West*. London.

Grubb, M. (1989). *The Greenhouse Effect*. Negotiating Targets. London.

Hahn, E. and U. E. Simonis (1991). "Ecological Urban Restructuring. Method and Action." *Environmental Management and Health*, Vol. 2, No. 2, pp. 12-9.

IPCC (Intergovernmental Panel on Climate Change) (1990). *Climate Change*. The IPCC Scientific Assessment. Report prepared for IPCC by Working Group I. Edited by J. T. Houghton, G. J. Jenkins, and J. J. Ephraums. Cambridge (reprinted 1991).

Lashof, D. A. and D. Tirpak (eds.) (1990). *Policy Options for Stabilizing Global Climate*. U.S. Environmental Protection Agency. Washington, D.C.

Oodit, D. and U. E. Simonis (1992). "Water and Development." *Productivity*, Vol. 2, No. 4. New Delhi, pp. 677-92.

Sand, P. H. (1990). *Lessons Learned in Global Environmental Governance*. Washington, D.C.

Strong, M. (1992). According to *Frankfurter Rundschau*, March 5, 1992.

Wilson, E. O. and F. M. Peter (eds.) (1988). *Biodiversity*. Washington, D.C.

World Commission on Environment and Development (1987). *Our Common Future*. Oxford.

World Resources Institute (1988). *World Resources*. Washington, D.C.

Sustainable Development: How to Allocate CO_2 Emission Reductions?

Udo E. Simonis

Among all of today's global environmental problems, climate change is the most urgent and the most threatening one. Climate change must be addressed because it will exacerbate all other problems such as deforestation, species extinction, loss of topsoil, etc. One could, however, easily argue that all other major environmental problems of today must be addressed primordially because they all end up having effects on climate.

Eco-Currents, January 1992

Introduction

Sustainable development implies that in the future, economists and development planners, diplomats and politicians will not only have to deal with growth and development processes, but will have to pay increasingly more attention to reduction and redistribution processes. This is particularly true with regard to the most important global environmental problem so far, climate change. Up to the present, this problem has been mainly caused by the industrial countries, and the debate is about how much the North should give up in climate relevant emissions. The developing countries might, however, follow suit if they keep to the "standard development path." Ecologically, it will be the developing countries which will suffer most from the effects of climate change. Economically, cost incidence will depend on the kind of preventive or adaptive measures taken, on institutional arrangements made, and on the wisdom of global environmental diplomacy. Some of these measures, arrangements and diplomacies will be dealt with in this chapter.

Greenhouse gas emissions

In analyzing global climate change and in formulating a corresponding policy (*global climate policy*), three categories of emissions are important: absolute emissions, per capita emissions, and emissions per unit of gross domestic product (GDP) or gross national product (GNP).

Table 1 shows the net national emissions of carbon dioxide, methane and chlorofluorocarbons (*absolute emissions*) for 30 countries and entails a "greenhouse index" in form of an unweighted component index.

Table 2 shows the corresponding net emissions per capita (*per capita emissions*).

Figure 1 shows the greenhouse gas emissions per unit of gross national product for three groups of countries (*emissions per unit of GNP*).

From these few (but still weak) basic statistical data it already becomes clear what a formidable task the reduction of, or adaptation to, climate change will present to the world in general, and to industrial and developing countries, respectively. Negotiations on this task are presently under way, concrete results, however, are still lacking. These negotiations center around a new distribution problem, the solution of which is extremely difficult. Some points of orientation have emerged, but a final solution is not yet in sight.

Ideally, all greenhouse gases should be comprised by an international agreement on their reduction (*climate convention* and *respective protocols*). This, however, would be a quite unrealistic proposition. Technical, economic, social and political aspects of emission reductions for individual gases differ quite remarkably from country to country. While the industrial countries are responsible for approximately 80 percent of the global CO_2 emissions (among them the USA, with its rather inefficient energy and transport structures), the developing countries are mainly responsible for methane emissions (from paddies and cattle ranching). While for some of the greenhouse gases it is easily possible to control (capture) emissions, for others this can only be achieved through adjustments of the product mix and of production technology. While for some gases a quick and complete phasing out (e.g., CFCs) seems necessary and possible, for others (e.g., methane, nitrogen oxide) a reduction is conceivable only as a slow step-by-step process.

Table 1:   *Greenhouse Index: The 30 countries with the highest greenhouse gas net emissions, 1987*

(Carbon dioxide heating equivalents, 000 metric tons of carbon; unweighted index)

Country	Greenhouse Index rank	Carbon dioxide	Greenhouse gases Methane	CFCs	Total	% of total
United States	1	540,000	130,000	350,000	1,000,000	17.6
U.S.S.R.	2	450,000	60,000	180,000	690,000	12.0
Brazil	3	560,000	28,000	16,000	610,000	10.5
China	4	260,000	90,000	32,000	380,000	6.6
India	5	130,000	98,000	700	230,000	3.9
Japan	6	110,000	12,000	100,000	220,000	3.9
Germany, Fed. Rep.	7	79,000	8,000	75,000	160,000	2.8
United Kingdom	8	69,000	14,000	71,000	150,000	2.7
Indonesia	9	110,000	19,000	9,500	140,000	2.4
France	10	41,000	13,000	69,000	120,000	2.1
Italy	11	45,000	5,800	71,000	120,000	2.1
Canada	12	48,000	33,000	36,000	120,000	2.0
Mexico	13	49,000	20,000	9,100	78,000	1.4
Myanmar	14	68,000	9,000	0	77,000	1.3
Poland	15	56,000	7,400	13,000	76,000	1.3
Spain	16	21,000	4,200	48,000	73,000	1.3
Colombia	17	60,000	4,100	5,200	69,000	1.2
Thailand	18	48,000	16,000	3,500	67,000	1.2
Australia	19	28,000	14,000	21,000	63,000	1.1
German Dem. Rep.	20	39,000	2,100	20,000	62,000	1.1
Nigeria	21	32,000	3,100	18,000	53,000	0.9
South Africa	22	34,000	7,800	5,800	47,000	0.8
Ivory Coast	23	44,000	550	2,000	47,000	0.8
Netherlands	24	16,000	8,800	18,000	43,000	0.7
Saudi Arabia	25	20,000	15,000	6,600	42,000	0.7
Philippines	26	34,000	6,700	0	40,000	0.7
Laos	27	37,000	1,000	0	38,000	0.7
Vietnam	28	28,000	10,000	0	38,000	0.7
Czechoslovakia	29	29,000	2,200	2,700	33,000	0.6
Iran	30	17,000	6,400	9,000	33,000	0.6

Source: World Resources, 1990-91, p. 15. On the methdology used, see p. 16

Table 2:   *Per capita Greenhouse Index: The 30 countries with the highest per capita greenhouse gas net emissions, 1987*

Country	Rank	Tons per capita
Laos	1	10.0
Qatar	2	8.8
United Arab Emirates	3	5.8
Bahrain	4	4.9
Canada	5	4.5
Brazil	6	4.3
Luxembourg	7	4.3
United States	8	4.2
Ivory Coast	9	4.2
Kuwait	10	4.1
Australia	11	3.9
German Dem. Rep.	12	3.7
Oman	13	3.5
Saudi Arabia	14	3.3
New Zealand	15	3.2
Netherlands	16	2.9
Denmark	17	2.8
Costa Rica	18	2.8
Germany, Fed. Rep.	19	2.7
United Kingdom	20	2.7
Singapore	21	2.7
Finland	22	2.6
U.S.S.R.	23	2.5
Ireland	24	2.5
Belgium	25	2.5
Switzerland	26	2.4
Nicaragua	27	2.4
Colombia	28	2.3
Trinidad and Tobago	29	2.3
France	30	2.2

Source: World Resources 1990-91, p. 17

Figure 1:   *Net greenhouse gas emissions per U. S. Dollar of Gross National Product, 1987*

A. OECD countries
Carbon dioxide heating equivalents (kilograms of carbon per $US of GNP)

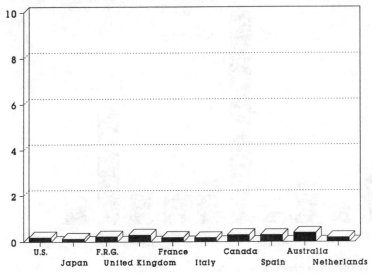

B. Planned economies
Carbon dioxide heating equivalents (kilograms of carbon per $US of GNP)

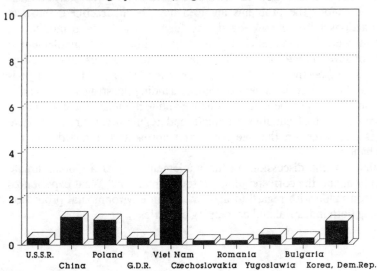

C. Developing countries

Carbon dioxide heating equivalents (kilograms of carbon per $US of GNP)

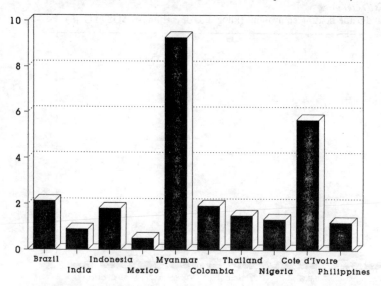

Source: World Resources 1990-91, p. 19.

Accordingly, in drafts for a framework convention on global warming (*climate convention*) the problems involved have been described, the necessary actions were acknowledged, and further research and monitoring programs were initiated. Such a convention will have to be implemented by one or several *protocols*, specifying targets and measures for the reduction of the respective greenhouse gas emissions (CO_2, CH_4, N_2O). It is here that the real work on details begins, including the struggle for the distribution of costs and benefits, on finance and technology transfer, and on the employment of suitable economic and regulatory instruments, like charges and taxes, on the one hand, and norms and standards, on the other hand.

What can the discussion on the implementation of a global climate convention, and the corresponding protocols, build on? What experiences have been made with regard to agreements on environmental protection involving both industrial and developing countries?

Global environmental policy: experiences so far

The number of effective international agreements on environmental protection comprising more than a single region (like, for example, river basins) and more than individual projects (like debt-for-nature swaps or the tropical forest action plan), and having been signed both by industrial and developing countries, i.e., agreements whose structure is relevant with regard to the climate convention, is rather limited. Volkmar Hartje who investigated this question, names only four of them (Hartje, 1989): the London Dumping Convention (1972), the Convention for the Prevention of Sea Pollution by Ships (1973 and 1978), the UN Conference on the Law of the Sea (1973-1982), and the Vienna Convention (1985) together with the Montreal Protocol on the Protection of the Ozone Layer (1987).

These agreements contain innovative regulations and instruments, including not only technical provisions, but also fiscal incentives and quota systems. The Montreal Protocol (with the succeeding revisions) is even considered a model blueprint as regards international environmental regimes (Gehring, 1990), an example of intelligent "ozone diplomacy" (Benedick, 1991).

Up to the present, however, these agreements were only of minor significance for the developing countries, in that they hardly had to fulfill any obligations for the reduction of harmful emissions. In this respect, too, the Montreal Protocol is a new beginning—modified, though, by a ten-year grace period for and by provision of information and technology transfer to the developing countries. A functioning global climate convention, by contrast, will imply significant economic adjustments not only for the industrial countries but also for the developing countries, with regard to production as well as technology.

Theoretically speaking, a relative and/or an absolute reduction of all the relevant greenhouse gases is to be aimed at. In doing so, basically all conceivable mechanisms and instruments could be used: *negative lists* (London Dumping Convention), *technical provisions* (Marpol Agreement), *property rights* (the Law of the Sea Conference), *rates of reductions or cancellation of production* (Vienna Convention, Montreal Protocol), etc. In view of a continuing high population growth in the developing countries, on the one hand, and urgent economic needs (i.e., necessary increases of income), on the other hand, *relative* limitations (with regards to population or gross domestic product) or *absolute* limitations of greenhouse gases would generate quite different consequences. These consequences, of

274   *Udo E. Simonis*

course, will influence the readiness of countries to cooperate or to oppose in the process of negotiating the climate convention and the respective protocols.

Regarding only the major greenhouse gases, these are probably the most important measures to be considered:

- relative *or* absolute limitation of carbon dioxide emissions (CO_2) resulting from the combustion of fossil fuels;
- cancellation *or* conversion of the trends of CO_2 emissions from biotic sources (i.e., reduced deforestation and increased reforestation, respectively);
- phasing out consumption *and/or* not taking up production of chlorofluorocarbons (CFCs);
- relative *or* absolute limitation of methane emissions (CH_4);
- relative *or* absolute limitation of the use of nitrogen fertilizers (N_2O).

Taking the formulation of the CFC reduction plan (not its implementation) as basically solved, the further negotiations on the global climate convention will focus on a CO_2-, a CH_4- and a N_2O-Protocol, or a combination of them, and a supplementation by other protocols (on reforestation and dersertification). At this point in time, there is only one greenhouse gas (apart from CFCs) which has been discussed seriously on the international level (leaving aside some detailed individual suggestions regarding other factors) and whose regulation can possibly be achieved in the current decade. That is carbon dioxide (CO_2). In the following, I shall, therefore, concentrate on this gas.

Reduction and redistribution processes: theoretical considerations

In the process of the Montreal Protocol three steps, or targets, emerged: *freeze, reduction*, and *phasing out*. The negotiations centered on rules to reach a quantitative reduction, while a solution via fiscal disincentives ("CFC tax") was not pursued. The volume of funds made available ("CFC Reduction Fund") is rather modest and sufficient at best to cover the costs of information transfer. With regard to the other greenhouse gases, especially CO_2, however, a further *growth* of emissions must be expected; freezing or reduction seem technically feasible, phasing out is impossible.

With regard to global environment policy, solutions via price and quantitative regulations are basically "ideal," as far as mechanisms of stimulation and/or sanctioning are concerned (Bonus, 1991). At the very beginning of all environment policy, the market mechanism is being changed. There are two approaches: One is to fix prices for environmental services, while it is left to the market mechanism to decide what emission level is economical (*price solution*); or a quota is fixed for the quantity of emissions allowed, while the prices for using the environment are left to develop in the market (*quantity solution*). These two basic approaches are symmetrical to one another, but they are not equivalent. One parameter, price or quantity, is fixed while the other is left to the market mechanism. The real question is which of these parameters should be fixed with regard to which environmental problem!

The crucial problem with price solutions (*taxes, charges*) is to determine the correct level of the price to be fixed (*shadow price*). The crucial problem with quantity solutions is to determine the appropriate quantitative ceiling (*quota*) of emissions to be permitted. In either case, if the determination is wrong, permitted emissions may exceed the absorption capacity of the ecological system (in our case, the climate system). Price as well as quantity solutions may, therefore, miss the actual target, i.e., conservation, stabilization or restoration of the ecological system. With regard to a CO_2 protocol it is to be expected that in the course of the negotiations, both types of solutions will be introduced. Up to date, quantity solutions are in the forefront, while the discussion on price solutions (*global resource tax, national CO_2-charge, "climate tax"*) has only just begun.

Moreover, with regard to quantity solutions legal rules (*reduction duties*) do prevail. However, the use of market-based instruments (*certificates or tradeable permits*) seems to be gaining ground. This suggests the implementation of certain framework parameters (for example: a certain rise in temperature) by emission quotas (see Tietenberg, 1985). These systems would have to be transformed into specific certificates which entitle the holder (country, group of countries) to an (annual) emission of a certain amount of a specified pollutant (in this case: CO_2). These certificates (or tradeable permits) could be regionally or globally transferable (*exchange*). They would be exchanged in the market at prices corresponding to their scarcity, and the ensuing income might then be used for substituting high emission products and technologies by low emission products and technologies. The certificates would add up to the set framework parameters (*global emission limit*). The certificates traded could thus be interpreted as a compensation for partial renunciation of production or use, respectively.

A special problem in regard to the implementation of a CO_2 protocol is the uncertainty as far as cause-effect-relations between emissions and impacts on climate (rise in temperature) are concerned. This problem could, however, be forestalled by corresponding (yearly) devaluations of the certificates. This would lead to either reduced emissions or to the need to purchase additional certificates.

It appears that CO_2 emissions qualify for a quantity solution, in the form of certificates to be traded at the firm, the national, the regional and even the international level. Specific conditions, however, would have to be met to implement this theoretical option smoothly in actual practice. There are also alternative instruments of global climate policy, like a tax on fossil fuels or a CO_2-charge. The related questions of these solutions, however, cannot be addressed in this chapter.

Global CO_2-emission reductions: three scenarios

In the following, three global emission reduction-scenarios are briefly compared. They include all important greenhouse gases. For reasons of clarity, however, only the CO_2 data are considered in detail.

Bach derives drastic reduction duties from the (catastrophic) projections of climate models, whereas Mintzer and EPA define the emission reductions from possible or probable changes of relevant parameters (especially energy intensity, mileage efficiency, energy tax). Accordingly, the three scenarios differ quite a bit (see *Table 3*).

- *Scenario A* can be called a strict "preventive strategy," i.e., a drastic reduction of CO_2 emissions from the burning of fossil fuels and also from biotic sources (clearing of forests, burnings, losses of vegetation);
- *Scenario B* occupies a "middle position." A reduction of CO_2 emissions from fossil fuels of less than 40 percent is expected, and an active reforestation policy is envisaged, leading to negative net emissions (via an enlargement of CO_2 sinks);
- *Scenario C* may be regarded as "modest policy." Prevention fails, emissions from the burning of fossil fuels double, changes in land use have only minor relieving effects; the resulting increase of average temperature (2075/1860: = 2.3 up to 7° Celsius) makes far-reaching adaptive measures necessary.

Table 3: *Scenarios of CO$_2$ reduction (1975-2100)*

Scenario A: "Preventive Strategy"; Bach, 1988

	Real emissions 1980	Estimated emissions 2100
CO$_2$ (million tons)		
- Fossil fuels	18,000	6 - 9
- Change of land use	4,000	0 - 4
Total	22,000	6 - 13

Δ T 2100/1860 = 1.5 to 4.5 degrees Celsius

Scenario B: "Intermediate Position"; EPA, 1989

	Real emissions 1985	2025	Estimated emissions 2050	2075	2100
CO$_2$ (billion tons)					
- Fossil fuels	19.4	20.5	n.a.	n.a.	12.2
- Change of land use	3.0	-1.1	n.a.	n.a.	-0.4
Total	22.4	19.4	16.0	14.1	11.8

Δ T 2100/1860 = 1.4 to 2.8 degrees Celsius

Scenario C: "Modest Policy"; Mintzer, 1987

	Real emissions 1975	2025	Estimated emissions 2050	2075	--
CO$_2$ (billion tons)					
- Fossil fuels	17.1	21.3	28.3	34.6	--
- Change of land use	3.8	3.0	2.7	2.5	--
Total	20.9	24.3	31.0	37.1	--

Δ T 2075/1860 = 2.3 to 7 degrees Celsius

Source: Compiled from Hartje, 1989

Of course, it is difficult to predict which of these scenarios will be taken as reference for the global climate convention, and the respective protocols. According to recent climate conferences of scientists and politicians, a limitation of average global warming to below two degrees Celsius might develop as a reference point. The implied "mixed strategy" of precaution (*prevention*) and adaptation (*cure*) actually will be determined by three major factors: (1) the real or supposed costs and benefits of the corresponding measures, (2) the perception of the irreversibilities caused by climate change, and (3) the institutional and instrumental measures which can be agreed on in the North-South-context.

The current discourse over the reduction of CO_2 emissions is an indicator of an already existing *common interest* in sustainable development of both North and South. In fact, there are interesting and surprisingly coincident plans, summarized in the following section.

CO_2-emission reduction plans: three examples

At the Second World Climate Conference in Geneva 1990, two plans on CO_2-emission reduction for the time until 2050 were presented: the IPCC proposal and the Ministers' proposal. The "International Panel on Climate Change" (IPCC) called for drastic and rapid reductions of CO_2 emissions in the OECD member countries, whereas overall global emissions will decrease only after the year 2005, and shall then fall by 46 percent until 2050, below the level of 1987 (see *Table 4*).

Table 4:   *CO_2-emissions plan - Second World Climate Conference*
               - The IPCC proposal (base year 1987, in percent)

Year	Industrial countries			Developing countries	World total
	OECD	others	total		
1990	+5	+5	+5	+11	+6
1995	+7	+8	+7	+24	+11
2000	-4	+5	-1	+37	+7
2005	-20	-10	-16	+50	-3
2020	-50	-30	-43	+60	-21
2050	-80	-70	-76	+70	-46

Source: WMO/UNEP, 1990

The Ministers' proposal was less drastic and with some temporary delay (see *Table 5*). The ministers, however, followed the scientists' notion, whereupon a further increase of CO_2 emissions should be accorded to the developing countries because of their need for further economic growth.

Table 5:   *CO$_2$-emissions plan - Second World Climate Conference*
- The Ministers' proposal (base year 1987, in percent)

Year	Industrial countries	Developing countries	World total
1990	+5	+11	+6
1995	+8	+24	+11
2000	+5	+37	+12
2005	0	+50	+10
2020	-20	+60	-4
2050	-60	+70	-33

Source: WMO/UNEP, 1990

The plan of the "Enquête-Kommission" of the German Parliament might be taken as a third reference case (see *Table 6*).

Table 6:   *CO$_2$-emissions plan*
- The German Enquête-Kommission (base year 1987, in percent)

| Year | Industrial countries | | | Developing countries | World total |
	economically strong	economically less strong	economically weak		
1990	+5	+5	+5	+11	+6
1995	+5	+7	+8	+24	+10
2000	-10	-4	+5	+37	+4
2005	-30	-15	-5	+50	-5
2020	-50	-35	-25	+60	-20
2050	-80	-80	-80	+70	-50

Source: Enquête-Kommission, 1990

This proposal differentiates the industrial countries according to their gross domestic product and suggests CO_2-emission reductions to be accorded to the developing countries. Thus, implicit criteria for the allocation of reduction duties, and the related redistribution goals, between industrial and developing countries, North and South, can be inferred from the three plans. In the following, special features of these sensitive issues for a global CO_2 protocol are addressed more explicitly.

Possible criteria for the distribution of CO_2-emission reductions between North and South

The allocation of the duties of the climate convention, and the accompanying protocols, between industrial and developing countries depends on various factors. Especially, to what degree should a certain greenhouse gas be reduced in relation to other gases, and what criteria should be applied for the reduction? A comprehensive strategy for reducing *all* greenhouse gases would probably focus on their relative importance for climate change, respectively on the global benefits of a climate stabilization. A partial strategy for one *single* greenhouse gas will probably focus less on possible benefits but on the technical options, the costs of emissions reduction, or on the substitution of the reduction duties vis a vis other gases.

For example, a total phasing out of CFC production in the industrial countries theoretically would allow for a less strict reduction of CH_4 or N_2O, which is technically difficult to achieve in the developing countries. At this stage, however, there is no need to go deeper into such "substitution dispute." Instead, I shall focus on CO_2 only - which, as noted earlier, causes more than 50 percent of the greenhouse effect. The remainder of the chapter attempts to illustrate the range of possible and realistic criteria for CO_2 reduction policies.

Two successful international environmental agreements may be the points of departure for the decision on such criteria: The ECE Convention on Long-Range Transboundary Air Pollution (1979), and the Montreal Protocol (1987). With the signing of the ECE convention a small number of ECE countries joined a "30-percent Club" as regards the reduction of sulfur dioxide (SO_2). Other ECE countries joined the "club" subsequently. Decisive for this success in beginning to control acid rain was not only the pressure ensuing from the observed damage to the forest ecosystems ("*Waldsterben*"), the formation of the electorate, the generation of technical and financial solutions, but also the consensus achieved by the "club" over a simple distribution criterion: "Every country shall reduce its SO$_2$ emissions by the *same* rate of 30 percent!" (This consensus had been reached after an intense discussion of the questions, whether the current or the accumulated emissions, the size of the country, its emission export/ import situation, etc. should be taken into account or not). In this way, the given departure point was "legitimized," prior accomplishments or geographic and other peculiarities were not considered. Thus, this case exemplifies

Allocation criterion I:
A proportionally equal reduction rate for all countries
referring to the starting point (and a base year)

The Montreal Protocol also requires a proportionally equal reduction rate (50 percent at first, 100 percent later on), but permits a temporary exemption from this rule for the developing countries. The developing countries were relieved from the reduction duty, because it was judged as being unfair: The industrial countries had caused the damage to the ozone layer with their accumulated CFC emissions, thus developing countries could not be expected to assume a proportional part of the duties. They might even have a right to emit in the future. On this line of argument is founded the

Allocation criterion II:
A proportionally equal reduction rate for one group of countries
(industrial countries), and fixation of a limited permissible increase
of emissions for the other group (developing countries)

The Montreal Protocol concedes the developing countries a CFC production of up to 0.3 kilogram per capita for ten years, and then requires a reduction to 50 percent. In comparison with CO$_2$ emissions, the reduction of CFC emissions needs but slight adjustment measures, because of quasi oligopolistic production and an initial level. The adjustments necessary for a CO$_2$ protocol will be much more extensive, as many technologies, products and economic branches are at stake. The industrial countries may bargain their own absolute reduction duties against the relative reduction duties (rate of growth of CO$_2$ emissions) of the developing countries. Apart from disparities in current emissions, the developing countries might also point at the historical emissions accumulated in the Earth's atmosphere. The more such allocation arguments (and others) are brought into the arena, the higher the probability that no common (mutual) reduction formula can be agreed on. This may make a criterion of equal treatment attractive. One that could be accepted as fair by the developing countries is *equal CO_2 emissions per capita of population*. This is the

Allocation criterion III:
Every country has a right to emit, resulting from the fixed (reduced)
global limit of emissions per capita of the world's population,
multiplied by the country's population number.

According to this criterion, countries exceeding the fixed limit of emissions per capita (the industrial countries) would have to reduce emissions drastically; countries falling below this limit (the developing countries) could emit additionally. This criterion is geared to fairness, not legitimizing the present emissions situation but requiring considerable redistribution in the North-South-context.

By introducing this criterion, peculiarities like the geographic situation, size of the country, resource endowment, differences in costs, etc. would not be taken into consideration. This, in turn, might open up corridors for bargaining in the negotiations on a CO_2 protocol.

Applying the distribution criteria I to III on the three scenarios presented in *Table 3*, reveals quite different magnitudes of the reduction duties and, respectively, the resulting *redistribution* between industrial and developing countries, as summarized in *Table 7*.

Technically speaking, there exists a wide range of possible measures to reach a reduction of current CO_2 emissions (cf. Goldemberg, *et al.*, 1987; Kats, 1989; Enquête-Kommission, 1991); the most important of them are probably the following:

- Reduction in the use of fossil fuels by way of energy saving, or increase in the efficiency of energy use, especially with regard to transport, electricity, heating;
- substitution of high-emission fuels by low-emission fuels;
- installation of new power generating technologies, like co-generation, district heating, district cooling, gas turbines;
- substitution of fossil fuels by renewable energy, like biomass, wind energy, photovoltaics, solar hydrogen;
- technical improvement or refitting of fossil fuel based power plants and engines.

Table 7: *Distribution of admitted CO$_2$-emissions from fossil fuels between industrial and developing countries: Three Scenarios, three distribution criteria*

	Global emissions billion tons	Industrial countries billion tons	Industrial countries (percent)	Developing countries billion tons	Developing countries (percent)
		Allocation of emissions			
Scenario A: Bach, 1988					
Departure point 1982:	17.4	12.6	(72.4)	4.8	(27.6)
Target 2100:	0.008				
Allocation according to					
Criterion I		0.0054	(72.4)	0.0021	(27.6)
Criterion II		0.0022		5.3[a]	
Criterion III[b]		0.0019	(25.3)	0.0056	(74.7)
Scenario B: EPA, 1989					
Departure point 1982:	17.4	12.6	(72.4)	4.8	(27.6)
Target 2100:	12.2				
Allocation according to					
Criterion I		8.8	(72.4)	3.4	(27.6)
Criterion II		6.9	(56.5)	5.3[a]	(43.5)
Criterion III[c]		3.1	(25.3)	9.1	(74.7)
Scenario C: Mintzer, 1987					
Departure point 1982:	17.4	12.6	(72.4)	4.8	(27.6)
Target 2075:	34.6				
Allocation according to					
Criterion I		25.1	(72.4)	9.5	(27.6)
Criterion II		19.0	(54.9)	15.6	(45.1[e])
Criterion III[d]		8.7	(25.3)	25.9	(74.7)

Notes:

a = absolute increase of 10%; b = 1.6 kilogram CO$_2$ per capita; c = 2.5 tons CO$_2$ per capita; d = 7.2 tons CO$_2$ per capita; e = increase of share by 100%.

Source: Compiled from Hartje, 1989

That is to say, more is needed than just a relative decoupling of energy consumption from the GNP, what actually has already happened in several industrial countries. For ecological reasons, economic growth in the medium and long term should be possible only if the reduction in energy consumption and in environmental damage is *absolute*. (It's not in the range of this chapter to address these basic questions of changes in economic structure, technology, and lifestyle.)

Up to now, only CO_2 emissions from *fossil fuels* have been dealt with. In their case, *freezing* and *reduction* are the issues. With CO_2 emissions from *biotic sources*, however, *phasing out* and a *reversal of trends*, i.e., negative growth rates must come into the picture.

To strive only for a reduction in emissions would be too modest in view of a possible net-assimilation of carbon in the biomass. Even the introduction of distribution criterion III mentioned above would not make sense here, as positive emissions fall very much behind the possibility of negative per capita emissions (by enlarging carbon-sinks through reforestation, for instance). An *additional* criterion might therefore consist in linking the obligation to stop deforestation in the developing countries with the obligation of afforestation in the industrial countries.

Another possibility consists in a direct link with the right to CO_2 emissions from fossil sources: *Biotic* emissions (resulting from slash-and-burn agriculture, deforestation, changes in land use) reduce the right to per capita emissions of CO_2 from *fossil* sources—and *vice versa*: reforestation and afforestation increase it.

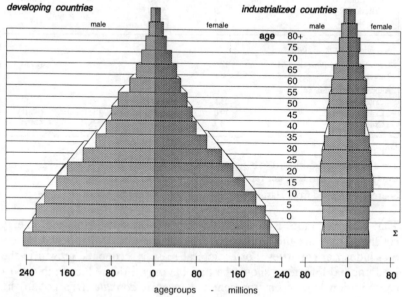

Figure 2:   Population pyramid, mid-1980s

Source: United Nations

There is *another* allocation criterion which might come into prominence in the process of negotiating the CO_2 protocol, i.e., an age *criterion* (cf. Grubb, 1989). As is well known, the population structure of the developing countries differs widely from that of the industrial countries; *Figure 2* shows the dimensions involved. In view of the fact that the population of the developing countries in average is much younger, an equal per capita emission right might prove ecologically counterproductive, i.e., giving an incentive to keep a high level of population growth. The industrial countries might, therefore, tend to introduce a *minimum age criterion* ("adults emission right"), by which their CO_2 reduction duties could be reduced, or their per capita emission rights be increased. *Figure 3* gives an impression of the dimensions that are at stake if an age criterion is to be considered in the negotiations of a CO_2 protocol between North and South.

Similarly, it could be arranged that the emissions of 1970 and not 1992 should be taken as the basis for defining the reduction duties, so that the incentive for keeping high population growth rates is neutralized.

Of course, distributional questions are political questions that require the exercise of social values beyond the individual preferences expressed in the market place. The problem of climate change is so complex that debates on allocation may never come to an end. Therefore it seems to me that a guiding criterion has to be postulated that is as simple as possible and, at the same time, can win a majority in the international political arena. The respective options have been presented above. Some of them seem easier to implement than others. But how to get from here to there?

From here to there: confrontation or cooperation

With regard to global environmental problems, Peter M. Haas recently formulated a "theory of epistemic consensus" (Haas, 1990, pp. 347 ff.). According to his (and my) view, substantial changes have occurred in the process of negotiating international agreements. This evolution of environmental policy competence can be understood as a collective learning process, an evolution that might refute Hardin's thesis of the *"tragedy of the commons"* (Hardin, 1968). Within this process, *"epistemic communities"* have formed transnational networks which are politically relevant because of their authoritative knowledge. If such networks develop, and if they get

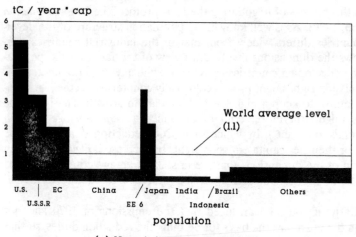

(a) No minimum age restriction

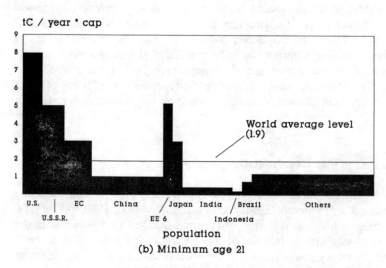

(b) Minimum age 21

Figure 3:   Per capita emissions, permit ratios and the effect of a minimum age restriction

Source: Grubb, 1989, p. 38

and maintain access to policy makers, global conventions and protocols might have an "efficiency guarantee." Neither "common interests" *per se* (upon which the Brandt Report was based), nor the notion of "sustainable development" (the Brundtland Report), nor "responsibility for our own future" (the Nyerere Report) alone will sufficiently enlarge the chances for international cooperation. Rather, cooperation depends upon the kind and strength of consensus within the "epistemic" community, and that consensus can be strengthened through improved cooperation among the community members.

This theory, it seems, has been verified by the Montreal Protocol process: Political action was prompted by an ecological crisis ("ozone hole"); international experts established the scope of political alternatives, then negotiated by diplomats; and when the members of this *community* had consolidated their position with the national governments, the latter supported the agreements.

Whether this theory will hold true for the "greenhouse effect," and whether it can be verified by the formulation and implementation of a CO_2 protocol, remains to be seen. While a loosely cohering *epistemic community* does exist, the internal consensus is not (yet) nearly as strong as in the ozone case. There even is a rift within the *greenhouse community*: There are (1) the preventionists, pleading for precaution and immediate action in order to avoid or at least confine climate change, and there are (2) the *adaptionists*, arguing for slow and gradual adaptation to a climate change which cannot be avoided anyway. Who will win, who will have the final say? And, to what extent are the elite *epistemic communities* dependent from and/or can rely on vernacular popular understanding of and will for, sustainable development?

References

Arrhenius, E. A. and T. W. Waltz (1990). *The Greenhouse Effect. Implications for Economic Development*. World Bank Discussion Paper 78. Washington, D.C.

Ayres, R. U. (1989). *Energy Efficiency in the US Economy. A New Case for Conservation*. IIASA Publications. Laxenburg.

Bach, W. and A. K. Jain (1988). "Von der Klimakrise zum Klimaschutz." *Institut für Geographie* (extended manuscript of 1988). Münster.

Benedick, R. E. (1991). *Ozone Diplomacy. New Directions in Safeguarding the Planet.* Cambridge, MA.

Bonus, H. (1991). "Umweltpolitik in der Sozialen Marktwirtschaft." *Aus Politik und Zeitgeschichte*, B 10/91, March 1, 1991, pp. 37-46.

Brown, L. et al. (1985). *State of the World. A Worldwatch Institute Report on Progress Towards a Sustainable Society.* New York.

Brown-Weiss, E. (1989). *In Fairness to Future Generations. International Law, Common Patrimony, and Intergenerational Equity.* New York.

Burtraw, D. and M. A. Toman (1991). *Equity and International Agreements for CO_2 Containment.* RFF Discussion Paper. Washington, D.C.

Carrol, J. (ed.) (1988). International Environmental Diplomacy. Cambridge, MA.

Chandler, W. U. (ed.) (1990). *Carbon Emission Control Strategies. Case Studies in International Cooperation.* Washington, D.C.

Committee on Science, Engineering, and Public Policy (1991). *Policy Implications of Greenhouse Warming.* National Academy of Sciences. Washington, D.C.

Council of the European Communities (1988). *Directive on the Limitation of Emissions on Certain Pollutants into the Air from Large Combustion Plants.* 88/609/EEC.

Daily, G., P. R. Ehrlich, H. A. Mooney, and A. H. Ehrlich (1991). "Greenhouse Economics. Learn Before You Leap." *Ecological Economics*, Vol. 4, No. 1, pp. 1-10.

Enquête-Kommission "Vorsorge zum Schutz der Erdatmosphäre" des Deutschen Bundestages (ed.) (1989). *Protecting the Earth's Atmosphere. An International Challenge.* Bonn.

—— (1990). *Protecting the Tropical Forests. A High-Priority International Task.* Bonn.

—— (1991). *Protecting the Earth. A Status Report with Recommendations for a New Energy Policy.* Vols. I and II. Bonn.

EPA (1989). *Policy Options for Stabilizing Global Climate.* Draft Report to Congress. Executive Summary. Washington, D.C.

Gehring, Th. (1990). "Das internationale Regime zum Schutz der Ozonschicht." *Europa Archiv*, Vol. 23, pp. 703-12.

Glantz, M. (ed.) (1988). *Forecasting by Analogy. Societal Responses to Regional Climate Change.* Boulder, Col.

Goldemberg, J. et al. (1987). *Energy for a Sustainable World.* World Resources Institute. Washington, D.C.

Grubb, M. (1989). *The Greenhouse Effect. Negotiating Targets.* London.

Haas, P. M (1990). "Obtaining International Environmental Protection Through Epistemic Consensus." *Millennium Journal of International Studies*, Vol. 19, No. 3, pp. 347-63.

Hahn, R. W. and G. L. Hester (1989). "Marketable Permits: Lessons for Theory and Practice." *Ecology Law Quarterly*, Vol. 16, No. 36, pp. 361-406.

Hardin, G. (1968). "The Tragedy of the Commons." *Science*, Vol. 162, pp. 1243-8.

Hartje, V. J. (1989). *Studienbericht E9a. Verteilung der Reduktionspflichten. Problematik der Dritte-Welt-Staaten*. Enquête-Kommission »Vorsorge zum Schutz der Erdatmosphäre«. Berlin.

Hekstra, G. P. (1989). "Global Warming and Resing Sea Levels. The Policy Implications." *The Ecologist*, Vol. 19, No. 1, pp. 4-15.

Hoeller, P., A. Dean, and J. Nicolaisen (1990). *A Survey of Studies of the Costs of Reducing Greenhouse Gas Emissions*. OECD, Department of Economics and Statistics. Working Papers No. 89, Paris.

IPCC (Intergovernmental Panel on Climate Change) (1990). *Policymakers Summary of the Scientific Assessment of Climate Change*. Report prepared for IPCC by Working Group I. June 1990; *Policymakers Summary of the Potential Impacts of Climate Change*. Report prepared for IPCC by Working Group II. June 1990; *Policymakers Summary of the Formulation of Response Strategies*. Report prepared for IPCC by Working Group III. June 1990, edited by J. T. Houghton, G. J. Jenkins, and J. J. Ephraums, Cambridge.

Japanese Council of Ministers for Global Environment Conservation (1990). *Formulation of the Government's Policy on Global Warming*. Tokyo.

Juda, L. (1979). "International Environmental Concern: Perspectives and Implications for the Developing States." In: D. W. Orr and M. S. Soroos (eds.), *The Global Predicament. Ecological Perspectives on World Order*. Chapel Hill, pp. 90-107.

Kats, G. H. (1990). "Slowing Global Warming and Sustaining Development." *Energy Policy*, Vol. 18, No. 1, pp. 25-33.

Keepin, W. and G. H. Kats (1988). "Greenhouse Warming. Comparative Assessment of Nuclear and Efficiency Abatement." *Energy Policy*, Vol. 16, No. 6, pp. 538-61.

Kelly, M. et al. (1990). *Cities at Risk*. London.

Lashof, D. A. and D. Tirpak (eds.) (1990). *Policy Options for Stabilizing Global Climate*. U.S. Environmental Protection Agency. Washington, D.C.

Manne, A. S. and R. G. Richels (1991). "International Trade in Carbon Emission Rights. A Decomposition Procedure." *American Economic Review*, Vol. 81, No. 2, pp. 146-50.

Mathews, J. T. (ed.) (1991). *Greenhouse Warming. Negotiating a Global Regime*. WRI Publications. Baltimore, MD.

Maumoon Abdul Gayoom, President of the Republic of the Maldives (1987). *Address to the 42nd Session of the UN General Assembly on the Issues of Environment and Development*, 19. October 1987. New York.

Mintzer, I. M. (1987). *A Matter of Degrees. The Potential for Controlling the Greenhouse Effect*. World Resources Institute, Washington, D.C.

Morgenstern, R. D. (1991). "Towards a Comprehensive Approach to Global Climate Change Mitigation." *American Economic Review*, Vol. 81, No. 2, pp. 140-5.

Morrisette, P. (1989). "The Evolution of Policy Responses to Stratospheric Ozone Depletion." *Natural Resources Journal*, Vol. 29, No. 3, pp. 793-820.

Morrisette, P. M. and A. J. Plantinga (1991). *How the CO_2 Issue Is Viewed in Different Countries*. RFF Discussion Paper. Washington, D.C.

Nitze, W. A. (1990). *The Greenhouse Effect: Formulating a Convention*. London.

Nordhaus, W. D. (1990). "Greenhouse Economics. Count before you leap." *The Economist*, pp. 19-22.

Oates, W. E. and P. R. Portney (1991). *Policies for the Regulation of Global Carbon Emissions*. RFF Discussion Paper. Washington, D.C.

Ogawa, Y. (1991). "Economic Activity and the Greenhouse Effect." *Energy Journal*, Vol. 12, pp. 23-36.

Okken, P. A., R. J. Sorart, and S. Zwerver (1989). *Climate and Energy. The Feasibility of Controlling CO_2 Emissions*. Dordrecht.

Ominde, S. H. and C. Juma (eds.) (1991). *A Change in the Weather. African Perspectives on Climatic Chance*. African Centre for Technology Studies. Nairobi.

Princeton Protocol on Factors that Contribute to Global Warming, 15. December 1988. Princeton University.

Robertson, D. (1990). "The Global Environment: Are International Treaties a Distraction?" *The World Economy*, Vol. 13, No. 1, pp. 111-27.

Rosenberg, N. J. et al. (1989). *Greenhouse Warming. Abatement and Adaptation*. Washington, D.C.

Sand, P. H. (1990). *Lessons Learned in Global Environmental Governance*. Washington, D.C.

Schneider, S. H. (1989). "The Greenhouse Effect. Science and Policy." *Science*, Vol. 243, pp. 771-81.

Simonis, U. E. (1990). *Beyond Growth. Elements of Sustainable Development*. Berlin.

Skolnikoff, E. B. (1990). "The Policy Gridlock on Global Warming." *Foreign Policy*, No. 79, pp. 88 ff.

Smith, D. A. and K. Vodden (1989). "Global Environmental Policy. The Case of Ozone Depletion." *Canadian Public Policy*, Vol. 15, No. 4, pp. 413-23.

Smith, J. and D. Tirpak (eds.) (1988). *Potential Effects of Global Climate Change on the United States*. U.S. Environmental Protection Agency. Washington, D.C.

Solomon, B. D. and D. R. Ahuja (1991). "International Reductions of Greenhouse-Gas Emissions." *Global Environmental Change*, Vol. 1, No. 1, pp. 343-50.

Speth, J. G. (1989). *Coming to Terms. Towards a North-South Bargain for the Environment*. World Resources Institute. Washington, D.C.

Streeten, P. P. (1989). "Global Institutions for an Interdependent World." *World Development*, Vol. 17, No. 9, pp. 1349-59.

The Nordwijk Declaration on Climate Change. Atmospheric Pollution and Climate Change Ministerial Conference, Nordwijk, The Netherlands, November 1989.

Tietenberg, T. H. (1985). *Emissions Trading. An Exercise in Reforming Pollution Policy*. Baltimore, MD.

Tolba, M. K. (1990). "A Step-by-Step Approach to Protection of the Atmosphere." *International Environmental Affairs*, Vol. 1, No. 4, pp. 304-9.

Topping, J. (1991). *Global Warming. Impact on Developing Countries*. Overseas Development Council. Washington, D.C.

Trexler, M. C. (1991). *Minding the Carbon Store. Weighing U.S. Forestry Strategies to Slow Global Warming*. WRI Publications. Baltimore, MD.

Tyson, J. L. (1989). "Why China Says Ozone Must Take Back Seat in Drive to Prosperity." *Christian Science Monitor*, Vol. 23, p. 8.

UNEP (1985). *Vienna Convention for the Protection of the Ozone Layer*. Vienna.

_____ (1987). *Montreal Protocol on Substances that Deplete the Ozone Layer*. September 16, 1987. Montreal.

United Nations (1983). *Conference on the Law of the Sea. Convention on Law of the Sea*. New York.

United Nations Economic Commission for Europe (ECE) (1979). *Convention on Long-Range Transboundary Air Pollution*, 13. November. Geneva.

_____ (1985). *Protocol to the 1979 Convention on Long-Range Transboundary Air Pollution on the Reduction of Sulphur Emissions or Their Transboundary Fluxes by At Least 30 Per Cent*, July 8. Helsinki.

_____ (1988). *Protocol to the 1979 Convention on Long-Range Transboundary Air Pollution Concerning the Control of Emissions of Nitrogen Oxides or Their Transboundary Movements of Hazardous Fluxes*, October 31. Sofia.

_____ (1990). *Energy Efficiency, Action for a Common Future*, May 8-16. Geneva.

Williams, R. H. (1990). "Low-Cost Strategies for Coping With CO$_2$ Emission Limits." *Energy Journal*, Vol. 11, No. 3, pp. 35-59.

World Commission on Environment and Development (1987). *Our Common Future* (= *Brundtland Report*). Oxford.

World Resources Institute (1990). *World Resources 1990-91*. New York.

Subject Index

The Authors

Gerhard Angerer, born 1943; physicist, Dr.-Ing.; head of the group on environmental research of the Fraunhofer-Institute for Systems and Innovation Research in Karlsruhe, Germany.

James T. Baines, born 1951; BE (Hons) chemical; consultant at Taylor Baines and Associates for Management, Research and Policy Analysis for Natural Resources and Sustainable Development in Christchurch, New Zealand.

Frank J. Dietz, born 1956; Msc., Drs. in economics; lecturer at the Department of Public Administration, Erasmus University of Rotterdam, The Netherlands.

Michael D. Everett, born 1938; Ph. D. in economics; associate professor of economics at East Tennessee State University in Johnson City, United States.

Jonathan M. Harris, born 1948; Ph. D. in economics; adjunct assistant professor of international economics, Fletcher School of Law and Diplomacy at Tufts University, Medford, MA, United States.

Johanna M. Kasperkovitz, born 1968; Drs. in economics; contract researcher, presently with Stichting Natuur en Milieu in Utrecht, The Netherlands.

Peter H. May, born 1952; Ph. D. in resource economics; coordinator of the Program in Ecological Economics and Agrarian Policy at the Federal Rural University of Rio de Janeiro, Brazil.

Deonanan Oodit, born 1940; economist; Deputy Secretary of the Committee for Development Planning of the United Nations, New York, United States.

Johannes B. Opschoor, born 1944; Ph. D. in economics; professor of environmental economics at the Free University of Amsterdam, The Netherlands. He is also Chairman of the Dutch Council for Environment and Nature Research.

John Peet, born 1938; Ph. D. in engineering; senior lecturer at the Department of Chemical and Process Engineering at the University of Canterbury, Christchurch, New Zealand.

Udo E. Simonis, born 1937; Ph. D. in economics; professor of environmental policy at the Science Center Berlin, Germany. He is also member of the German Council on Global Change.

Jan van der Straaten, born 1935; Ph. D. in economics; senior lecturer at the Department of Leisure Studies at Tilburg University, The Netherlands.

Paul P. Streeten, born 1917; Ph. D. in economics; professor of economics at Boston University, Boston, MA, United States.